ADVANCE PRAISE FOR

THE SEVEN KEYS TO INVESTING SUCCESS

"Markets give you a serious education, and *The Seven Keys to Investing Success* shows why trying to outguess the market can be a very expensive education."
—David Booth, founder and executive chairman,
Dimensional Fund Advisors

"If someone were to hand you the key to a treasure chest, would you hesitate to take it? P.J. DiNuzzo's *The Seven Keys to Investing Success* unlocks the most critical tenets that every investor should understand and assimilate before jumping into the shark-filled waters of developing an appropriate portfolio for your situation. A scan of the table of contents will allow you to quickly find answers to your biggest worries or most pressing questions. It is tough to place a dollar amount on the peace of mind that comes with a long-term investment plan that will see you through the rest of your life, but I assure you it will be well worth your time to read at least some of the sections of this book. Either on your own, with another advisor, or with P.J. himself, develop your personal plan and execute it."
—James Lange, CPA, attorney, and author of *Retire Secure! Pay Taxes Later*

"P.J. DiNuzzo cuts through the 'today's financial noise' with his empirically based and four-decade market tested investment process to help you build an amazing life of significance. *The Seven Keys to Investing Success* is a straight-forward and detailed, step-by-step roadmap for accelerating your success even more."
—John Bowen, founder and CEO, CEG Worldwide, LLC and author
of *Becoming Seriously Wealthy: How To Harness The Strategies
Of The Super Rich And Ultra-Wealthy Business Owners*

"Deep, intimate knowledge of the client and the ability to truly act in the client's best interest are necessary ingredients in delivering a great client experience. In *The Seven Keys to Investing Success*, P.J. DiNuzzo lays out what that experience means to today's investor."

—Dave Butler, co-chief executive officer, Dimensional Fund Advisors

"*The Seven Keys to Investing Success* is a thorough but lucid and enjoyable prescription to a comprehensive financial and lifestyle plan. It is written in the spirit of the late John C. 'Jack' Bogle but tempered in light of modern finance, empirical research, and investment technology, as well as decades of P.J.'s experience, including leadership of the successful and highly respected wealth management firm he founded 30+ years ago. I know from personal experience that P.J. 'eats his own cooking' when it comes to investing, practices what he preaches, and holds his advice to high standards, always with the client's fiduciary process first and foremost. Especially impressive is chapter 7, 'Managing Emotions with a Plan and Discipline,' which is a gem I have not experienced in other investment books."

—Dr. Robert F. Sekerka, University Professor Emeritus, physics and mathematics, Carnegie Mellon University department of physics, and author of *Thermal Physics: Thermodynamics and Statistical Mechanics for Scientists and Engineers*

"P.J. DiNuzzo's *The Seven Keys to Investing Success* is a valuable resource based on highly acclaimed research and extensive professional experience that provides investors effective strategies to use at every stage of their investment journey to increase the likelihood they will meet their personal financial goals."

—Dr. Jon A. Shank, professor of education, emeritus, Robert Morris University, and author of *Century 21 Computer Skills and Applications, 11th Edition*

"P.J. DiNuzzo's hands-on experience of over 30 years, guiding every type of client and investment goal, whether sophisticated or not, has been combined with extraordinary access to the most successful investment gurus to produce a highly engaging and action-oriented work. *The Seven Keys to Investing Success* should serve as a saving and investing North Star."

—William Haney, chair of the board of Alva, and a director of Big Win Philanthropy, former CRO and director of Credit Benchmark and BISAM, and a senior executive at Thomson Reuters

"If you are reading P.J. DiNuzzo's *The Seven Keys To Investing Success* hoping that it will confirm that your existing long-term financial plan is sound, or are hoping your advisor has your back, you will likely be disappointed. There are too many gems and valuable processes, and the odds are you derive enormous benefit from reading and implementing some or all of the recommended steps to financial security."

—James Lange, CPA, attorney and author of *Retire Secure! Pay Taxes Later*

THE SEVEN KEYS TO INVESTING SUCCESS

P.J. DiNuzzo

President, Founder, Chief Investment Officer

CPA, PFS, AIF, MBA, MSTX

DiNuzzo Private Wealth, Inc.

DiNuzzo Wealth Management

LIONCREST
PUBLISHING

THE SEVEN KEYS TO INVESTING SUCCESS

ISBN   978-1-5445-0802-3   *Hardcover*
         978-1-5445-0804-7   *Paperback*
         978-1-5445-0803-0   *Ebook*

THIS BOOK IS DEDICATED TO

Pasquale (Patsy) and Rose
Joe and Anna
Natale (Ned) and Phyllis
Nick and Renee
Mike, Jessica, and Stella
Patsy, Michaela, and Lucca
Renee and Avery

Thank you for your authenticity, genuineness, gratitude, appreciation, heritage, tradition, legacy, guidance, wisdom, time, patience, passion, understanding, support, and listening. If you weren't you, I could never be me.

I love all of you and am forever IN Gratitude for the immeasurable gifts you have provided me during my life.

CONTENTS

ABOUT THE AUTHOR

P.J. DiNuzzo is the Founder, President, Chief Investment Officer (CIO), Chief Compliance Officer (CCO), and Director of Business Development for DiNuzzo Private Wealth, Inc. (DPW)/DiNuzzo Wealth Management (DWM), which has operated as an SEC Registered Investment Advisory Firm since 1989 and currently manages $760 million as of November 30, 2019. P.J. has devoted his entire professional career to helping and empowering others to make smart money and life choices through financial life planning, indexing/efficient market theory, retirement planning, and educating the public regarding their benefits. He has been on the leading edge of Fiduciary advice, financial life planning, and indexing research for decades and approved as one of the first 100 Advisors in the United States with Index Research/Development Leader and Institutional Mutual Fund Manager, Dimensional Fund Advisors (DFA) in the early 1990s. Additionally, he was a pioneer in providing Fiduciary-based objective financial advice and removing prevalent industry-wide conflicts of interests by founding his firm, DiNuzzo Private Wealth, Inc. (DPW)/DiNuzzo Wealth Management (DWM), in 1989 as one of the first few hundred fee-only practices in US history.

DiNuzzo Private Wealth, Inc. (DPW)/DiNuzzo Wealth Management (DWM) has been consistently ranked as one of the top 500 Wealth Management firms in the country on numerous occasions by national publication *Financial*

Advisor (FA) magazine. Under P.J.'s leadership, DiNuzzo Private Wealth, Inc. (DPW)/DiNuzzo Wealth Management (DWM) has regularly been recognized as one of the "Best Places to Work" and was awarded the honor of "#1 Best Place to Work" in Pittsburgh and Western Pennsylvania in 2008, 2013, and 2016 by the *Pittsburgh Business Times*.

P.J. DiNuzzo has earned the distinguished Personal Financial Specialist (PFS®) designation. The American Institute of Certified Public Accountants (AICPA), a national professional organization of CPAs has only awarded the PFS® accreditation to less than 5% of CPAs nationwide. Candidates must meet six necessary requirements including an arduous technical exam and a peer review of their ability to demonstrate significant experience in a wide range of comprehensive personal financial planning disciplines.

Mr. DiNuzzo has appeared and been interviewed on numerous occasions regarding Financial Wellness LifePlanning, Strategic Asset Allocation, Portfolio Diversification, Indexing, Rebalancing, and Retirement Income Planning on various television and radio programs including: OPRAH & Friends with Jean Chatzky on XM Radio; CNBC-TV Power Lunch; KDKA-TV2 Sunday Business Page with Jon Delano; The Lange Money Hour radio show with Jim Lange; and The Street.com TV.

P.J. has also been interviewed and quoted on numerous occasions regarding Financial Wellness LifePlanning, Strategic Asset Allocation, Portfolio Diversification, Indexing, Rebalancing, and Retirement Income Planning in various national, regional, and local magazines including: *Kiplinger's Personal Finance Retirement Planning*; *MarketWatch* from Dow Jones; *Morningstar*; *SmartMoney*; *BusinessWeek*; *Investment Advisor*; *Financial Planning*; NAPFA *Advisor*; *The Wall Street Transcript*; *Wealth Management Exchange*; *Wealth Manager*; *Bottom Line Personal*; and IARFC.

He has also been interviewed and quoted on numerous occasions regarding Financial Wellness LifePlanning, Strategic Asset Allocation, Portfolio

Diversification, Indexing, Rebalancing, and Retirement Income Planning in various national, regional, and local newspapers including: *The Wall Street Journal*; *Barron's*; *Reuters*; *Bankrate.com*; CBS News; YAHOO! Finance; *Pittsburgh Post-Gazette*; *Chicago Sun-Times*; *FT.com Financial Times*; Smart Money Select.com; *The Atlanta Journal Constitution*; *St. Louis Dispatch*; *Chicago Board Options Exchange*; *Investment News*; *Pittsburgh Business Times*; *The Sharon Herald*; *The Christian Monitor*; *The Beaver County Times*; *Pittsburgh Tribune Review*; The Mutual Fund Wire.com; *Gulf News – the United Arab Emirates (UAE)*; TMC.net; Comcast.net Finance; Rydex Investments; Free Real Time.com; Individual.com; Lockheed Federal Credit Union; Invest n Retire; ABC-TV9 *WCPO.com*; *Fort Worth Star Telegram*; KY Post.com; *Wealth Advisor*; Jim Prevor's Perishable Pundit; *Reading Eagle*; *The Toledo Blade*; Horsesmouth; DemocraticUnderground.com; The Community Investment Network; *Daily Herald*; *Scripps News*; *The Modesto Bee*; *Hitched*; *Prime*; El Paso times.com; *Paladin Advisor*; *Advisor Max*; Denverpost.com; *Oswego Daily News*; *The Dollar Stretcher*; *Financial Advisor*; *The Ledger*; Post-Gazette. now; *The Columbus Dispatch*; *Savannah Morning News*; and Hampton Roads News Channel.

Mr. DiNuzzo is a member of the Financial Planning Association (FPA), American Institute of Certified Public Accountants (AICPA), the Pennsylvania Institute of Certified Public Accountants (PICPA), the AICPA's National CPA Financial Planning Insights Panel, The National Association of Tax Professionals (NATP), the Pittsburgh Stock and Bond Club, and the regional DFA Study Group.

P.J. chose football in lieu of a Major League Baseball offer from the Houston Astros to play with their Class A Minor League Team, as he attended and played football at Indiana University under Head Coach Lee Corso in the "Big Ten" (Bloomington, Indiana) and also at the University of Pittsburgh under Head Coach Jackie Sherrill. He later received his BS in Business Administration from Geneva College in Beaver Falls, Pennsylvania. His graduate studies culminated in an MBA (Masters in Business Administration) from the Katz Graduate School of Business at the University of Pittsburgh and an MSTX (Masters of Science in Tax Law) from Robert Morris University at the downtown Pittsburgh Campus. P.J. received his Certified Public Accountant (CPA) designation from the State of Delaware. Additionally, he earned his Accredited Investment Fiduciary® (AIF®) from the Center for Fiduciary Studies.

P.J. was a member of the Investment Committee on the Endowment Board for Valley Care Associates, a nonprofit organization providing adult day care, home safety consulting, and physical modifications for the elderly in Allegheny and Beaver Counties. He has served as Finance Council board member for St. Blaise Church. He is a volunteer and supports Habitat for Humanity, Pittsburgh's Red Door Program for the homeless, and has commitments to his churches in Midland, Beaver Falls, and Pittsburgh's Southside. He also advises The P.J. DiNuzzo Family Charitable Fund at The Pittsburgh Foundation, dedicated to food, clothing, shelter, healthcare, education, and transportation for less fortunate individuals in Pittsburgh, Beaver County, and Allegheny County. He is a lifelong resident of Pittsburgh and its suburbs. He devoted more than twelve years to helping and assisting numerous young men in the inner city and Pittsburgh area by supporting and coaching more than 1,000 basketball games at the AAU, elementary, middle school, junior high, and high school levels attempting to teach and instill in them teamwork, trust, structure, discipline, and hard work. Weather permitting, he typically rides his bicycle to and from work, logging a few thousand miles per year.

Important Disclosure Information

ACKNOWLEDGMENTS

My book, *The Seven Keys to Investing Success*, could not have been written without the contributions and input over my lifetime of many family members, team members, individuals, organizations, and the Dimensional Fund Advisors (DFA) team and research department.

Special thanks to my advisory team and their areas of expertise: Mark S. DiNuzzo, Executive VP, CFP, AIF, MBA, Retirement Planning/Risk Management, Wealth Advisor; Carl J. Hartman, Senior VP, Senior Investment Officer, ChFC, AIF, Retirement Planning/Investment Management, Wealth Advisor; Michael V. DiNuzzo, Sr. VP, CFP, ChFC, MSFS, AIF, Retirement Planning/Risk Management, Wealth Advisor; Robert F. Graham, VP, AIF, MBA, VP Retirement Planning, Wealth Advisor; Jacob R. Potts, VP, CFP, ChFC, AIF, Portfolio Management Trade Team Leader, Wealth Advisor; Leslie D. Taylor-Neumann, VP, Wealth Planning Team Leader, Wealth Advisor; Jennifer B. Reddinger, VP, CFP, AIF, Wealth Advisor; Andrew C. Pursel, AVP, Wealth Advisor; and Ken McDaniel, EA, Tax Advisor.

Additional special thanks to my fellow team members in our operations department: Jackie DiNuzzo, Compliance Officer/HR Manager; Lisa Faulkner, Senior Client Service Specialist; Terri Tepsic, Executive Administrative Assistant/Marketing Manager; Mikey Ronacher, Client Performance Team

Leader; Brooke McMaster, Senior Client Service Specialist; Cliff Smith, IT Director; Heather Dunbar, Director of Operations, Operations Team Leader; Marjorie Patterson, Client Service Specialist; Ken Aikens, Client Service; Renee Foody, Administrative Assistant; Marjorie Patterson, Client Service Specialist; Denise Lyons, Bookkeeping Manager; Nick DiNuzzo, Video/Internet Manager; Rose Dessler, Compliance Officer/HR Manager; and the Matriarch of our family, Phyllis Nutz (DiNuzzo), Client Service (Emeritus).

Attorneys: James Lange, Matt Schwartz, Karen Mathias, C.J. Jacques, Cori Siri, Mary Jane Jacques, Andy Sykes, Tom Giachetti, Jennifer Johnson, and John Montoya.

Certified Public Accountants (CPAS): James Lange, Ken Herrmann, Glenn Venturino, Steven T. Kohman, Diane Markel, Shirl Trefelner, Robert Keebler, Sheryl Rowling, Paul Demharter, David Campsey, and Steve Klemash.

Operations and Technical Specialists: Sandy Proto, Daryl Ross, Alice Davis, and Donna Master, Eric Emerson, Carol Palmer, Beth Gardner, Bryan Tann, Erika Hubbard, and Ed Mittleman.

Wealth Advisors/Financial Advisors: Patsy DiNuzzo, Kevin Kroskey, Phil Henry, Sheryl Rowling, Mark Hebner, Michael Kitces, Mario Giganti, Glen Hahlen, Roger Gibson, Ross Levin, Joyce Schnur, Nancy Skeans, Glenn Kautt, Cheryl Holland, Rebecca Pomering, Shaun Kapusinski, Ron Carson, Mark W. Ambrose, and Tony D'Amico.

Consultants: Lee Brower, Dan Sullivan, Bob Veres, Angie Herbers, Gary Klaben, Barb DaCosta, Gene Fama Jr., Phillip Palaveev, David Blanchett, Dr. Joseph Bosiljevac, Sharon Epperson, John Furey, Brenda Winslow, John Bowen, Russ Alan Prince, Jonathan Powell, and Sharla Hamil.

Image Artist: Sue Abrams.

Professors: Gene Fama Sr., Nobel Laureate; Kenneth French; Ed Lazear; Terrence Thomas Odean; Michael Finke; Wade Pfau; Robert Novy-Marx, Myron Scholes, Nobel Laureate, and Merton Miller, Nobel Laureate (deceased), and Harry Markowitz, Nobel Laureate.

Publishing Manager, Kayla Sokol; Editor, Susan Paul; and Executive Editor, Jessica Burdg.

Dimensional Fund Advisors (DFA): David Booth, Rex Sinquefield, James L. Davis, Weston Wellington, Dave Plecha, Dan Wheeler (retired), Dave Butler, Gerard O'Reilly, Joel Hefner, Rob Bessett, Mike McCann, Ron Krisko, John Wilson, John "Mac" McQuown, and Marlena Lee.

Companies/Organizations: Dimensional Fund Advisors (DFA), Indexed Fund Advisors (IFA), Morningstar, TRX, TD Ameritrade Institutional, Fidelity Investments Institutional, Charles Schwab and Co. Institutional, AICPA, PICPA, NATP, Dalbar, Social Security Timing (SST), Vanguard Investments, Envestnet/Tamarac, FI 360.

FOREWORD

by

JAMES LANGE, CPA/ATTORNEY

I am a CPA, a retirement and estate planning attorney, and a respected voice in IRA (and just about every other kind of retirement plan) and Roth IRA conversion planning. In addition to my work for my clients, I travel around the country offering my analysis and recommendations to other lawyers and investment advisors—teaching long workshops on the intricacies of helping clients achieve a secure retirement—as well as workshops for individuals nearing or in retirement who are also seeking a secure retirement. This is an issue near and dear to my heart. P.J. is a kindred spirit. He places an equal emphasis on financial education and in particular he shares my belief that an informed and knowledgeable client sets the foundation for a long and successful client/Wealth Advisor relationship.

His book, *The Seven Keys to Investing Success*, fulfills both objectives: for the reader who is seeking good advice and a path to thinking critically about investing and preparing for a long life without undue anxiety about finances, you could not find a better analysis of the process; one that clearly articulates his philosophy and his methods. If you are a client or a potential client, here is almost all of the information you will need to carry on constructive and informed discussions with your advisor. At this point, I would like to offer a round of applause for P.J.'s determined efforts to advance the cause of healthy long-term financial life management!

I feel obligated to disclose that I am not independent with regard to P.J. because we do have a fee-sharing agreement with certain clients. That said, I would not risk my reputation as a CPA, attorney, and a registered investment advisor by saying anything that isn't true.

One of the problems that consumers face is distinguishing between advisors who provide credible advice, manage money intelligently, and act in the client's best interest, and advisors who, to put it bluntly, put their financial interests first. I have seen him turn down opportunities because they were not a good fit. And I have seen him morph a big opportunity into a modest opportunity because it was the right thing to do for the client.

Virtually all advisors, including P.J. DiNuzzo and I, come equipped with graphs and charts and reasons why our recommendation and analysis are so valuable. This book goes beyond persuasive charts and graphs. He takes you inside his head and his heart. His family's influence on his life has been and is immeasurable and formative in a good, if not always easy, way. But this is not his only motivation for writing this "inside baseball" look on what he does and how he thinks about it.

P.J. has worked long and hard to develop his practice: He founded DiNuzzo Private Wealth, Inc. (DPW)/DiNuzzo Wealth Management (DWM) in 1989 with the Security and Exchange Commission (SEC) with $0 AUM, removing prevalent industry-wide conflicts of interest with its founding business model. His was one of the first 300 Fiduciary-based firms in the US, one of the first 300 fee-only firms in the US, one of the first 100 Registered Investment Advisory firms in the US approved by Dimensional Fund Advisors (DFA) in the early 1990s, and one of the pioneer firms in the US to lead with financial planning instead of myopically just managing money. DiNuzzo Private Wealth, Inc.

(DPW)/DiNuzzo Wealth Management (DWM) now manages $760 million as of November 30, 2019. The man has something to say and people should listen. *The Seven Keys to Investing Success* is an invaluable resource.

I have heard P.J. modestly say something to the effect that he is just a mouthpiece for the Nobel Prize winners at Dimensional Funds Advisors, his favorite low-cost set of index funds. (I might add, one of the things I like about the book is that it is based on sound peer-reviewed and often Nobel Prize-winning research.)

I beg to differ. *The Seven Keys to Investing Success* articulates P.J.'s original thinking. He doesn't explain particular investments or funds, but rather his methodology for managing money. This book represents his cumulative knowledge and wisdom gained from 30+ years in the field. Furthermore, as someone who has seen how he manages his clients' money—and perhaps more importantly, how he and his team manage their clients' financial lives—his book really reflects how the entire team at DiNuzzo Private Wealth, Inc. (DPW)/DiNuzzo Wealth Management (DWM) practices what they preach.

I have often heard P.J. say, "No two people are alike, just as no two snowflakes are alike." Each client is treated as an individual case study. There are no pat answers. No lumping people into predefined categories, and no rote recommendations.

Many advisors feel pressure to write a book. They slap something together and get it out there and claim they are a published author. I have watched P.J. sweat and toil over this book, literally for years, and I can tell you with absolute certainty no one in the world other than P.J. could have written this book. This book reflects his thinking and his philosophy.

P.J. thinks everyone needs a financial plan—a detailed plan—a customized plan the quality of a "DiNuzzo Financial Wellness LifePlan™." He asks questions, listens, and then executes and fills in the tables for all the things he writes about: the "DiNuzzo Money Bucket Stack Analysis™," the Cash Flow Plan, the Balance Sheet Asset and Liability Plan, the "DiNuzzo Tax Bucket Strategy Analysis™," the "DiNuzzo Withdrawal Buckets Sequence Analysis™," Social Security Maximization, and identifying your unique "High-Net-Worth Personality."

When he asks clients how much they spend per month, he doesn't take that number at face value. He digs deeper. His team often finds things the clients overlooked. The difference between what the clients thought they were spending and what they really are spending can have a profound impact on P.J.'s recommendations. If he simply accepted the clients' number at face value and planned an investment strategy accordingly, the client might not, for instance, have a sufficient weighting in fixed income and would be exposed in the event of a downturn. It's all in the details.

The other thing *The Seven Keys to Investing Success* brings to the party is protecting older investors with his DiNuzzo Glidepath™. Yes, if the market has a 30-year bull market after you retire, you would not do as well by following P.J.'s Glidepath. But, if the market takes a major downturn and takes many years to recover, there will always be food on the table, a shelter over your head, gas in the car, and a little money for Saturday night. That is what he calls his Risk Capacity. I never worry that a client that I refer to P.J. will end up broke because he didn't sufficiently plan for a potential downturn. That said, he presents a compelling case against too much money in fixed income because of the danger of taxes and inflation and lost opportunity.

In a world of jokers and boasters, P.J. DiNuzzo and *The Seven Keys to Investing Success* are the real thing.

—James Lange, CPA and Attorney

I Believe...

That money is not the most important thing on earth, but...

It is the most important tool to align yourself with your future and who you are in this world along with what you want to accomplish for your family and your desire to live the life you truly want.

I also believe your lifetime of hard work and sacrifice can serve as the momentum for you to achieve the most meaningful and Best-Life you and your loved ones were meant to experience.

This journey started for me as a child growing up and witnessing firsthand the angst my high school educated father, Ned, experienced while trying to save, invest appropriately, and develop a financial and retirement plan to provide one day for him and my mom, Phyllis.

My father died entirely too young at the age of fifty-one. Ostensibly, he died from excessive financial stress and the daily pressure of being a 25-year veteran "steel mill hunky" turned entrepreneur and managing two businesses through challenging economic times (exorbitantly high interest rates AND massive steel mill closings in our hometown of Midland, Pennsylvania, as well as the nearby towns of Aliquippa and Beaver Falls from the late 1970s through the early 1980s) without sufficient financial guidance or coaching.

Decades ago, once I had acquired a critical mass of financial planning and investment knowledge, it hit me like a ton of bricks that if my father had a Wealth Advisor at my, or any of my peers', level of personal finance expertise that he, in all likelihood, would not have died from the monumental financial stress and weight on his shoulders at the young age of fifty-one.

Someone to coach and guide him with managing his Balance Sheet (Assets and Liabilities) and most importantly his Cash Flow (Income and Expenses) would literally have made all of the difference in the world to him and his family.

I think of him all of the time and how his tragic outcome could have been avoided if he had a good "financial coach." He is my constant inspiration and the sole reason I founded my firm: to help people.

Over the decades I have developed numerous proprietary tools to assist my team on our mission, many of which I am sharing with you in my book.

Starting in 1989 with only one employee, myself, and $0 in assets under management, all I had was my guiding "North Star" principle of helping others. At the time of my book being published we have over twenty team members, approximately three-quarter billion dollars in assets under management, and clients in over thirty states across the USA.

I have been blessed to find like-minded team members who have and share this vision along with me to run, not the largest, but rather the best and ever-evolving client-centric Fiduciary Standard Wealth Management firm possible operating with a laser focus on my original and my team's #1 ongoing goal to this day:

Helping people.

THERE IS A BETTER WAY TO INVEST

Every less-than-optimal investment decision I have made in my retail (1979–1988) and institutional (1989–2020) investment lifetime has occurred when I have disregarded or veered away from any of the fundamental philosophies espoused in my book.

—P.J. DiNuzzo

We'd all love to flip a switch, shut off the lights, and go home. But it's more complicated than that.
—Keith Brainard, Research Director, National Association of State Retirement Administrators, *Wall Street Journal*, June 21, 2013

No one in his right mind would walk into the cockpit of an airplane and try to fly it, or into an operating theatre and open a belly. And yet they think nothing of managing their retirement assets. I've done all three, and I'm here to tell you that managing money is, in its most

critical elements (the quota of emotional discipline and quantitative
ability required) even more demanding than the first two.
—Dr. William Bernstein, Journal of Indexes, July/August 2008

I have always had an interest in numbers. As a kid, I'd memorize hundreds and hundreds of major league baseball player statistics in my extensive baseball card collection. Later, I discovered investing, stocks, bonds, and mutual funds, so even early on, I had an inkling that I might end up in the field of investment management.

My interest was heightened, I believe, as I was growing up, by the many telephone conversations about numbers, specifically as they related to *money*, that I overheard between my father and the stockbrokers he had hired.

My father was a stereotypical Italian man and a fireball at five feet, nine inches tall, with olive skin, jet-black hair—and the ill-famed, Italian temper to boot. His parents, my paternal grandparents, had come to the United States from Naples, Italy as teenagers, met here, and had thirteen children. They never really learned to speak English. My grandfather worked at a steel mill on the outskirts of Pittsburgh in Midland, Pennsylvania, for forty years, and my father followed suit, graduating from Midland high school and going to work in that same mill. He never went to college. In the middle of his life, after twenty-five years in the steel mill, my father bought a small restaurant and began to save some money.

Money management—and investing, in particular—were new and foreign concepts to my father, so when he started to save some money he hired a stockbroker to make all his investment decisions. It did not go well, and so he'd fire one and then hire another, but the result was always the same. This was the 1970s, and his *very* loud phone conversations with the stockbrokers sounded like a broken record: "You call me, saying 'Hey Ned (my father's name was Natale, but he went by "Ned"), you have to sell now to take your gains *or* sell right now and cut your losses,' but all I know is I do not have any more money today than I gave you three years ago." My father, trusting his hard-earned cash to half a dozen brokerage firms over the years, never made a dime off of their "advice."

The sad part of it was that he knew they weren't investing his money properly, yet he didn't know what else to do. My father may not have had a college degree, but he did have a PhD in common sense and was nobody's fool. He knew he was being taken for a ride—that what these brokers were doing was what he called "highway robbery" back then. He also suspected their investment "guidance" would have a serious and detrimental effect on his retirement plans.

He had left the steel mill with no pension, so any money he was able to put away by running that restaurant was all he had for retirement. That nest egg—wrongly invested—never had the opportunity to grow. As a teen, I could not help but wonder how his portfolio was being managed. I had no idea what "world-class institutional portfolio management" was, but I did know one thing: it was not what these brokers were doing with my father's money.

There was no way that institutions, foundations, endowments, and family dynasties managed their money like this. I began to research investments on my own, and that led me to my current career as a Wealth Manager, and my lifelong journey to research the best strategies for portfolio management.

I was not drawn to the retail investment world, but rather to the academic community. Retail brokers and advisors had consistently provided poor advice to not only my father, but also to every family member and friend I had known. Their recommendations, I discovered, were precisely the opposite of many successful strategies of institutional investment managers who manage the largest portfolios on earth. The successful world of investing includes no front-end loads, no back-end loads, no 12b-1 fees, no exorbitant expense ratios, no surrender charges, no redemption fees, and no excessive portfolio turnover. It was literally a *completely* different world than the brokers and advisors of the retail investment world that my father had entrusted his hard-earned money to.

Growing up and throughout my life, I have always been driven to and enjoyed helping others. When you enjoy doing something, you consistently see opportunities to take advantage of your interests, and my interest and aptitude for numbers, statistics, probabilities, and my innate desire to help other people drew me to my profession, and to become the man I am today. Being a "giver" rather than a "taker" has always felt more natural and comfortable for me as my natural place in the universe. I believe this part of my personality and who I am, my inner compass, was the impetus that inspired me to start my Wealth Management practice in 1989. I began with *zero* dollars under management, yet I had a burning desire to help others, so they would not experience the same horrendous experience with their life savings as my father, who is now deceased.

On my journey, I soon discovered that there were two common denominators to these large portfolios directed by the top institutional asset managers: (1) they held, on average, an approximately 65% stock exposure; and (2) of that stock exposure, they held approximately two-thirds in domestic stocks and one-third in international markets. As you will learn in my book, the two initial most important challenges you must get right in long-term portfolio management are the Asset Allocation "Risk Allocation" (stocks vs. bonds), and full and proper diversification utilizing the desired Asset Classes and market Premiums, which I will identify.

After obsessive personal research, my *most exciting discovery* at that time, during the late 1980s, was Efficient Market Theory (EMT) and the power of indexing, especially over long periods of time. This was probably most articulately described to me in a one-on-one conversation decades ago with Rex Sinquefield, co-founder of Dimensional Fund Advisors (DFA), as an "epiphany." Efficient Market Theory, strongly supported by over ten decades of academic research and financial data, simply states that all available information regarding the market value of a company (e.g., "Price Discovery") is efficiently reflected in its market price, and that index funds are the best way to take advantage of available stock Premiums (i.e., potential extra return via Equity, Value, Small, and Direct/Expected Profitability Premiums). By and large, the media and popular investment gurus encourage the *opposite* approach by promoting active investing—attempting to "outpick" and/or "outsmart" the entire market and, in effect, try to predict the future by investing in select or single companies (e.g., market timing) or active mutual funds. As you'll discover in my book, the last ten decades of data prove that attempting to predict the future is a *loser's game*.

Once I became sold on Efficient Market Theory and the superiority of index investing, my journey through the academic world led me straight to Dimensional Fund Advisors (DFA) and the University of Chicago's Booth Graduate School of Business, and I became one of the first 100 advisors in the United States approved with them in the early 1990s (thank you, Dan Wheeler!) to access and utilize their institutional funds for my clients, as only less than one-half of one percent of advisors nationally were approved to work with DFA. When I started my practice in 1989, I was also one of the first few hundred firms in the United States founded as a fee-only Fiduciary-based practice. To me, this approach was not only ethical, but a matter of common sense, as the largest, best, and brightest institutions, foundations, and endowments operate this way. I wanted to build a practice for my "family of clients" that contained *no inherent conflicts of interest*.

DiNuzzo Private Wealth, Inc. (DPW)/DiNuzzo Wealth Management (DWM) is a Wealth Management firm licensed by the Securities and Exchange Commission (SEC) in Washington D.C. according to and operating under a *Fiduciary Standard*. A Fiduciary Standard requires the advisor to analyze, make recommendations, and provide advice as if the situation, challenges, and investments *were his or her own*. In other words, we are ethically, legally, and morally bound to advise you what we would do if we were in your shoes. We embrace our Fiduciary Standard and are dead serious about it, to the point that we view it as our "sacred responsibility" to our clients. Therefore *every* penny I and my family have invested is invested in exactly the same investment funds and vehicles as what I recommend to my clients.

In contrast, the vast majority of individuals are receiving conflicting advice from brokers and advisors who are bound by what can be interpreted as a *suitability standard* rather than a Fiduciary Standard. This means an investment just has to be "suitable" for you. Typically the average stockbroker or advisor providing you with this type of advice *does not own anything* that they are recommending to you in their own portfolio. Which advisor would you rather work with?

When prospective clients come into one of our offices and I explain the *Seven Keys* that lead to long-term success, they are often befuddled since it is typically different from what they have been exposed to. They wonder why they haven't heard these principles before. The primary reason is that the financial media and investment "gurus" make their money from encouraging an active investing approach and attempting to *ignite* your emotions accordingly, with no basis in the data or even common sense, creating needless stress in your investing and personal finance decisions.

Why Successful Investing for LifePlanning and Retirement Planning Is So Stressful

When most people think of "retirement," they think of resting in a hammock in the backyard, traveling at their leisure, and being free from the constraints of a job. In short, they think of "relaxing." When most people think of *planning* for life and retirement, however, they think of the opposite. Why does investing and LifePlanning tend to be so stressful? There are at least three reasons:

1. Most companies no longer provide defined benefits (pensions) to their employees, therefore most individuals must now be

responsible for their own retirement investing. In short, they've been thrust into a new position with virtually no training but tremendous responsibility: I refer to this newly identified position as the Family Chief Investment Officer (FCIO).

2. In direct proportion to the number of individuals taking responsibility for their investments and retirement planning, media noise has increased dramatically—very often giving the Family CIO the wrong "advice" about building a successful strategy.

3. Few clear roadmaps exist for LifePlanning and retirement investing—and the few that do have difficulty breaking through the media noise.

If you are reading my book, whether you know it or not, you have most likely accepted the position of Family CIO. As your family's new CIO, new challenges have arisen in your life, which were previously not present. With so many questions, so much information, so many conflicting "talking heads," and so much financial "noise," just what should you do? Family CIOs need keys to a clear roadmap to successful Financial Wellness LifePlanning.

THE FAMILY CHIEF INVESTMENT OFFICER (FCIO) = TREMENDOUS RESPONSIBILITY

I don't feel like the Chief Investment Officer. Who gave me that title?
—Typical Reader

Some of our parents and grandparents did not need to understand the difference between a stock and a rock when they retired because they had Social Security and, in many cases, a monthly pension check from the company they worked for. Today, whether or not individuals accept it or understand it, the responsibility of Family Chief Investment Officer (CIO) has shifted from the employer to the employee. The Family CIO has the same responsibilities as would the CIO for a major endowment, foundation, or institutional portfolio. However, the importance of success for every family's CIO is arguably more important than that of any major organization. "You cannot afford free advice."

—Ed Slott, author of *The Retirement Savings Time Bomb and How to Defuse It* (Penguin, 2012) and host of the PBS show *Ed Slott's Retirement Rescue!*

FIGURE 0.1. **Challenges for the Family CIO (Chief Investment Officer)**

Defined Benefit "Pensions"

Investment "Media Noise"

| 1970's | 1980's | 1990's | 2000's | 2010's | 2020's |

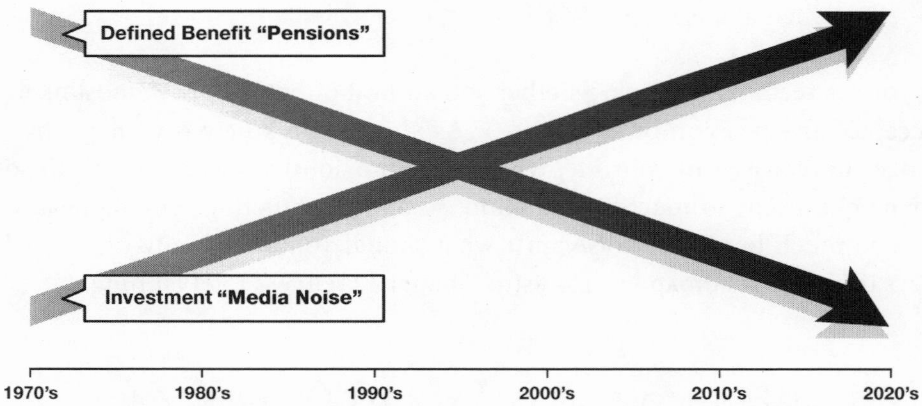

Source: DiNuzzo Private Wealth, Inc. (DPW)/DiNuzzo Wealth Management (DWM).

In Figure 0.1, *Challenges for the Family CIO*, I shine a light on the challenges individual investors face as their Family Chief Investment Officer. While a *defined benefit* (i.e., pension plan) historically covered the retirement needs of the majority of employees over the past 60+ years, these benefits have been gradually reduced to a smaller and smaller percentage each year while *defined contribution* (i.e., 401(k)s and 403(b)s) percentages have increased each year. "Guaranteed income" for households across the US has been declining since the 1970s, such that the majority of households retiring today have zero pension income coming into their household. Also, at the same time, you could see that investment "media noise" has been escalating consistently since the 1970s via social media, TV, radio, print, magazine, and the internet. Not only does the Family CIO now have full responsibility for developing their own "personal pension plan," it's getting harder and harder to receive objective advice and maintain an uncluttered mind.

After a lifetime of picking stocks, I have to admit that Bogle's arguments in favor of the index fund have me thinking of joining him rather than trying to beat him. Bogle's wisdom and common sense (are) indispensable...for anyone trying to figure out how to invest in this crazy stock market.

—James J. Cramer, from *The Little Book of Common Sense Investing* by John C. Bogle

FIGURE 0.2. **Inflation vs. Capital Risk**

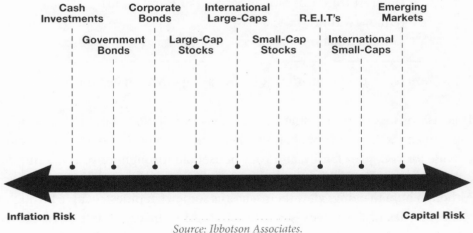

Source: *Ibbotson Associates.*

In Figure 0.2, *Inflation vs. Capital Risk*, I have illustrated the continuum of investment options listing a number of broad Asset Classes. A significant number of Family CIOs, when looking at risk, look strictly at capital risk and not inflation risk. After the financial meltdown in 2008 and 2009, we saw a flight to perceived "safety" (i.e., cash) by many individual investors. In this flight to safety, the residual effect was that many individual investors were simply "losing money safely"—or, in other words, "losing money slowly." Remember, if an individual has their portfolio invested in money market funds that are yielding a 1.0% interest rate, and inflation is 3%, their real rate of return is a negative 2.0% per year!

In the real world, I have seen countless examples of individuals who "invest" their portfolio during retirement at 1% or 2% in "safe" investments while taking a 4% or 5% withdrawal out of the portfolio, thinking they are just invading their principal by 2% or 3% per year. But if I add the effects of inflation and the loss of purchasing power to their portfolio, they are falling behind dramatically on an annual basis. Here's the simple retirement income math

2% (interest from CD, Money Market, or Bond Fund)
− 5% (annual withdrawal)
− 3% (annual inflation)

_____

−6% real rate of return/loss of purchasing power in just one year!

This risk of loss of purchasing power *vis-à-vis* inflation should be of *equal* concern and weight in your analysis when building a portfolio to support and provide for you, your family, and your household throughout your lifetime.

Although human beings view themselves as somewhat indestructible through many decades of their lives, you cannot afford to incorporate this risk bias into your retirement planning. To more fully understand the risks inherent in retirement planning, it's helpful to think of retirement in three stages, shown in Figure 0.3, *The Three "Stages" of Retirement*:

FIGURE 0.3. The Three "Stages" of Retirement

GO-GO:
Retirees maintain lifestyle, travel, the group that does not consider themselves "old".

SLOW-GO:
Between the ages of 70 and 84, brought on by the body saying "Slow-Down," 20% - 30% budget decline.

NO-GO:
85+, significant changes in retirement lifestyle generally brought on by health issues.

Source: The Prosperous Retirement, Guide to the New Reality *by Michael Stein.*

1. **Go-Go.** During this stage, you tend to maintain your preferred lifestyle. You don't view yourself in any way as a senior citizen. I recommend that clients plan their highest amount of entertainment, travel, and vacationing during this stage.

2. **Slow-Go.** This stage generally occurs between ages 70 and 84. While still active, travel and activity begin to slow down during this phase, accompanied by a commensurate reduction in expenses. I recommend that clients plan their *second* highest amount of entertainment, travel, and vacationing during this stage.

3. **No-Go.** At age 85 and older, significant changes in retirement lifestyle typically arise due to declining health. This is the primary reason I recommend planning more entertainment, travel, and activity during the first two-thirds of your retirement.

FIGURE 0.4. **Key Retiree Risks**

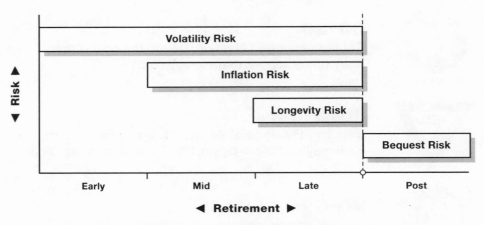

Source: "Building Efficient Retirement Income Portfolios"
Morningstar Working Paper by David Blanchett.

Figure 0.4, *Key Retiree Risks*, shows the big picture of the risks you will face over your household's "retirement lifetime." As you progress through time, you will face *four* significant risks throughout retirement (and beyond). The first is "Volatility Risk," which permeates your entire retirement plan, but is especially acute during the first five to ten years of retirement. For example, imagine the stock market dropping 20% or more right after you retire. (In future chapters I will cover in more detail the specific "Needs" Bucket in my DiNuzzo Money Bucket Stack Analysis™ (DMBSA™) which specifically addresses this challenge.)

Next comes "Inflation Risk." Over the course of an archetypal 30-year retirement plan, inflation risk is not lucidly as noticeable during the first 10 years, but escalates rapidly as a formidable obstacle during the remaining 20 years. Often individual investors are over-weighted on conservative sources for retirement income, such as CDs, money market funds, and bonds. These types of investments predominantly have a short-term negative "real rate of return" when you subtract inflation from the investment's rate of return. This negative rate of return reduces the retirees' purchasing power *every year* they are alive. In other words, again, they are "losing money safely and slowly." Future chapters will explain more about how the "Wants" Bucket in the DiNuzzo Money Bucket Stack Analysis™ (DMBSA™) provides a solution to this retirement nemesis.

"Longevity Risk" is, ironically, the risk inherent in living a long life. The longer you live, the more money you will need to support yourself/household. The multifaceted analysis you will find throughout the remainder of my book specifically takes this risk into account. In my investment strategy, this risk will be managed with my "Needs," "Wants," and "Dreams/Wishes" Buckets of the DiNuzzo Money Bucket Stack Analysis™.

The remaining testamentary/legacy risk is one that manifests itself *after* you and your spouse/partner are deceased—"Bequest Risk." Many individuals desire that a specific amount of money or range of assets be left to their beneficiaries, heirs, and/or charities. Bequest Risk increases as a result of poor investing and/or retirement income planning, resulting in underfunding your legacy goals. The "Dreams/Wishes" Bucket of my DiNuzzo Money Bucket Stack Analysis™ addresses this risk.

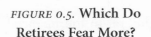

FIGURE 0.5. **Which Do Retirees Fear More?**

As you can easily observe in Figure 0.5, *Which Do Retirees Fear More?*, addressing your investment plan and retirement income plan is no casual matter. For the typical retiree, a suboptimal outcome is literally feared more than death itself. My entire book is dedicated to ameliorating this challenge that stands before you.

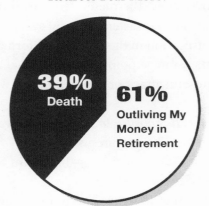

Source: *Allianz Life Insurance Companies of North America.*

Media "Noise" Is Everywhere

By day we write about "Six Funds to Buy Now!"...By night we invest in sensible index funds. Unfortunately pro-index fund stories don't sell magazines.
>   —Anonymous, *Fortune*, April 26, 1999

It is difficult to get a man to understand something when his salary depends upon his not understanding it.
>   —Upton Sinclair, 1935

You make more money selling advice than following it. It's one of the things we count on in the magazine business—along with the short memory of our readers.
>   —Steve Forbes, publisher of *Forbes* magazine, from
>   a presentation at the Anderson School, University
>   of California—Los Angeles, April 15, 2003

In addition to the financial challenges of investing a portfolio successfully over time, the media tends to promote an investing approach that leads to financial disaster, virtually every time. During a presentation at an academic institution in the state of California (quoted above), Steve Forbes summed up the vantage point of the financial media quite well. Media noise and its purposeful attack on your emotions will provide another formidable foe.

It is absurd to think that the general public can ever make money out of market forecasts.
>   —Benjamin Graham, *The Intelligent Investor* (1949)

The traditional model of investing has historically focused on many factors beyond and outside of your control, such as stock picking, hot managers, market timing, and the financial press. As you will discover in my following chapters, there is no crystal ball and no one has tomorrow's newspaper—but the good news is that you do not need either to be successful. My mantra for investing success is "control what you can control" and then relax.

FIGURE 0.6. The Traditional View of Investing

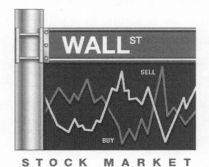

The traditional model focuses on factors you ... can't control:

- **STOCK PICKING**
- **HOT MANAGERS**
- **MARKET TIMING**
- **FINANCIAL MEDIA**

There is no crystal ball or tomorrow's newspaper, but the good news is ... *You don't need it!*

I think the most important factor in getting out of the recession actually is just the regenerative capacity of American capitalism, and we had many recessions of the history in this country when nobody ever heard of fiscal policy or monetary policy. The country always comes back.

—Warren Buffett, CNBC's Squawk Box, September 23, 2010

FIGURE 0.7. "Capitalism 101"

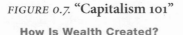

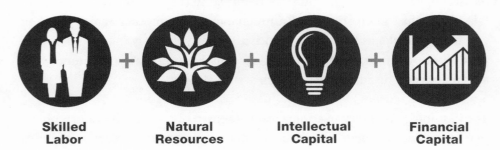

In Figure 0.7, "*Capitalism 101*," I have represented the most successful economic model in the history of mankind: capitalism. By capitalism I mean open and free markets in which a free people engage in commerce by producing goods and services for their fellow man. Not only has this model been the most successful economically and produced the highest level of lifestyle wealth in history, it has also done more to enhance the human condition and assist the less fortunate than any other model in world history. My investment strategy for investing, LifePlanning, and retirement income success will be based upon this model, which has enabled our country, the United States of America, to go from "worst to first" in less than 250 years. Through an ever-evolving process of "creative destruction," American capitalism remains the most successful model for economic growth across the globe.

> *Experience conclusively shows that index-fund buyers are likely to obtain results exceeding those of the typical fund manager, whose large advisory fees and substantial portfolio turnover tend to reduce investment yields. Many people will find the guarantee of playing the stock-market game at par every round a very attractive one. The index fund is a sensible, serviceable method for obtaining the market's rate of return with absolutely no effort and minimal expense.*
> —Burton G. Malkiel, from *The Little Book of Common Sense Investing* by John C. Bogle

In Figure 0.8, *Active vs. Passive Investment*, I have juxtaposed a direct comparison of active investing and passive investing (i.e., index investing). I will talk about this much more in future chapters, but another major decision you need to make as the Family CIO is whether you are going to index your portfolio or attempt to beat the market. This Figure helps you compare the advantages and disadvantages of each systematically.

The first major category of comparison is return objective. The return objective for active managers is to beat the market, where the objective of index investing is to obtain the market rate of return for the index or Asset Class (segment of the market) targeted for investing and holding in your portfolio.

FIGURE 0.8. **Active vs. Passive Investment**

	ACTIVE INVESTMENT	**PASSIVE INVESTMENT**
Return Objective	Beat a market	Obtain the return of a market, index or asset class
Style Definition	55% drift from classification	Pure and consistent classification
Average Equity Fund Investor Return over 20 yrs.	5.29% per year according to Dalbar for 20-year period ending 2017	S&P 500 = 7.20% annualized return
Approach	Stock Picking, Time Picking, Manager Picking, or Style Drifting	Buy, hold and rebalance a globally diversified portfolio of index funds
Taxes	Higher Taxes (about 20-40% of return over 10 years)	Lower Taxes (about 10% of the return over 10 years)
Portfolio Turnover	Turnover of approximately 65% in 2017 for 100% in stock mutual funds	Turnover of approximately 16% in 2017 for a 100% stock index portfolio
Net Performance	Expected to lag the index return by expenses and mistakes. Higher taxes may result from more frequent realizing of capital gains	The index return minus low fees, low taxes, and sometimes, tracking error
Proponents	Virtually all brokerage firms, mutual fund companies, market timing services, hedge funds, investment press and brokerage training programs	The Univ. of Chicago, Nobel Prize recipients, Vanguard Group, Dimensional Fund Advisors, Barclays Global Investors, Warren Buffett, and Charles Schwab
Analytical Techniques	Art – Qualitative, disregard for risk, forecasting, predicting the future, feelings, intuition, luck, betting, gambling and speculation	Science – Quantitative, risk management, long-term statistical analysis, accurate performance measurements, rules based
State of Mind	Stressed	Relaxed

Source: Index Funds, The 12-Step Recovery Program for Active Investors.
Mark T. Hebner, Dalbar, SPIVA, Greenwich Research, John Bogle.

Regarding style definition, active mutual fund stock managers generally have approximately a 55% drift from their classification, which means that if they are classified as a US Large Cap Value manager, they generally only have 45% of US Large Cap Value stock holdings in their portfolio, while 55% of their holdings would be in a different stock Asset Class (think oranges, bananas, and pears mixed into your supposedly all-apple basket). The indexing style definition provides purer and more consistent exposure, which is what you will desire for success.

When you look at the track record of the average equity (stock) return for the average individual managing their own all-equity portfolio, you see an annual return of 5.29% per year, according to Dalbar Research, for the 20-year period ending 2017. When compared to the s&p 500® index return over the same period of 7.20%, index investing has provided significant benefits. The approach of active investing focuses on stock picking, time picking, manager picking, and/or style drifting. In contrast, my approach regarding index investing and strategic allocation is to buy, hold, and with discipline systematically rebalance a globally diversified portfolio of index funds customized to your unique situation.

Regarding taxes, active investing funds generally produce high taxes, ranging from 20% to 40% of the total return over a recent 10-year period. Index funds, on the other hand, generally produce low taxes, about 10% of the total return over the same recent 10-year period ending on December 31, 2017. The portfolio turnover for 100% in active stock mutual funds in the year 2017 was approximately 65%, while index stock fund turnover that same year was around 16%. The net performance of active managers was materially below their comparable index due to the amount of fees, expenses, taxes, and mistakes. Index funds' higher returns have been enhanced due to lower fees, lower taxes, and low tracking error.

Individual investors recently held approximately 74% of their stock mutual funds in active equity/stock funds, whereas index/passive investments for individual investors is currently approximately 26% and growing.

Active stock mutual fund investors, or those who attempt to "outsmart" or "beat" the stock market, and index investors are diametrically opposed in approach. Regarding active investing, the proponents are virtually all brokerage firms, mutual fund companies, market timing services, the investment press, newsletters, social media, and brokerage training programs. Proponents of index investing, as you will see reinforced many times throughout my book, include the University of Chicago Booth Graduate Business School and its related research, Nobel Prize recipients, Dimensional Fund Advisors (DFA), the Vanguard Group, Barclays Global Investors, and Warren Buffett.

Regarding analytical techniques, active investing is more of a subjective "art," based on qualitative formulas, disregard for risk, forecasting, predicting the future, feelings, intuition, luck, betting, gambling, and speculation. Index investing is more of an objective science, based on quantitative formulas, risk management, long-term statistical analysis, accurate performance measurements, and evidence.

> *Fiduciaries should strongly consider index funds as an alternative to actively managed funds. Index funds incur about 80% less in transaction costs than actively managed funds...long-term returns for actively managed funds trail their respective indexes.*
> —Michael C. Keenan, "The Elephant in the Living Room," *Financial Advisor* magazine

FIGURE 0.9. **Why Invest in a Portfolio of Indexed Funds?**

Because You *OBTAIN*...	Because You *AVOID*...
Market rates of returns, less fees, expenses and taxes	Speculation through stock, time, manager and style picking
Increased Diversification	Unrewarded Concentration
More than 90 years of Risk and Return Data	Silent Partners and below market rate of returns
Style Purity, Asset Allocation Consistency	Style Drift, Asset Allocation Shift
Relaxation	Stress

Source: ®2018 Index Fund Advisors. Inc. Sources, Updates, and Disclosures: ifabt.com.

Figure 0.9, *Why Invest in a Portfolio of Indexed Funds?* includes a summary of the benefits of index investing: you can obtain market rates of returns with lower fees, expenses, and taxes; increased diversification, style purity, and consistency in Asset Allocation; and an extraordinary long track record with reliable data going back to before the Great Depression. You get to avoid speculation through stock, time, manager, and style picking; unrewarded concentration and concentrated positions within an active portfolio; the high expense of "silent partners" (who siphon off fees and expenses) that result in below-market rates of return; and the style drift and Asset Allocation shift that characterizes active management. Because my *Seven Keys to Investing Success* is based on index investing, it can produce a more relaxed investor state of mind, versus the stress which often accompanies frenetic, active investing.

FIGURE 0.10. **The Big Picture of Your Roadmap for Retirement Success (The Remainder of This Book)**

Source: *DiNuzzo Private Wealth, Inc. (DPW)/DiNuzzo Wealth Management (DWM).*

Figure 0.10, *The Big Picture of Your Roadmap for Retirement Success*, provides a bird's eye view of the successful strategy you will follow throughout the rest of my book. The largest variables to manage are emotions management (Behavioral Coaching), financial life planning, and investment management, which, if handled properly, can allow you to enjoy personal financial success. My book will show you how to consistently choose the most probable pathway for success among dozens and dozens of decisions at every "crossroad" or "fork" in the road along your retirement planning/investment "highway."

Making the most well informed and best decision at every crossroad materially increases your chance of arriving successfully at your destination.

FIGURE 0.11. **Your Personal Finance House™**

"Yes, You Have One...Everyone Does!"

Source: DiNuzzo Private Wealth, Inc. (DPW)/DiNuzzo Wealth Management (DWM).

When I meet with individuals, spouses, or partners, I typically like to remind them that it's my belief that everyone in life is or has the opportunity to be an expert, great, or very good at *something*, but typically does not have the ability to be an equal expert at multiple and/or other different disciplines in life. I have enjoyed professional relationships with extremely intelligent clients over my decades in business—such as professors, engineers, scientists, attorneys, accountants, and entrepreneurs—and they are truly experts in their respective fields, but typically not experts anywhere *near* the same level regarding the discipline of personal finance and the elements that comprise optimal investing and Financial Wellness LifePlanning.

I remind every one of my clients that they have a "Personal Finance House™," and yes, you have one, too. Everyone does. However, even the brightest individuals I have met with have often been remiss in having even a basic understanding of what it means to create the proper foundation and structure to keep their personal finances in order.

You have a one-of-a-kind personal finance house. The good news is, as in most things in life, knowing the challenge is over half the battle. In this instance, knowing you have a personal finance house and that you need a plan to create the proper structure is the beginning of understanding how to put your financial house in order.

FIGURE 0.12. **Your DiNuzzo Customized Personal Finance House™: The Four Corner Rooms**

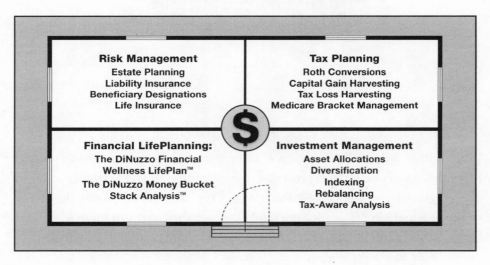

Source: *DiNuzzo Private Wealth, Inc. (DPW)/DiNuzzo Wealth Management (DWM).*

Once you have acknowledged that you have a personal financial house that's unique to you, the next step is to take a good look at, and study, the "rooms" inside. If you had a bird's eye view and were to lift the roof and take a look inside, you'd notice there are four primary rooms in your house, as shown in Figure 0.12, *Your DiNuzzo Customized Personal Finance House™: "The Four Corner Rooms."*

Starting in the upper left-hand corner is what I refer to as the "Risk Management" corner room. This room handles any and all topics around risk management, the most important of which would certainly be Estate Planning and all related documents, wills, trusts, power of attorneys, living wills, and so on. The next category in this room is Insurance, including but not limited to auto insurance, homeowner's insurance, umbrella insurance, and of course life insurance. The final, major category in this room is Beneficiary Designations such as those on IRAS, Roth IRAS, 401(k)s, and 403(b)s. Remember, these are the "controlling legal documents" regarding the ultimate distribution of these assets. If your beneficiary designation conflicts with language in your will, the beneficiary designation on these types of accounts that you have entered is going to take precedence. Simply, these beneficiary designations are more powerful than the language in your will.

You will enter the Risk Management room the least frequently compared to the other rooms in your personal finance house, but any decisions in here have an exceptional magnitude of importance and need to be thought over long and hard. There are *significant* strategic decisions that need to be made in this room. There are typically other items in the Risk Management room, but these are the most important ones you need to consider first.

Moving to the right, you'll see the Tax Planning room. In tax planning, there are approximately 80 to 90 major tax planning strategies available, but normally only a couple dozen that are applicable to the average investor. These topics are well beyond standard tax return preparation. In tax planning, you will benefit from a proactive mentality, working on strategies before the end of the year and prior to the end of the tax season to reduce taxes when the return is compiled the following year. I've listed some major categories again, but there are typically two to three dozen topics that are applicable for the average investor and of course, some of them are not applicable year-to-year. There may be an opportunity that comes up once every 10 years, but nonetheless, the major considerations for tax planning are Roth IRA Conversions, Capital Gain Harvesting, Harvesting Capital Losses, Tax Bracket Management,

Medicare Bracket Management, Income Smoothing, Tax-Aware Investing, and Nonqualified Tax Deferred Annuities just to list a few of the more common tax planning strategies.

There's sort of a bright line running horizontally across the middle of the house with two rooms representing "DiNuzzo Financial Wellness LifePlanning™" and "Investment Management." Our Registered Investment Advisory practice averages 50 to 60 hours in these rooms every week from start to finish.

I consider the "DiNuzzo Financial Wellness LifePlanning™" room, in the bottom left-hand side of my image, to be the most important room. It's the "General Manager" and *strategic driver* for the entire house. There has to be a centralized plan and strategy, and that is where the "The DiNuzzo Financial Wellness LifePlan™" resides, and the point of collaboration where all the decisions are made for the other rooms in the house. It's where we practice our fundamental goal of "empowering our clients to make smart money Best-Life choices." "The DiNuzzo Financial Wellness LifePlan™" is the vehicle that allows people to travel proactively through the Financial Wellness LifePlanning process.

I will talk at length throughout my book regarding Efficient Market Theory (EMT) and the power of indexing in stock mutual funds, as well as bond mutual funds. Here in the Investment Management room, I've listed five macroeconomic categories of utmost importance for a successful Financial Wellness LifePlan: customized Asset Allocations, full and proper diversification, indexing, Tax-Aware investing, and a structured and disciplined rebalancing strategy.

All four rooms in your personal financial house are of mission-critical importance, but the "magic happens" when there is harmony and synergy between these four rooms and when they work together with a single mission of empowering smart money and Best-Life choices under a strong Fiduciary Standard.

FIGURE 0.13. **Your DiNuzzo Customized Personal Finance House™: The Foundation**

"The Foundation" = Assets, Liabilities, Income & Expenses

Source: DiNuzzo Private Wealth, Inc. (DPW)/DiNuzzo Wealth Management (DWM).

Coming out of the "bird's eye" view, we'll take a look at the final view of your customized personal finance house—the "worm's eye" granular view illustrated in Figure 0.13, *Your DiNuzzo Customized Personal Finance House™: "The Foundation."* Remember the basic concept that any structure is only as solid as its footer, or foundation. The foundation for every individual's personal finance house is their unique assets, liabilities, Net Worth, income, and expenses. Knowing the specific values, and equally important "flavors" of these various key elements is mission critical to your long-term success. The footer and foundation provide your unique base information that we use in compiling every client's customized "DiNuzzo Financial Wellness LifePlan™."

The DiNuzzo Financial Wellness LifePlan™ or "DFWLP™" is a comprehensive plan that we develop for our clients. This book does not intend to cover that entire plan but rather the investment component of the plan, with a focus on financial planning, tax planning, and cash flow management, specifically as it relates to financial independence and retirement.

I believe everyone deserves to know and follow the financial advice of the best minds in the field of Modern Finance, and that's what you'll find in my book. My research and information "stands on the shoulders of giants," and some of these giants include Nobel Laureates William F. Sharpe, Merton Miller, Harry Markowitz, Paul Samuelson, Daniel Kahneman, Myron Scholes, and Eugene Fama; Professors Kenneth French, Terrence Thomas Odean, and Burton G. Malkiel; financial luminaries David Booth, Rex Sinquefield, Benjamin Graham, Warren Buffett, John C. "Jack" Bogle, Roger Ibbotson, Charles D. Ellis, Dr. William Bernstein, and Mark T. Hebner; Dimensional Fund Advisors' research department; and the University of Chicago Booth Graduate Business School.

My book follows a somewhat unusual format, as you may have noticed. Each chapter will begin with a clear explanation of the key in the process and the principles behind it. The remainder of the chapter will present the data and insights directly from the expert sources to provide the evidence. In my experience working with many different client personalities, I have found over my four-decade professional career that some people learn best through text and stories. Some learn best through images. And still others learn best through numbers, charts, and graphs. My goal is to present this information in as many ways as necessary in order to connect it to *your unique learning style.*

Also, you'll see many quotes directly from Nobel Prize winners, academics, and investment luminaries—far more than is typical. This is intentional. I often tell clients that I'm doing my job well when they don't hear my voice coming out of my mouth—they hear the voice of the "giants" I've learned from. I want to be sure you also hear the voices of these "giants" directly from their own mouths—it's best you hear it directly from them, in some cases over and over, because I know from experience it is likely the opposite of what you have heard all of your life. My primary goal is *financial education*, and I want you to learn it directly from the source, the same way that I did. You just don't know what you don't know. This book can be your sourcebook and reference book for investing and retirement income success that you can return to again and again, especially when the media "noise" gets loud and you may need a reminder of the well-paved path to investing success and enjoy your investment experience.

Although every individual's personal finance situation is as unique as their DNA, my approach always includes the same *Seven Keys to Investing Success*. These "seven keys," and the principles behind them, not only come from Nobel Prize-winning research, nearly a century of financial data, and ethical principles, but they also come from the school of hard knocks. Every less-than-optimal investment decision I have made in my retail (1979–1988) and institutional (1989–2019) investment lifetime has occurred when I have disregarded or veered away from any of the fundamental philosophies espoused in my book.

Specifically, *Seven Keys* and related chapters will comprise your roadmap to a successful investment experience:

1. **The First Key**: Are You a Do-It-Yourselfer or a Delegator?

2. **The Second (and Most Important) Key**: Have a Plan

3. **The Third Key**: Strategic ("Buy and Hold") vs. Tactical ("Market Timing") Asset Allocation: *Placing the Odds in Your Favor*

4. **The Fourth Key**: Diversification to Maximize Reward vs. Risk

5. **The Fifth Key**: Indexing vs. Active Investment Management: *Making Efficient Market Theory Work for You*

6. **The Sixth Key**: Rebalancing: *Rules for Buying and Selling Your Investments*

7. **The Seventh (and Equally Most Important) Key**: Managing Your Emotions: *With a Plan and Discipline*

Relax. That's what investing and retirement should be like. Planning for it doesn't have to be stressful. If you take your responsibility seriously as the Family Chief Investment Officer (FCIO), and simply follow my "keys" step-by-step, you can rid yourself of investing anxiety and be free to enjoy your investment experience…and…relax.

ARE YOU A DO-IT-YOURSELFER OR A DELEGATOR?

The Seven Keys to Investing Success apply to every investor, from Do-It-Yourselfers to Delegators. Knowing your "Investor DNA" is the first key toward making the best decisions for your household and a successful retirement.

People normally do not describe themselves in terms of their Investor DNA, and you may not even be aware of the type of investor you are. However, understanding your strengths and weaknesses and what "makes you tick" can help you determine whether you're a Do-It-Yourselfer, a Delegator, or somewhere in between. To help you figure this out, let's look at the nine distinct High-Net-Worth Personality Types.

HIGH-NET-WORTH PERSONALITY TYPES

FIGURE 1.1. The Nine High-Net-Worth Personalities

FAMILY STEWARDS	THE ANONYMOUS	ACCUMULATORS
• Dominant focus to take care of their families. • Conservative in personal and professional life. • Not very knowledgeable about investing.	• Confidentiality is their prominent concern. • Prize privacy for their financial efforts. • Likely to concentrate assets with a financial advisor who protects them.	• Focused on making portfolios bigger. • Investments are performance-oriented. • Tend to live below their means and spend frugally.
INDEPENDENTS	MOGULS	GAMBLERS
• Seek the personal freedom money makes possible. • Feel investing is a necessary means to an end. • Not interested in the process of investing or wealth management.	• Control is a primary concern. • Investing is another way of extending personal power. • Decisive in decisions and rarely look back.	• Enjoy investing for the excitement of it. • Tend to be very knowledgeable and involved. • Exhibit a high risk tolerance.
PHOBIC	VIPS	INNOVATORS
• Are confused and frustrated by the responsibility of wealth. • Dislike managing finance and avoid technical discussions of it. • Choose financial advisors based on level of personal trust they feel.	• Investing results in ability to purchase status possessions. • Prestige is important. • Like to affiliate with institutions and financial advisors with leading reputations.	• Focused on leading-edge products and services. • Sophisticated investors who like complex products. • Tend to be technically savvy and highly educated.

Source: CEG Worldwide.

Each of the nine High-Net-Worth Personality Types exhibits unique traits, has specific priorities, and takes different approaches toward life, money, and investing. Three of these types comprise Delegators (the first column), three more comprise Do-It-Yourselfers (the last column), and in the middle column are three that can fall into either category.

The Delegators

Typical Delegator investor personalities are described as either *Family Stewards*, *Independents*, or *Phobics*. While each type displays distinct differences, all three investor personalities in the Delegator category prefer primarily to rely on a trusted advisor to help guide their investment decisions.

FIGURE 1.2. **Distribution of the High-Net-Worth Personalities.**

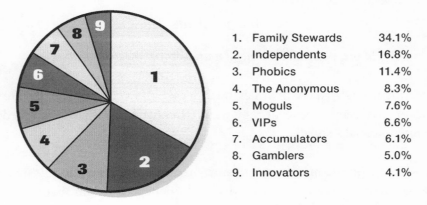

1.	Family Stewards	34.1%
2.	Independents	16.8%
3.	Phobics	11.4%
4.	The Anonymous	8.3%
5.	Moguls	7.6%
6.	VIPs	6.6%
7.	Accumulators	6.1%
8.	Gamblers	5.0%
9.	Innovators	4.1%

N = 1,417 affluent individuals

Source: Russ Alan Prince and David Geradoti, Cultivating the Middle-Class Millionaire, *2005.*

Family Stewards

"Good financial management lets me take good care of my family."

This is the largest group of affluent individuals, making up more than 34% of High-Net-Worth investors. The Family Steward's primary financial concern is taking care of their family. The majority of their financial goals are tied to larger family issues, such as assisting children and grandchildren, paying for college, or transferring wealth to the next generation.

This investor personality type is prudent, careful, and protective of their family and their milestones, goals, and objectives. They appreciate the importance of investment planning and management and want goal-based planning that will improve their financial position.

Family Stewards typically have not spent an excessive amount of time building their knowledge of Wealth Management. They need guidance from someone with a high level of expertise who can provide the services that will allow them to fulfill their primary goal of caring for their family.

Independents

"To me, successful financial management means freedom."

Independent High-Net-Worth Personalities overtly want the freedom to do whatever they want whenever they want. They seek to achieve this freedom through financial security.

Successful corporate managers and entrepreneurs often fall into this investor personality type. They dream of individual financial freedom that will allow them to pursue their desired lifestyle, hobbies, or travel. Independents often want to retire early to pursue their life's interests.

Like Family Stewards, Independent investor personalities also do not spend an excessive amount of time developing their financial knowledge and sophistication, and due to this shortfall, they often seek out a financial advisor to assist them. They understand the importance of investment planning and management, and their goal in delegating is to gain investment advice that will allow them to achieve financial freedom.

Phobics

"The last thing I want to talk about is my money."

Phobic investors don't want to deal with their money and they don't want to learn how to deal with their money. This High-Net-Worth Personality Type prefers to delegate the management of their financial affairs to a trusted Wealth Manager.

A common challenge for the phobic is that they tend to make decisions—including choosing a financial advisor—based on their emotions, or "gut feelings," rather than following a proper vetting process. Their aversion to discussing financial matters can make it a struggle for their trusted advisor to get them to participate in building a successful strategy that caters to their investing and retirement goals.

DELEGATORS: JOSEPH AND FREDA

Joseph is a supply chain manager and Freda is a teacher's aide. The married couple came to see me for a "Discovery Meeting," where prospective clients get to know me and the firm at DiNuzzo Private Wealth, Inc. (DPW)/DiNuzzo Wealth Management (DWM). The initial meeting allows us to see if we're a good fit for one another. If we are and if there's a possibility of collaborating, we set up a second meeting called a "Plan Presentation Meeting."

Halfway through the first meeting, Joseph stopped me. He turned to Freda and said, "Honey, I know you've always trusted me to handle our investments. Throughout our adult lives, I've been solely in charge of our investments. We've had relationships with three other investment firms that didn't work out, but none of those firms did what P.J. is describing right now. I've heard enough to know this is a perfect fit. It's what we need *right now*."

Freda agreed, and we were able to move forward and develop a customized DiNuzzo Financial Wellness LifePlan™ that satisfied all their life goals and retirement plans. More importantly, Joseph could rest easy, knowing that my Fiduciary-based firm has, for four decades, considered our work and client relationships a "sacred responsibility" and will place his and his wife's best interests first and foremost in their investment plan.

THE SEVEN KEYS TO INVESTING SUCCESS

Joseph was clearly a Delegator. Though he was an excellent supply chain manager, he wasn't comfortable making life planning, financial planning, tax planning, and investment decisions that would affect him and his wife, Freda, for the rest of their lives. Once he realized that we shared the same core beliefs, and that I was very capable of empowering him to make smart money and Best-Life choices regarding their financial future, Joseph was thrilled to accept my guidance.

If you've had a bad experience with a wealth manager, investment advisor, or stockbroker, do not let that color your attitude toward all advisors. Each firm is different, and trying to be a Do-It-Yourselfer when you are clearly a Delegator could cost you a lot of money *and* a lot of sleepless nights. If you are a Delegator, accept that it's in your DNA to rely on a trusted advisor. Then, perform your personal due diligence and find the advisor that's the right fit for you.

DO-IT-YOURSELFERS

Do-It-Yourself investor personalities include *Accumulators*, *Gamblers*, and *Innovators*.

Accumulators

"You can never be too rich or too thin, but being rich matters more."

Accumulators typically save more than they spend. They tend to live well below their means and not display any outward signs of wealth. Accumulators enjoy watching their investments grow and are most comfortable when their capital is appreciating. They often are averse to spending money and abhor paying professional fees and expenses. They are often described as being "tight with their dollars." Thus, they are very focused and obsessed with fees and performance and often their assessment and degree of success is tied directly and solely to their overall performance. Accumulators typically are self-directed Do-It-Yourselfers.

Gamblers

"You have better odds playing the market than in Vegas."

Gamblers love the excitement and drama of investing. For Gamblers, investing is part of their life and because of this, they are often the most performance-sensitive of all the High-Net-Worth Personalities. Gamblers are typically very knowledgeable about investing and confident in the concept of their ability to beat the market. Not surprisingly, they often have a higher than usual tolerance for risk. Gamblers are self-directed Do-It-Yourselfers when it comes to investing.

Innovators

"Options and derivatives are the best thing that ever happened."

Innovators are extremely knowledgeable and often at the cutting edge of investment management and technology. They enjoy new products, innovative services, and complex analytical methods. They typically have highly technical backgrounds. Like Accumulators and Gamblers, people with this High-Net-Worth Personality Type are self-directed Do-It-Yourself investors.

DO-IT-YOURSELFERS: FRED AND JANE

Fred is an engineer and Jane is an executive assistant for a large corporation. The married couple met with me for an initial "Discovery Meeting," and I knew from the start that they could benefit from the services of DiNuzzo Private Wealth, Inc. (DPW)/DiNuzzo Wealth Management (DWM) *immediately*, and over time. We were an excellent match for their needs.

From an investment perspective, 100% of their portfolios were in actively managed mutual funds, versus index funds. There was no rhyme or reason to their wide-ranging Asset Allocations across their various accounts, and plenty of red flags including under-diversification and high expenses.

In our second meeting, the "Plan Presentation," I presented them with a customized DiNuzzo Financial Wellness LifePlan™ tailored to their situation, which included a diversified investment strategy that would increase their growth probabilities, lower their risk, and *significantly* lower their investment expenses while putting them on a path to financial stability in retirement.

Though it was clear that Fred and Jane needed my help, we came to an impasse at the end of the meeting. They were not ready to move forward and Fred asked me to give him some time to think it over. I gave him a month and checked back in, and he was still thinking about it. A month later, I called again. The couple still was not ready to accept my Financial Wellness guidance. Here is what I told Fred on that call:

"Fred, I'm always looking to see if our firm is the 'right fit' for any prospective client that we meet. After getting to know each other very well, I am confident that our firm is a *great* fit for you and Jane, and your future. What are the obstacles at this time that are keeping you from engaging us at DiNuzzo Private Wealth?"

Fred said, "P.J., honestly, I *know* you can do better than I can. I *know* that, when it comes to life planning and investing, I'm not anywhere near as educated or experienced as you are, and I don't have the accumulated wisdom of your firm. It *does* bother me, and I *am* conflicted, knowing that not having the right strategy could end up costing me hundreds of thousands of dollars. It bothers me a *lot*. But the thought of paying you, or *anyone*, any money—no matter how much money your advice could make me or save me—just doesn't *feel* right to me. I would actually lose sleep over it."

"Well," I told him, "there's your answer, and it's the correct answer. You're self-directed, and you've been self-directed all your life. There's nothing wrong with that—it's just who you are."

Know your Investor DNA. Trusting your investment strategy to a Fiduciary-based advisor could save you hundreds of thousands of dollars, but you need to be comfortable with delegating.

DELEGATORS *OR* DO-IT-YOURSELFERS

Anonymous, *Moguls*, and *VIPs* comprise the final three High-Net-Worth Personality Types. People who represent these High-Net-Worth Personalities may be Delegators *or* they may be Do-It-Yourselfers, but all three have unique, specific traits that distinguish them from one another.

Anonymous

"My money is my business, and no one else's."

This type of investor is intensely private. They do not like to disclose their financial positions, or even any type of personal information, to anyone. The collaborative relationship required for them to work successfully with a financial advisor can succeed only if they have complete trust in their advisor and know that their information will be held in the highest confidence.

The Anonymous investors may be Do-It-Yourselfers or Delegators, and their decision often relies on whether they are able to find a Wealth Advisor they truly trust.

Moguls

"Being rich means power."

Moguls are motivated by control, influence, and power in their lives, and leveraging their life's work. By definition, if they choose to delegate, they are most comfortable having a feeling of being in total control of the investment relationship.

Mogul personalities understand the importance of Asset Allocation and investment management, and they enjoy wielding control over their investments—either by doing it themselves or delegating financial management to an advisor. Moguls typically have a keen interest in wealth protection. They can easily be Do-It-Yourselfers or Delegators.

VIPs

"There are a lot of ways to get respect, and having money is one of them."

These High-Net-Worth Personality Types have typically worked hard to gain prestige and the respect of others. Due to their lifestyle, they typically are in need of a focus on Wealth Management. The VIP's strongest interest often lies in wealth protection services and in charitable giving. Like the others in this category, they could be Do-It-Yourselfers or Delegators.

As in any management position, the first decision you need to make as Family CIO is how much of this responsibility you want to delegate and how much you want to do yourself. Before I get started on your *Seven Keys to Investing Success*, we need to identify what metaphorical car you're going to be driving.

In my experience with clients, I generally see three investment personalities: Delegators, Validators, and Do-It-Yourselfers.

FIGURE 1.3. **Types of Investors: The Importance of Your Seating Choice.**

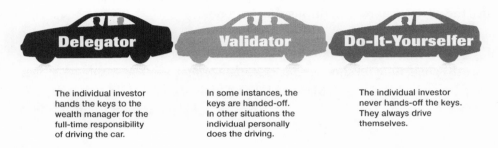

The individual investor hands the keys to the wealth manager for the full-time responsibility of driving the car.

In some instances, the keys are handed-off. In other situations the individual personally does the driving.

The individual investor never hands-off the keys. They always drive themselves.

Source: DiNuzzo Private Wealth, Inc. (DPW)/DiNuzzo Wealth Management (DWM).

Delegators are individual investors who prefer to fully delegate the responsibility of managing their portfolio or portfolios and providing Financial LifePlanning and Wealth Management advice to a Wealth Advisor or Wealth Advisor practice (approximately three-quarters of our clients). Delegators typically do not have the "will, skill, or time" to manage their own investments. Validators, meanwhile, are those who prefer to delegate some of the responsibility to a Wealth Advisor they have hired, making some of their portfolio investment choices and financial planning decisions themselves (approximately one-fourth of our clients). For example, with a $2 million portfolio, a Delegator client would give us the entire $2 million to manage, while a Validator would give us $1,000,000 and manage the other $1,000,000 personally. Finally, Do-It-Yourselfers are exactly what you'd expect: they delegate *none* of the responsibility to a Wealth Manager or a financial advisor and always manage 100% of their portfolio or portfolios. Although none of our firm's clients are Do-It-Yourselfers for obvious reasons, I have noticed that the Do-It-Yourself tendency *can* change over time. Some investors, for example, may start out as Do-It-Yourselfers, but as they get older, either due to unexpected burdens such as an illness in the family or simply due to the sheer size and complexity of Financial Wellness LifePlanning and their portfolio upon retirement, they may choose to fully or partially engage professional services as a kind of "insurance policy." Either way, it's very important that you identify the type of car you're driving down this road for investment management and retirement income success, because it will impact how you put into practice the advice you receive throughout my book.

> *Return generation is the responsibility of the market, which sets prices to compensate investors for the risks they bear.*
> —Marlena I. Lee, Dimensional Funds Advisors (DFA), "Rebalancing and Returns"

IDENTIFY YOUR INVESTOR DNA

Figure out if you're a Do-It-Yourselfer or a Delegator.

If you are a Do-It-Yourselfer, enjoy this book and I wish you the best of luck with your investments.

If you are a Delegator, you have a choice to make. You can choose to trust your investments to a product salesperson/retail broker, or an independent Fiduciary-based Wealth Manager.

Product Salespeople/Retail Brokers

Product salespeople and retail brokers are, typically, *commissioned* agents who are compensated by a third party or by their firm *for selling you investment products*. Despite the descriptions on their website such as "best interests" or the titles on their business cards, product salespeople and retail brokers should not be confused with independent Fiduciary-based advisors. Understanding the difference between how people in the two categories are compensated is mission critical.

The product salesperson/retail broker's first and foremost duty is typically to themselves and their firm and not to you, *even though you are the customer/ client*. Wealth management and planning work are incidental to their primary focus of selling products and or generating commissions and/or trades. This introduces an immediate and egregious conflict of interest. Historically, regulators have done a poor job of policing the myriad of titles and practices these people use. The more research you do to understand their firms and their products, the more likely you are to become confused about what, exactly, they are going to do for you.

Independent Fiduciary-Based Advisors

In contrast to product salespeople and retail brokers, independent Fiduciary-based Wealth Advisors are always morally and legally required to act as fiduciaries to their clients, meaning *they must always put their client's best interests first*. Because there is no inherent conflict of interest, independent Fiduciary-based advisors are significantly better aligned with their clients' goals.

Independent advisors do not receive a commission based on selling their clients' conflicted products. Instead, they typically calculate their fee as a percentage of the amount of money they manage for you, the client investor. Due to the benefits of economies of scale, the percentage fee typically declines as your account size increases.

An independent Fiduciary-based advisor's compensation may be described in a straightforward, transparent, and easy to understand fashion. This is how DiNuzzo Private Wealth, Inc. (DPW)/DiNuzzo Wealth Management (DWM) operates. Unlike salespeople, our Wealth Management Firm only receives compensation from you and no one else, allowing us to maintain our objectivity. For safety, the custody of your assets is with a "household name," third-party custodian such as TD Ameritrade, Charles Schwab & Co., or Fidelity Investments, who serve as the safe-keeper of your investments. These custodians are responsible for ensuring your investments and your money are in a *separate* account under *your* name, and that your advisor has no access to your account and only limited authority to manage and bill the account on your behalf, based on your signed Advisory Agreement with the firm.

With an independent Fiduciary-based advisor, you receive regular electronic or physical statements, trade confirmations, and other information independently and directly from the third-party custodian. You should *never* work with a broker or advisor who takes custody of your money themselves (e.g., Bernie Madoff et al.).

Salespeople and brokers work for their firm. Independent Fiduciary-based advisors work for you. Eliminating the financial incentive of generating more trades for higher commissions is an integral element of your long-term success. As Wealth Managers, the advisors at DiNuzzo Private Wealth, Inc. (DPW)/DiNuzzo Wealth Management (DWM) have been dedicating our Fiduciary Standard of placing your best interest ahead of our own for over thirty years.

Choosing an Independent Fiduciary-Based Advisor

If you are a Delegator, finding the best-fit Fiduciary-based advisor for you and your household is mission critical. You don't want to be saddled with a decision that results in buyer's regret for an extended period of time. Finding the right fit for you, as soon as possible, can materially enhance your and your family's lives.

Following are the key areas of consideration for finding the best match for you and long-term success with your advisor:

Firm Experience. Look for an advisor or firm with extensive investment experience culminating in a significant inventory of material wisdom. "Years in business" is a beneficial key litmus test, along with the combined years of Wealth Advisor experience on the team. These factors should be of the utmost importance in your advisor selection. DiNuzzo Private Wealth, Inc. (DPW)/ DiNuzzo Wealth Management (DWM) currently has 146 years (as of November 30, 2019) of combined Wealth Manager experience and offers clients the cumulative knowledge of its entire team.

Firm Size. Number of advisors and size of their investment portfolio. The size of the firms you interview will have a high correlation to the type of experience and services you will be provided.

It has been my experience that behemoth, national- and regional-type firms often have challenges with higher turnover, higher expenses, and customizing the client experience for each individual household. On the other end of the continuum, solo and small independent firms have the glaring challenge of being understaffed and having too small and shallow of a bench.

My belief that medium-sized firms are often the best fit for the typical Delegator household is related to firms that are large enough to have a full array of services available but still small enough to have the ability to work one-on-one and uniquely customize solutions on a household-by-household basis and maintain a closer more personal relationship from ownership through the Lead Wealth Manager relationship.

The Wealth Manager to number of client household ratio is mission critical as well. At DiNuzzo Private Wealth, Inc. (DPW)/DiNuzzo Wealth Management (DWM) we have historically averaged 100 to 150 households per "Lead Advisor." Many firms attempt to have their Advisors manage 400 to 600 households. Vanguard is less expensive than us on the surface but their advisors typically service a massive number of households similar, or greater, than this. There are also a material number of national firms which assign 700 to 900 households to each of their Advisors. This knowledge is of the utmost when performing your due diligence and considering taking action based on your Advisor's "advice" and how well it has been "customized" to fit your unique needs.

Education and Professional Qualifications. In searching for the best fit regarding investment management and Wealth Management, education is often a strong indicator of a good fit. Look for firms with credentials such as CFP, PFS, CPA, ChFC, AIFS, MBAS, MSFP and MSTX. Advisors who have spent a lifetime investing in professional development for themselves and their firms, striving to maintain leading edge and best practices are the key for what you're looking for.

Connectivity and Trust. Establishing a close and unique relationship with your firm and Lead Wealth Manager so that you can work in a *collaborative* manner sharing important personal, financial and emotional information will yield the highest results over time.

Current Clients. You should also evaluate the firm's culture, work history, and the type of clients they service. Ideally, you and your situation should be very similar to that of a significant number of the firm's existing clients.

Services Offered. Historically, Financial Advisors and Mutual Fund Managers have concentrated almost exclusively on attempting to "beat the market" in failed attempts to outperform various stock market indexes. Moving forward, especially regarding investing and Financial Wellness LifePlanning, more focus will rightfully be placed on the multiple factors that individually and collectively can provide significantly more benefit to individuals and households. This new approach is referred to as "Gamma/Advisor Alpha," and it can make your current investing, life, and retirement planning far more successful. It is the approach that I utilize and describe throughout my entire book.

My firm's value promise has always been easier to describe than to define. But, when you think about it, it makes sense—since value is a subjective assessment and varies from individual to individual. However, some aspects of investment advice lend themselves to an objective quantification of their potential added value. At best, I can only estimate the "value-add" of each personal finance, guidance, and advice tool we utilize, because each is affected by your unique situation and the market environments to which they are applied.

FIGURE 1.4. **Gamma/Advisor Alpha: How Leading Wealth Advisors Can Add Value for Their Clients**

Typical Annual Wealth Enhancement Benefit	"Gamma" Module	Chapter	Detail
1.5%	1. Behavior Coaching	2	Ongoing, annual or semi-annual progress meetings, communication, web meetings, emails, phone calls
.7%	2. Dynamic Withdrawal Strategy(s)	5	Ongoing, annual or semi-annual progress meetings. Withdrawal hierarchy, and customized evolving withdrawal strategy
0 – .7%	3. Spending Strategy(s)	5	Withdrawal sourcing and order
.45%	4. Cost Effective Portfolio(s)	8	Construction and implementation, low fees, low expenses, low turnover
.25 – .35%	5. Portfolio Rebalancing	9	Utilizing portfolio(s) and asset class "bands"
0 – .45%	6. Suitable (Liability Driven), Portfolio Asset Allocation Strategy(s)	5	Including proper diversification vis-à-vis personal financial statements. Descending/Ascending Glidepath.
.23 – .75%	7. Tax Management of Portfolio(s)	9	Asset location, tax-loss harvesting, capital gain recognition,low-cost tax-deferral strategies, tax planning/preparation,and tax-bracket; management, smoothing, and arbitrage
.10%	8. Guaranteed Income	5	"Needs" bucket; identification calculation and funding strategy
>0%	9. Social Security Maximization	9	Highly customized strategies often resulting in a 5 or 6 figure cash flow increase over your lifetime(s)
>0%	10. Roth IRA Conversions	9	Highly customized strategies often resulting in a 5 or 6 figure (or more) tax savings over your lifetime(s)
>0%	11. Beneficiary Designation Management and Strategies	1	Customized estate savings, tax savings, beneficiary benefits
.10%	12. Total Return & Income Investing	5	Customizing asset allocations and accessing benefit of blended: capital appreciations, dividends, and interest for withdrawal needs
>3%/year	TOTAL (Approximate)		

Source: Vanguard, Morningstar, Inc.

There is a great temptation to define a Wealth Manager's value-add as an annualized portfolio return number. This may seem appropriate, as fees deducted annually for our advisory relationship could be justified by the "annual value-add." However, although some of the strategies I describe in this and/or other chapters could be expected to yield an annual benefit—e.g., increasing performance, lowering risk, reducing expected investment cost, lowering anxiety, sleeping better, or reducing taxes—the most significant opportunities to add value do not present themselves consistently, but intermittently over the years, and often during periods of either stock market tribulation or euphoria. These opportunities can exacerbate an investor's fear or greed, tempting him or her to abandon a well-thought-out and personalized Financial Wellness LifePlan. In such circumstances, my firm has the opportunity to add tens of percentage points to our value-add, rather than mere basis points, and more than offset years of our advisory fees.

While the value of my firm's wealth creation is certainly real, the difference in my clients' performance if they stay invested according to their customized "DiNuzzo Financial Wellness LifePlan™," as opposed to abandoning it, does not show up on any specific client's statement. An unknown number of alternate histories may have happened had I made different decisions; yet, we only measure and/or monitor the implemented decisions and outcome, even though the other histories were real alternatives. Clients' statements don't keep track of the benefits of our talking to our clients to stay on plan and stay the course in the middle of a bear market, or convincing them to rebalance during a bull market contrary to their opinion that it doesn't "feel" like the right thing to do at the time by selling stocks and buying bonds. Although I am unable to precisely measure and show these other outcomes, their value and impact on my clients' wealth creation is very real.

Unlike money managers' traditional approach of focusing on "alpha," (attempting to outperform the market, which is a luck-based, zero-sum game), or "beta" (Asset Allocation), the higher potential value of "Gamma" (numerous techniques that Wealth Managers utilize to produce material Net Worth improvement for their clients) can be achieved by Wealth Managers instituting and following a leading edge Financial Wellness LifePlan strategy. It is estimated by Morningstar that the cumulative benefits for retirement income planning based on a Gamma approach can be up to an approximate 25% increase in income throughout retirement. I will let you be the judge of the "Gamma" value-adds a firm such as mine is able to bring to the table, as you analyze and internalize my firm's following "Top 12" list based on Morningstar and Vanguard's research. Key value-adds by Fiduciary-standard Wealth Managers specializing in a comprehensive financial life planning process include: (1) Behavior Coaching, (2) Dynamic Withdrawal Strategy(s), (3) Spending Strategy(s), (4) Cost-Effective Portfolios, (5) Portfolio Rebalancing, (6) Suitable "Liability-Driven" Portfolio Asset Allocation(s), (7) Portfolio(s) Tax Management, (8) Guaranteed Income, (9) Social Security Maximization, (10) Roth IRA Conversions, (11) Beneficiary Designation Management and Strategy(s), and (12) Total Return vs. Income Investing. Some of these topics are discussed in detail in the following chapters, while others are beyond the scope of this book but are critical topics for you to address with guidance from your Wealth Manager.

HAVE A PLAN

Human beings on average show little evidence of being planners or of acting intentionally when it regards matters of personal finance.

—P.J. DiNuzzo

Think "marriage" in lieu of "dating."

—P.J. DiNuzzo

A fool with a plan can outsmart a genius with no plan.

—T. Boone Pickens

The important thing about an investment philosophy is that you have one you can stick with.

—David Booth, co-founder and CEO,
Dimensional Fund Advisors (DFA)

The beginning is the most important part of the work.

—Plato (circa 428–348 BC)

The journey of one thousand miles begins with a single step.

—Lao Tzu

FINANCIAL WELLNESS LIFEPLANNING: IDENTIFY AND SET YOUR UNIQUE MILESTONES, GOALS, AND OBJECTIVES

Most people think planning a successful retirement only has to do with your investment strategy. The first step to planning a truly successful retirement and financial independence is to identify and set your milestones, goals, and objectives both now and in retirement.

When it comes to creating a successful investment plan, nothing could be truer than the above quote by Plato—the beginning truly is the most important part of the work.

Successful investing and the "DiNuzzo Financial Wellness LifePlan™" require a marriage of "art" (emotions) and "science" (numbers). Most of the chapters ahead deal with the science of investment planning and management because they are, in plain English, "numbers oriented." However, in this chapter I begin with the art of identifying and setting our milestones, goals, and objectives. Since these milestones, goals, and objectives are unique to each individual, family, and household, this is a very subjective but critical process. In life, as we all know, if you don't know where you're going, any path can get you there. To create a successful investment plan, you must first define what a successful "investment experience" means for *you*.

Investing for Your Unique Financial Wellness LifePlan

If you want to know what your financial independence and retirement plan looks like...look in the mirror. *You* are the key variable. How you save and invest over your lifetime has the highest correlation to the quality of "living richly," retirement, and financial independence success you will enjoy.

When I first talk with individuals about getting ready for financial independence and/or retirement, many times I start by asking them, "What did you do last Saturday?" At first, they're surprised by that question, but when they start to think about it, they often say something like, "Well, the weather was nice that day. I did a little bit of stuff around the house, and then I went out golfing with my buddies for most of the day. Then I came back. My wife and I had dinner, and then I read a novel until bedtime. That's what I did last Saturday." And then I would say, "Well, just look at retirement as a life full of Saturdays." This sounds like fun at first, but as you will see, it also may present unforeseen challenges.

When most individuals imagine how they would define a successful retirement, they just want to do what they enjoy doing. But if we're talking about a life full of Saturdays instead of just one Saturday a week, you'll likely want to put some structure around your activities for the long term. Once they go through a year or two of "Saturdays" just doing what they enjoy, a lot of retirees become bored, and the skills and wisdom they spent a lifetime building begin to go dormant and eventually fade away. I believe a truly successful retirement is mentally challenging, physically healthy, and lasts a long time. To have this kind of retirement, you need to plan for three basic types of activities:

1. **Activities you enjoy doing.** This is what most people think of when they think of their lifetime of Saturdays: relaxing, traveling, or hobbies like gardening or other physical activities. These kinds of activities are certainly important, but they shouldn't make up the whole of your retirement.

2. **Activities that challenge you.** Everyone goes through life with a set of skills. I maintain the philosophy that everyone is, or has the gifts to be an expert at something, and whatever skills you have accumulated over the course of your life, you'll want to continue using those skills and challenging yourself in retirement. For example, if you were a top engineer or architect who spent thirty or forty years perfecting a highly refined acumen, it will be very

difficult to just flip that part of your life off like a light switch and not share your expertise with others in need. For a long and successful retirement, you'll want to challenge yourself to apply your strengths and your skills from the beginning and throughout your retirement to keep yourself vibrant and healthy—mentally as well as physically.

3. **Activities supporting a charity or cause.** It's very important to focus at least part of your time toward something that's fulfilling and has meaning to you. Many of our clients have been very involved in specific causes during their retirement. I think of one of our clients in her 80s who is very involved in politics, environmental causes, and a variety of organizations.

You might even find some type of part-time employment. A lot of times, individuals look at me a little cockeyed when I mention that, because they're thinking, "Well, I'm retiring to get away from work." So I just tell them to keep an open mind. What if you were to run into a consulting opportunity that is something that you enjoy doing, and it's for a cause or organization you strongly believe in? You may be reenergized, and it might be the greatest thing on earth to get paid for something that you love doing. Maybe you could help this organization five, ten, fifteen, or twenty hours a week. Remember…the #1 activity that enhances gratitude and appreciation for "off" days is…work! Even one day of work or volunteering per week can be a tremendous catalyst for happiness during your off days. The bottom line is that being successful in retirement is more than just doing what you enjoy doing. A successful retirement can also include building personal relationships, challenging your skills, and contributing to a meaningful cause that is larger than yourself. As an extra bonus, this additional income has a dual benefit as it can also enhance the financial success of your retirement.

So, how do you envision your ideal life in retirement? What relationships, experiences, principles, and material items are most important to you? How would you like to spend your time—what activities would you want to prioritize, in all three categories listed above? Open your mind and think big.

Why You Need to Plan for Retirement

The probable is what usually happens.

—Aristotle

FIGURE 2.1. **Why You Need to Plan for Retirement**

The Likelihood of a Person (Age 65) Living to the Following Ages:

AGE	Surviving Spouse	Single Female	Single Male
75	96%	83%	76%
80	87%	68%	58%
85	68%	50%	37%
90	40%	28%	17%
95	14%	10%	4%

Source: IRS Actuarial Tables.

Before I move on, we need to address something that may seem obvious, but is often overlooked. Your primary objective is to not run out of money before you run out of breath. Many individuals say they want to "live for today" and "won't even buy green bananas," so to speak. However, studying the average lifespan for individuals retiring at age 65 can be an eye-opening experience for anyone with that philosophy. Many are surprised by how long they are likely to live. For a married couple or partners, there is a one-in-four (25%) chance that at least one spouse/partner is going to live into their early to mid-90s. Also, because this is an average lifespan, you need to remember that approximately 50% of individuals live longer than the lifespan represented by the data in Figure 2.1, *Why You Need to Plan for Retirement.*

An additional challenge with predicting mortality is that the longer you live, the longer you are likely to live, due to the statistical likelihood of improvements in medical treatments, lifestyle changes, etc. The bottom line is that individuals *often underestimate* their personal life expectancy. Therefore, when we meet with clients, we desire to typically create a DiNuzzo Financial Wellness LifePlan™ for a lifespan longer than what they may often have had in mind. Typically, our plans average approximately 30 years in retirement for our clients. If someone were to retire at 65, they would typically have a plan approximately through age 95. If you had to use a quick "rule of thumb" when building a plan, *I would recommend using 95 years of age as your benchmark.* Subtracting your age at retirement from the number 95, then, provides you with the target length of your retirement income plan.

THE DANGERS OF NOT HAVING A PLAN: BILL AND SUSAN

Bill is seventy years old and an accountant. His wife, Susan is seventy-five and a professor at a major university. The couple's High-Net-Worth Personality is primarily Family Steward and secondarily Independent. They have approximately $100,000 in taxable accounts including checking and savings accounts and FDIC-insured money market funds. The couple has a combined investment of close to $2 million in traditional, tax-deferred IRAs. They also have $300,000 in another IRA, invested in a variable annuity that has a Guaranteed Lifetime Withdrawal Benefit (GLWB), also known as a living benefit income rider.

During our Discovery Meeting, I identified their strong Family Steward tendencies and legacy desires for their children and grandchildren. I immediately brought up the advantage and possibility of a Roth IRA Conversion opportunity which would be a win for their heirs, while lowering their federal taxes over their lifetimes and their children's lifetimes.

Having a plan is the most important key in your roadmap to a successful retirement. In all their years of employment, Bill and Susan had neglected to create a plan, so I worked with them to develop a DiNuzzo Financial Wellness LifePlan™ customized to their unique lives and goals. We quickly discovered they did not have enough cash on hand to pay the taxes required for the recommended Roth IRA Conversions.

Here is where Bill and Susan had gone awry: Without having a plan, they had made investments that would not serve them well in retirement. Their variable annuity came with approximately 2% *higher* than average costs. The Guaranteed Lifetime Withdrawal Benefit rider also came with costs that were absolutely unnecessary. Because the couple did not have a plan, they fell into the common trap of being distracted and being "sold" an investment that was a terrible fit for their retirement on a number of fronts.

My longtime saying is "Annuities are never bought; they're always sold." Because they're sold, individuals do not do the necessary research before they invest in them, nor do they typically understand even the *basic* elements of the annuity they purchase. Before making any major purchase—a home, a car, or even a kitchen appliance—people do their homework. They look at more than one house, vehicle, or refrigerator. They study and weigh the options and the costs, and after deliberating, they choose whatever is best for them and their household.

People don't do that with annuities. They don't understand all the aspects of the annuity and how it benefits (or does not benefit) their financial plan.

The initial, obvious effect of having $300,000 in the annuity was that it was invested in the wrong "Account Type" and should have remained in their traditional IRA account. The long-term effect of this decision was unnecessarily exorbitant expenses and a rider that was an ill fit for their plan.

There was more bad news. Bill and Susan were guaranteed income with their pensions and Social Security benefits. Due to the IRA's Required Minimum Distributions (RMDS) along with the GLWB of their IRA annuity, they were looking at approximately $5,000 a month in surplus income—*$60,000 a year in excess income.*

If Bill and Susan could wave a magic wand, they would want to prevent *any* withdrawals from their IRA accounts because they're going to have to pay taxes on every penny. They don't need the money and would rather leave it where it is so they can pass it on to their children and grandchildren. Withdrawing it will put them in a higher tax bracket, forcing them to pay more taxes on *any* income they receive.

From a cash flow perspective, Bill and Susan's situation doesn't look so bad. They have more money than they need to live on. Unfortunately, they will not be able to keep as much of it as they could have if they had had a plan and invested wisely to support that plan.

Adding insult to injury, had they known the value of Roth IRA Conversions and how good a fit it is for their plan, they would have saved more money in their taxable accounts to pay for the federal taxes. Paying the IRS tens or even hundreds of thousands of dollars or more in lifetime taxes than was necessary makes my head want to explode.

It's important to identify and analyze any "gaps" in your plan and address them before you can move forward with your investment strategy. In Bill and Susan's case, the approximately 2% per year in additional expenses on their annuity was costing them $6,000 a year. Assuming a 30-year life expectancy after retirement, that amounts to $180,000—money they could have used to pay for a grandchild's first car, college education, and down payment on a first home.

Ideally, as Family Stewards with the priority of transitioning their wealth to the next generation, they would have transitioned their IRA into a Roth IRA to leave to their children, instead of locking it into that tax-deferred annuity. With money in the Roth IRA for their children, and money in a taxable account to pay for the Roth IRA Conversion taxes on their traditional IRA, they would have gone into retirement secure in the knowledge that they had a strategy that benefited them and their family and a plan to support it.

When couples come to see me this late in the game, I regret not having met them earlier in their lives. A lot of progress can be made in just a few years, but ideally, I like to start planning 10 years or at least 5 years before a person's projected retirement date. Everyone's plan should be based on their unique goals and each investment should have a clear purpose that supports the plan and places them in a better situation for retirement.

Set Your Lifetime Financial Milestones, Goals, and Objectives

Now that you have a clear sense of what some of your "DiNuzzo Financial Wellness LifePlan™" variables for success look like (and how long you are likely to be there), you'll need to think about your lifetime financial milestones, goals, and objectives. Simply stated, these milestones, goals, and objectives are the items you want to accomplish financially from now until the end of your life, and beyond (e.g., Legacy), that will lead you step-by-step to your destination of "living richly," however you defined it above.

Below are some sample milestones and goals for consideration. Use these as examples to jump-start and stimulate your mental creativity.

Sample Milestones and Goals

- Buy a first, new, bigger, or second home.
- Increase vacation and travel.
- Buy a new car.
- Save for a personal or family celebration.
- Educate children or grandchildren.
- Fund graduate-level or higher education for children or yourself.
- Save responsibly for retirement.
- Pay off debt.
- Save for wedding(s).
- Retire and relax.
- Save for home improvements.
- Grow your portfolio(s).
- Fund Roth IRA Conversion(s).
- Reduce income and estate taxes.
- Start a new business.
- Make living gifts or leave assets to beneficiaries or charity.
- Protect your spouse, family, and/or significant other in case of your death.
- Fund final expenses.
- Prepare for retirement: enjoyable activities, challenging tasks, and supporting cause(s).

I like to walk clients through this process of setting DiNuzzo Financial Wellness LifePlan™ milestones, goals, and objectives during our first meeting, and one thing I've learned over the decades is that spouses/partners often *have never* or barely discussed these topics together before coming in for an initial "Discovery Meeting." Why? Most self-appointed Family Chief Investment Officers (FCIOs) tend to be autocratic and independent. They are prone to tell their spouse/partner, "I'll take care of it, you don't have to worry." And, often times, the non-CIO spouse/partner is comfortable with that structure. But, very often the non-CIO spouse doesn't truly understand what their mate is doing. That's why I tend to be more sensitive to the non-CIO spouse/partner during this process.

If you are your family's FCIO, talking to your spouse/partner in detail about your financial milestones, goals, and objectives before enacting any sort of plan is part of your responsibility and "job description." You need full and equal input from your spouse/partner when you set your joint Financial Wellness LifePlan goals, because the goals drive the whole plan. Perhaps one of you wants a vacation home and the other doesn't, or one wants to pay for your grandchildren's education and the other feels like that is the parent's responsibility. If financial emotions are running high, honesty is always the A-plus answer. These impasses *never* improve with time by sweeping them under the carpet.

Create a Comprehensive Financial Checklist

After identifying your major financial life planning milestones and goals, it is important then to focus on the significant financial categories you need to manage and leverage in order to achieve these goals, and create a comprehensive financial checklist. Think of this checklist as your job description as family CIO. Your comprehensive financial checklist includes the tasks required to meet your financial goals and objectives. Note: some items in your comprehensive checklist will be applicable while you are working, while others will apply during retirement. Like your milestones, goals, and objectives, the entire checklist will be built around a Financial Wellness LifePlan, with some items not being directly applicable to your financial situation at any given time, and different items having varying levels of importance through the cycles of your life. The good news is that 99% of items on the following pages can be addressed by the techniques we'll cover in my book.

Personal Finance and Cash Management

- At a minimum, contribute to qualified plans, such as 401(k)s or 403(b)s, at work, at least up to the "company match" amount and ideally contributing the maximum amount.
- Audit Health Savings Account (HSA) contributions.
- Audit potential Roth IRA Conversion opportunities.
- Balance retirement savings with cash flow at a comfortable level.
- Build an "Emergency Reserve Fund" 6 to 12 times monthly expenses (while still working).
- Build an "Emergency Reserve Fund" 12 to 36 times monthly expenses "when retired."
- Contribute to a Roth IRA.
- Eliminate credit card debt.
- Eliminate Private Mortgage Insurance (PMI).
- Establish Home Equity Line of Credit (HELOC) as an emergency option and for emergency cash flow protection.
- Manage "discretionary" expenses on Retirement Cash Flow Statement (RCFS) and contribute to savings, if possible.
- Manage Automated Teller Machine (ATM) spending and avoid foreign ATM fees.
- Negotiate and/or reduce unreimbursed employee expenses.
- Perform, at a minimum, a comprehensive "annual financial checkup"—either self-directed or with your Wealth Manager.
- Refinance mortgage.
- Review Alternative Minimum Tax (AMT) effects for major financial decisions.
- Review line-item expenses on your cash flow statement.
- Review permanent record file and document retention.
- Set mortgage amortization schedule: pay off mortgage and other debt prior to retirement.

Investment Planning

- Analyze pros/cons of establishing a Reverse Mortgage in retirement to buttress your cash reserve bucket and especially to protect your safe withdrawal rate(s).
- Avoid front-end loads, back-end loads, 12(b)-1 mutual fund fees, and mutual funds with excessive turnover.
- Build DiNuzzo Money Bucket Stack Analysis™ (DMBSA™) to identify proper Asset Allocations for various taxable, tax-deferred, and tax-free portfolios.
- Build or move toward an All-Index portfolio and eliminate or reduce active and alternative investments.
- Consider safekeeping physical stock and bond certificates in brokerage accounts at national firms, such as TD Ameritrade, Fidelity Investments, or Charles Schwab, instead of at home or in a bank safe deposit box.
- Establish monthly or quarterly dollar cost averaging (DCA) into investment accounts whenever possible.
- Have a lucid understanding of you and your spouse/partner's joint and individual "time horizon(s)" regarding your aggregate investments as well as your individual investment accounts.
- Have a clear understanding of you and your spouse/partner's joint and individual "Risk Capacity," and "Risk Tolerance" regarding your investment "Buckets" for: "Needs," "Wants," and "Dreams/ Wishes" for your aggregated investment assets.
- Identify cash reserve goal through DMBSA™ analysis.
- Identify, if applicable, and invest "second-tier" cash reserves through DMBSA™ Cash Reserve bucket for higher yield achievement, such as high-quality short-term bonds.
- If so inclined, invest a *maximum* of 5% of your aggregate investment assets, based on your Personal Balance Sheet (PBS) totals, into your "Las Vegas" portfolio for personal observation/ hunch/investment newsletter/"hot stock tip" trading schemes.

- Improve/optimize returns on cash investments within your Cash Reserve bucket in your DMBSA™.
- Invest surplus discretionary cash for long-term goals.
- Maintain low fees and seek out low-expense index funds.
- Maintain low investment turnover, both in portfolio and within individual mutual funds.
- Manage "Asset Location" (e.g., hold income-generating investments in tax-deferred accounts, and growth investments in taxable accounts), if applicable, regarding portfolio size and taxes.
- Manage taxable portfolios within a tax-efficient strategy.
- Fully and properly diversify portfolio(s).
- Rebalance your portfolio(s).
- Review Asset Allocation, diversification, expenses, and historical data on fund-by-fund basis in qualified retirement accounts at work—e.g., 401(k)s and 403(b)s.
- Review stock option strategies annually.
- Review your stock option's agreement regarding disability and mergers.
- Set and maintain a lifelong "DiNuzzo Glidepath™" for your DMBSA™ Risk Capacity/Income Gap (your "Needs," for your food, clothing, shelter, transportation, healthcare, and education expenses); Risk Tolerance (your "Wants," for all other discretionary expenses); and investment portfolio, which will be paying for nearly all expenses in retirement.
- Set appropriate Asset Allocation for various milestones, goals, objectives, "Needs," "Wants," "Dreams/Wishes," and time horizon(s).
- Verify and update beneficiary designations on all qualified accounts, such as IRA, 401(k), 403(b), life insurance policies, and on taxable accounts with Transfer on Death (TODs), if applicable.
- When investing in individual municipal (muni) bonds, invest for quality and safety first, and yield second. Do not purchase bonds below a single "A" rating and be sure they are General Obligation (GO) bonds, which have mandatory municipality tax increases embedded in them to protect your investment.

Tax Planning and Preparation

- Analyze life insurance policies (e.g., second to die) which can potentially provide the same basic income tax advantages as a Roth IRA.
- Analyze borrowing from permanent life insurance policies.
- Analyze, typically for entrepreneurs with medium-sized businesses, "Captive Insurance Company" applicability and options.
- Analyze IRC Section 199A "QBI"(Qualified Business Income) deduction regarding specifically defined: Sole Proprietorship, Partnership, LLC, S Corporation, Rental Real Estate, Trusts, and Estates.
- Analyze tax benefit of Roth IRA Conversion(s).
- Analyze tax bracket management, smoothing, and arbitrage.
- Apply investment tax management to taxable accounts.
- Billing strategy regarding investment management fees: taxable accounts fees to taxable accounts, Roth IRA investment management fees to taxable accounts, and IRA(s) (typically) to identical IRA(s). Note: client and financial advisor should discuss pros and cons. Also discuss with your tax advisor.
- Consolidate debt into tax-deductible loans (if appropriate), such as a Home Equity Line of Credit (HELOC).
- Donate appreciated securities in lieu of cash.
- Donate non-cash items to charity.
- Estimate taxes and withholdings either up or down in taxable accounts and IRA accounts with withdrawals due to annual federal and state tax law changes.
- Have a Net Investment Income Tax (3.8%) "NIIT" plan.
- Have a plan for the additional 0.9% Medicare tax on earned income.
- Have a Medicare "IRMAA" tax bracket plan.
- Hire local, experienced Certified Public Accountant (CPA) firm in state of residence, if possible.
- Plan for "income smoothing strategies," especially between retirement and age 70.

- Review benefits of utilizing Charitable Remainder Trust if you have significant unrealized capital gains and "NIIT" implications to spread over an extended period.
- Review federal and state quarterly estimates.
- Review federal and state tax withholding on your work paycheck(s).
- Review impact of incentive stock options with CPA regarding AMT.
- Review income-shifting strategies.
- Review potential favorable impact of Non-Qualified tax deferred annuities, "faux IRAs," for taxable investments for income smoothing and proactive tax mitigation.
- Review tax deduction/tax preparation worksheet with your CPA.
- Review unreimbursed employee expenses.
- Understand beneficial timing of Tax-Loss Harvesting.
- Understand effects of income from the seven "Tax Asset Classes": taxable interest income, dividend income, capital gain income, tax-exempt interest income, pension and IRA income, Real Estate/oil/gas income, and Roth IRA/insurance income.
- Understand when capital gains harvesting strategies are beneficial.
- Review potential benefits of Qualified Charitable Distributions (QCDs).

Estate Planning

- Bypass Trust—consider pros and cons of adding provision to wills.
- Consider changing custodian on children's accounts.
- Consider establishing a Revocable Living Trust (RLT).
- Consider irrevocable trust for asset protection or estate tax reduction.
- Draft and execute advanced medical directives.
- Draft and execute financial durable power of attorney.
- Draft and execute healthcare durable power of attorney.
- Draft and execute living will.
- Draft and execute will.

- Equalize estates to take advantage of unified credit.
- Estate tax liquidity—consider additional life insurance.
- Gifting—consider annual program to reduce estate tax.
- Gifting—pay tuition and medical bills directly.
- Hire an attorney who specializes in elder care law.
- Hire an attorney who specializes in estate planning law.
- Meticulously evaluate irrevocable life insurance trusts.
- Analyze benefits of reducing or avoiding jointly held property.
- Retain appreciated securities to get step-up basis.
- Review beneficiary designations with an attorney.
- Shift assets by changing titles.
- Understand pros/cons of Bypass Trust vs. Portability.
- Verify beneficiary designations on retirement accounts and life insurance.

Risk Management (Insurance)

- "Umbrella" (excess liability) coverage. Establish and/or consider increasing. Should normally be at least equal to your "Net Worth." Typically purchase *at least* $1 million.
- Obtain appraisals for collectibles, antiques, artwork, and valuables—verify adequate insurance coverage.
- Audit benefits of consolidating auto, home, and umbrella insurance policies with a single insurance company.
- Audit maximizing full advantage of life insurance Cash Value balance(s).
- Audit need for additional uninsured motorist insurance.
- Audit replacement of existing life insurance policy(ies) with 20-year term possibility.
- Beneficiary designations—verify and update on all documents.
- Consider increasing auto and homeowner's deductibles.
- Consider dropping collision and comprehensive auto insurance on older model cars.

- Homeowner's insurance policy—consider purchasing guaranteed replacement cost coverage.
- Household inventory—list, videotape, or photograph and store offsite.
- Liability coverage—integrate auto and homeowner policies.
- Life insurance ("Risk Management") coverage—audit annually.
- Long-term care (LTC)—typically defer purchase decision until retirement (or within five years of retirement).
- Long-term disability insurance (LTD) with Cost-of-Living Adjustment (COLA).
- Medicare insurance coverage—purchase supplemental, price high-deductible policy.
- Second-to-die life insurance—consider adding.
- Term life insurance policies—evaluate applicability and/or replacement of existing policies.

Retirement Planning

- Consider partial conversion if income qualifies for a Roth IRA.
- Consider using ultra low-cost tax-deferred annuity for surplus taxable savings earmarked for retirement.
- Consolidate multiple retirement accounts into one account to reduce annual fees.
- Contribute maximum each year to Roth IRAs, if possible.
- Decide how you rate and feel about each key retirement risk: volatility risk, inflation risk, longevity risk, and beneficiary/legacy risk.
- Develop a plan and stick with it.
- Establish company retirement plan or 1401(k) (Individual/Solo 401(k)).
- Increase/maintain cash flow targets for retirement savings.
- Invest maximum annually in deductible IRA.
- Know your unique financial independence/retirement "number/ range."

- Maintain a lifelong "DiNuzzo Glidepath™" for your DMBSA™ "Risk Capacity"/"Income Gap" ("Need" expenses, such as food, clothing, shelter, healthcare, transportation, and education) and "Risk Tolerance" ("Wants," or discretionary expenses).
- Understand the importance of the two primary unknowns (investment returns and life expectancy) when forecasting financial independence and retirement income.

Education Planning

- Accumulate education savings in parents' name.
- Consider establishing section 529 plans.
- Establish systematic investment plan.
- Gradually reduce Asset Allocation toward less volatility to match time horizon.
- Retain existing US Series EE Bonds for education.

Don't be overwhelmed by the number of items I have asked you to consider, but remember, being Family CIO is serious stuff! I will address a number of these throughout my *Seven Keys*. The most important thing is to take the time from the beginning to set your milestones, goals, and objectives. You have to know where you're going in order to get there, and you want to be sure you're following a plan and roadmap that takes you where you want to go.

Successful investing is more than a lifetime of Saturdays, and a successful investment strategy and plan is more than just picking individual investments as/when the opportunity arises randomly over time. First decide what a full and meaningful Financial Wellness LifePlan will look like for you, including all of your major financial milestones and goals. Then create, refer to, or delegate to a professional a detailed financial checklist of everything that you will need to address to achieve those financial milestones and goals.

Preparations for Your "Money Bucket" Stack Analysis

Before you proceed to the second half of this chapter, "The DiNuzzo Money Bucket Stack Analysis™" (DMBSA™): Organizing Your Investments into Understandable "DiNuzzo Money Buckets," you must first prepare your Expenses and your targeted Retirement Cash Flow Statement (RCFS). These subjects are explained in the following sections.

Assets, Liabilities, and Net Worth
Your Personal Balance Sheet…Manage It, Don't Let It Manage You

The nicest house on the block is the house that is paid off free and clear.
—P.J. DiNuzzo

The greatest of all gifts is the power to estimate things at their true worth.
—La Rochefoucauld, *Reflexions, ou sentences et maxims morales*

A picture is worth ten thousand words.
—Ancient Chinese Proverb

Lay the foundation of your "DiNuzzo Financial Wellness LifePlan™" with a solid understanding of where you are today regarding your unique assets and liabilities by building your own Personal Balance Sheet (PBS).

There has historically been a common stereotype that stockbrokers are often asked questions regarding "hot stock tips" at "cocktail" parties. Although I have *never* been asked for hot stock tips or ever been invited to a cocktail party, since a lot of people know me and what I do, I am consistently asked the same question over and over: "Can I retire?" It happens to me in the middle of a Giant Eagle or Aldi grocery store, at a gas station, or in a Home Depot or

Lowe's hardware store. When I am approached regarding this topic, I always answer this question with a question: "Is your house paid off?" This initiates a much deeper conversation, which always leads to the logical conclusion that the size of one's liabilities is paramount and is a symbiotic variable when contemplating financial independence/retirement. My personal opinion, especially from my Italian upbringing, is that paying off debt is *never* a bad decision. Since you have accepted the challenge of Family Chief Investment Officer (FCIO), your first task is to build a balance sheet, listing assets, liabilities, and resulting "Net Worth."

The Foundation for Success: Your Personal Balance Sheet (PBS)

Hypothetically, if you were a member of the Investment Committee for a reasonably sized institutional organization, the initial critical piece of information you would need to know would be the assets, liabilities, Net Worth, and other key various aspects of the balance sheet for that organization. Even a lemonade stand has to follow the same foundational business principles to be successful. The same holds true for your personal finances. The Personal Balance Sheet is literally the "footer/foundation" of your working and retirement investment management and financial planning strategies. As I will illustrate, there are approximately a dozen or more significant areas of your Personal Balance Sheet you will need to understand and manage in order to position yourself, as securely as possible, for retirement income planning success.

Before you can even begin to consider how you are going to invest your lifetime savings, you must have a complete grasp of the strengths and weaknesses of your Personal Balance Sheet. Collecting the data to build your Personal Balance Sheet will reveal important variables that will lead to key observations and critical decisions that must be made. When approaching this exercise, as in everything else we will work through, maintaining an objective viewpoint makes all the difference in the world. Understanding your PBS keeps you in control of your financial future.

Fundamentally, this appears to be a standard, straightforward exercise. However, even the majority of Brokers/Financial Advisors do not prepare a Personal Balance Sheet for their clients. Rather than doing the "grunt work" of compiling personal financial statements such as the PBS, most brokers, mutual fund salespersons, and investment managers focus on just "running the money," "selling a product," and positioning themselves to maximize commission fees and "loads." If they do any "planning" at all it is typically founded on regional or national "guesstimates." Due to my background as a CPA (Certified Public Accountant), our firm has compiled this financial statement as a standard operating procedure for our clients for decades. The Personal Balance Sheet is integral to an individual's "retirement readiness ratio" percentage. If your Personal Balance Sheet is not strong and in good working order, retirement will be a distinct challenge in most cases. Of course, the PBS is simply numbers on paper, but the true value comes with the analysis of the various ratios, sizing, projections, and "Needs" anticipation. Also, as we shall see, there is a significant relationship between the Personal Balance Sheet and the Retirement Cash Flow Statement (Income and Expenses.)

Begin with the End in Mind: The Characteristics of the Typical American Retiree

An intuitive, pragmatic, and common-sense approach to the Personal Balance Sheet can be viewed from a reverse engineering perspective. First let's establish the basic characteristics of the average retiree in the United States. The average professional individual retires at approximately 66 years of age. The average individual has his or her house paid off and no other debt than perhaps an auto loan. And the average individual, who has had a professional career, has a typical "lump sum" distribution from their employer of multiple hundreds of thousands of dollars or more. (Keep in mind, these are individuals who have had a professional career and *not* individuals who have not been fortunate enough to go to college or enter into the workforce at a higher level.)

If you hold the target steady, then you can reverse engineer any question or observation you have when looking at your Personal Balance Sheet. For example, if you want to retire at an age materially younger than the average age of 66, then something "special" needs to have happened in your life. After all, without a unique circumstance, how would you expect to be able to retire at a younger age than the average worker in America? For instance, perhaps you have more material assets than other potential retirees. Or you have less debt, more guaranteed income, and/or lower monthly expenses. I will discuss guaranteed income later in my book, but as far as making an astute declaration, you would have to be "above average" somewhere else and/ or in numerous areas in your financial landscape if you are going to retire younger. Likewise, there needs to be something else "above average" if you have a mortgage and are going to retire, since the average individual who retires owes nothing on their residence. If one of the major building blocks of retirement success is not in place, such as no mortgage and no debt, then there simply has to be something else in your financial picture to offset what is placing you at a potential disadvantage. If not, you are plausibly placing your Financial Wellness LifePlan and retirement in jeopardy. Proceed with caution when seeking advice, as many financial professionals are eager to grab hold of your money in order to start "ringing their register." Remember my earlier comments about finding a Wealth Manager, Wealth Advisor, Financial Advisor, or Financial Planner who operates under a Fiduciary Standard/Oath *and* is serious about it.

Deciphering the Personal Balance Sheet (PBS)

Our detailed Personal Balance Sheet for each client is very customized and too expansive of a topic to review here so I will provide you with an executive summary.

If you look closely at my Figure 0.13, *Your DiNuzzo Customized Personal Finance House*™ earlier in the introduction, you will notice that the "foundation/footer" supporting it, and yours in real life, is Assets & Liabilities, Income & Expenses, and the "bottom line"…Net Worth.

Any Balance Sheet, business or personal, can be viewed as consisting of "two sides," a left-hand side and a right-hand side. The left-hand side, from top to bottom, would list all of your "Assets." While the right-hand side would detail all of your "Liabilities." The upper left, Assets, would start off with "Cash & Cash Equivalents" whose sum equals your total "Cash Reserves." These line items consist primarily of the following: checking accounts, savings accounts, CDs, Money Market Funds, US Savings Bonds, Cash, and potentially gold or silver coins. The next category directly below your "Cash Reserves" total is "Investment Assets." Investment Assets include the following "account types": Individual Taxable, Joint Taxable, Revocable Living Trust, Traditional IRA, SEP-IRA, Simple IRA, After-Tax IRA, Roth IRA, Rollover IRA, 401(k)s, 403(b)s, 401(a)s, 457(b)s, Health Savings (HSA)s, Pension Lump Sums, Cash Balance Plans, ESOP's, Stock Certificates, Bond Certificates, Variable Annuities, Fixed Annuities, Stock Options, Education Savings, and 529's. The final Asset category on the bottom left of your Personal Balance Sheet is "Use Assets." These line items include: primary residence, second residence, time-share, personal property, automobiles, life insurance cash value, expectancy/inheritance, business value, mineral rights, gas rights, commercial Real Estate, land, limited partnership, oil rights, loan receivable, deferred compensation, jewelry, collectibles, artwork, antiques, recreational vehicle, quad, motorcycle, boat, tractor, and farm equipment.

Listed at the bottom left of your Personal Balance Sheet would be "Total Assets." This line would be the sum of your "Cash Reserves" plus "Investment Assets" plus "Use Assets."

The right-hand side of your Personal Balance Sheet from top to bottom would list all of your Liabilities (and Net Worth). "Liabilities" line items with outstanding balances would include: credit card balances (over 30 days), personal line of credit, estimated deferred taxes (i.e., Roth IRA Conversion, Inheritance, Severance, Marcellus Shale, Realized Capital Gains, Unrealized Capital Gains), Private Elementary/High School Tuition/costs, Undergrad Loans, Graduate School Loans, Medical School Loans, Assisted Living/

Patio Home Down Payment, Long-Term Care Down Payment/Purchase, Providing Care/Caregiver For Parents, Co-Signed Obligations, Wedding, Kitchen/Bathroom/Roof/Deck/Windows/Wall/HVAC, 401(k) Loan, Margin Loan, New Automobile, New Auto Down Payment, Non-Budgeted Travel or Celebration, Life Insurance Loan, New/Second Residence Down Payment, Moving Expenses, Non-Budgeted Gifting/Donation, Bequest, Business Obligation, Startup Business, Alimony, Child Support, Final Expenses, Major Purchase, Mortgage Balance, Home Equity Line of Credit (HELOC), Auto Loan, and Auto Lease.

Listed toward the bottom right-hand corner of your Personal Balance Sheet would be "Total Liabilities." This line would be the sum of your Short-Term, Intermediate-Term, and Long-Term liabilities. Finally in the bottom right-hand corner would be listed "Net Worth." Net Worth is the most important product of your Personal Balance Sheet. It is calculated after all of your attention to detail and hard work simply by subtracting "Total Liabilities" from "Total Assets." An accurate assessment of your "Net Worth," and its elements, is mission critical to your plan.

INCOME AND EXPENSES

Your Retirement Cash Flow Statement (RCFS): Manage It, Don't Let It Manage You

Ninety-nine percent of retirement income challenges arise when individuals withdraw more than 5% per year from their investment portfolios. This is the most common element in challenging and sub-optimal retirement households...excessive portfolio withdrawals. Annual withdrawals greater than 5% (of the household's total investments) are the culprit and generally found at the epicenter of every draconian scenario.

—P.J. DiNuzzo

*Annual income twenty pounds, annual expenditure nineteen six,
result happiness. Annual income twenty pounds, annual expenditure
twenty pounds ought and six, result misery.*
                        —Charles Dickens, *David Copperfield*, 1850

**Capture every expected monthly expense of $10 or more on your Retirement
Cash Flow Statement (RCFS), and you will have the key to peace of mind.**

The second keystone, after your Personal Balance Sheet, for a successful
investment experience, Financial Wellness LifePlan, and retirement is your
Retirement Cash Flow Statement (RCFS).

Oh no, you may be thinking. *I'm going to have to do a budget.*

How about if we toss the word "budget" out for a minute and embrace the one
document that will make it possible to relax, enjoy life and, ultimately, have
peace of mind? Doesn't that prospect make the creation of a RCFS much more
appealing than creating a simple "budget?"

We can turn your financial frown upside down by looking at the RCFS in
the positive light with which it should be viewed. An annual or semiannual
"financial checkup" is as important or more than your yearly physical, dental
checkup, or eye exam. While most people would not consider skipping their
appointment with their doctor or dentist, often they do not give a second
thought to their semiannual or annual financial checkup. Your family's cash
flow knowledge is a powerful tool in your financial toolbox and until you
learn how to construct and leverage it properly, you are not likely to get a
comfortable handle on your financial wellness.

It will be obvious, once you have compiled a basic (retirement) cash flow statement, the need to either increase your income, decrease your expenses, save
more, and/or work longer. The key concept you want to internalize from this

chapter, just as in my other chapters, is another one of my investing, DiNuzzo Financial Wellness LifePlan™, and retirement success mantras: "Manage it… don't let it manage you."

Another key benefit of the RCFS is identifying your various savings targets. The savings targets are going to tie directly into your Financial Wellness LifePlan and retirement plan. Your financial independence planning number—i.e., your ultimate "nest egg"—is uniquely different from everyone else's. Each individual and each household needs and can tremendously benefit from a "DiNuzzo Financial Wellness LifePlan™" or similar process. Simply put, the RCFS will identify how much you need to save each month to reach your financial wellness and retirement goals.

Improving the Grade: Your Financial Report Card

Just as in grade school, high school, college, or grad school, the more time and focus you put on key areas by applying yourself, the better your "grades" are going to be. While earning a C or C- in a certain area is not optimal, even worse is not knowing you have a C or C-. The only way we can shift your priorities and improve your (financial wellness) grade is to know what that grade is. Whether it is your academic report card, or your financial one, identifying the problem areas are the first step toward material improvement.

Looking at the big picture from your cash flow statement, you want to identify your "income" and your "expenses." You need to know where you stand regarding what is coming in and what is going out on a monthly basis. As the Family Chief Investment Officer of your own family "corporation" or "organization," you have to be engaged in your role as a financial Fiduciary. It is your responsibility to pull the grades up and maintain an outstanding report card. My RCFS is designed to help you reach that goal.

It's All in the Details

One of the key aspects of the cash flow statement is the appreciation for detail. When you are working and have earned income (paycheck) coming into your household for one or both spouses/partners/individuals, you look at life differently. Your earned income "spigot" or "faucet" is turned on and wide open. Let's face it. When we are in full swing during our professional careers, we have a little bit more breathing room when it comes to our finances. If we make a mistake or misstep, we can always suck it in a little bit and watch our expenses for a few months to make up for it. We can work overtime to help compensate in that area for additional income to help amend our financial mishap. However, in retirement, which is the most important goal you will invest and save for, you simply do not have this luxury.

When you compile your RCFS, your goal is to capture any expense that is $10 per month or greater. This may seem a bit anal in its approach, but you need to appreciate your ultimate goal of financial independence, living richly, and retirement—that is, how important $10 or $100 or, especially, $1,000 per month can be. For example, if you were off on your cash flow statement by $1,000 per month entering retirement, thinking your monthly expenses totaled $8,000 per month when in reality they were $9,000 per month, based on today's current market, you would need to have approximately $300,000 in a portfolio for the average individual family unit. As always, I am basing this on an approximate 30-year retirement plan. So, if you looked at how much money you needed to be able to ensure that you can receive $1,000 per month, on an inflation-adjusted basis, for the remainder of your life in retirement, that requires approximately a $300,000+ portfolio. Considering this, the smaller dollar amounts mentioned take on new meaning. If you need $300,000 to provide that $1,000 per month in cash flow, then obviously you would need at least $150,000 for the remainder of your life to cover a $500 per month shortage.

Accuracy is vital, and although this may seem like a challenge, the hardest obstacle is actually one familiar to us all—procrastination. Just by getting started, you will have overcome 80% of your obstacles. Once you set up your first cash flow statement, the annual updates will be surprisingly easy to complete.

Pay Yourself First

A key criterion, and one of my most basic and fundamental cash flow recommendations, is the practice of *paying yourself first*. Control what you can control. If you were giving your children, who just graduated from college, any personal financial advice, this arguably would run a close race for the number one spot. Tell them to pay themselves first. What do I mean? Get in good savings habits now, by putting aside a minimum of 10% into savings. In many cases, they will have a 401(k) or 403(b) or some other type of qualified plan available to them at work. This allows them the additional tremendous benefit of being able to place money into those accounts *pre-tax* before federal taxes are withheld from their pay. The compounding benefits of this fact are dynamic and keeping the money away from Uncle Sam simply makes the savings process a lot easier.

So, you want to "pay yourself first"—one of my key mantras of successful personal financial planning. You want to save for retirement the smart way—save pre-tax. Remember, your ultimate goal is to be able to relax, enjoy life, and have peace of mind by planning ahead and staying on top of your personal finances with a Financial Wellness LifePlan and recurring "financial check-ups." You can, and will, remain in control of your personal finances, which is an extraordinarily liberating feeling, knowing that you can sleep at night without the stress of wondering, "Am I in good shape? Am I in bad shape? Am I behind? How far am I behind? How much more should I be saving? Is my income enough? Am I going to be able to retire… or am I going to have to work forever?"

Other than our health, concerns about our finances weigh heavily on many of us, consuming our thoughts 24/7, affecting our sleep, our eating habits, etc. A clearly defined cash flow statement will relieve you of the massive amount of anxiety that many individuals carry on their shoulders throughout life. It can free you of sleepless nights and a racing mind by placing you in control of your journey and destiny.

Will coming up with a personalized RCFS take a bit of work? Of course. However, the rewards, from a purely emotional perspective, will be of an exponential nature. Let's get started on your pathway to restful nights.

Italian Envelopes: Use the Cash Flow Management Process That Works for You

The key point of the RCFS, and the other processes I discuss in my book, is to develop a system you are comfortable with, something that works for you and your unique situation.

Most of my bedrock personal finance beliefs were taught to me by my parents and grandparents, who were all strong believers in consistently saving and having no debt. In awe at the real-world survival experience gained by my grandparents and great-grandparents growing up in the slums of Naples, Italy, and the ghettos of Warsaw, Poland, I heeded their advice at a young age. In particular, my Italian father, Natale (Ned), and his mother, Grandma Rose, had a "system" that worked for them. Remember, historically our country and economy had functioned as much more of a "cash" society, with no credit or debit cards and very little or no checking accounts.

My father and his mother ran their household budget and maintained their cash flow with what I called "Italian envelopes." Drawers were full of these envelopes with the names of particular categories: groceries, clothing, electric bill, savings, mortgage, etc. When I was growing up and exposed to this method, it seemed distinctly and uniquely Italian, as though this system had been handed down through the family from generation to generation. Since then, however, I have had numerous conversations over the years with clients of varying nationalities and ethnicities whose parents or grandparents also used the same system.

So whether it's "Italian envelopes," an Excel spreadsheet, or QuickBooks, I want to encourage you to use whatever tool makes you comfortable and successful in managing your cash flow.

The Retirement Cash Flow Statement (RCFS)

Our detailed (Retirement) Cash Flow Statement, as was the case above with our Personal Balance Sheet, is very customized and too expansive of a topic to review here so I will provide you with another executive summary.

As a reminder, your Cash Flow Statement is the other half of the footer/foundation for your Personal Finance House and another mission-critical element of your DiNuzzo Financial Wellness LifePlan™.

Your Cash Flow Statement can be thought of as being unique as to its "top" and "bottom." The top portion would list all of your income and sources. While the more voluminous bottom area would detail all of your expenses; Fixed Outflows, Variable Outflows, and Total Outflows.

The "Inflows" portion line items consist primarily of: Gross Salary, Social Security, Net Rental Income, Trust Income, Alimony, Child Support, Gas/Oil/Mineral Leases, Stock Options, Net Farm Income, Defined Benefit "Pension" Income, Annuity Income, Reverse Mortgage Income, Deferred Compensation, VA Benefits, Disability Income, and Portfolio Income.

Listed directly below your "Total Inflows" are your "Outflows," first "Fixed Outflows" followed by "Variable Outflows."

Typical "Fixed Outflows" are Mortgage, Rent, Home Equity, Second Mortgage, Condo Fee, Time-Share, HOA, Property Taxes-School/County/Local, Auto Payment, Auto Lease Payment, Homeowners Insurance, Renters Insurance, Umbrella Insurance, Flood/Mine/Wind Insurance, Auto/Boat/Motorcycle Insurance, Life Insurance Premiums, Healthcare/Hospitalization, Medicare,

Supplement, Long-Term Care, Long-Term Disability, Professional Liability, Malpractice, E & O, Union Dues, Federal Withholding, State Use Tax, and Payroll Taxes. The sum of these categories equals your "Total Fixed Outflows."

Next in line are "Variable Outflows." These include: Grocery, Household Supplies, Dining Out/Fast Food/Starbucks, Adult Beverages/Tobacco, Gasoline/Commute/Parking/Bus/Uber/Lyft, Auto Registration/Inspection/Taxes/AAA/EZPass, Auto Repair/Tires/Oil Change/Carwash, Pharmacy/Vitamins/Prescriptions, Credit Card/Student Loans/Alimony/Child Support, Tax Prep/Software/Legal/PT/Trainer/Chef/Chiropractor/Margin/Lifelock, Hair Stylist/Haircut/Nails/Salon/Spa/Massage, Clothing/Shoes/Linens/Dry Cleaning, Entertainment/Pitt/PSU/Steelers/Penguins/Pirates/Theater/Country Club, Movies/Concerts/Museum, Vacation/Travel/Visiting Family & Friends, Children & GC/Stipends/Tuition/Tutor/529s/Daycare/Sports/Lessons, Medical/Dental/Braces/Eye/Ambulance/CoPay/Deductible/Hearing Aid, Electric Budget, Heat Budget/Natural Gas/Oil/Propane, Water/Sewage/Trash/Recycle/Maintenance Contract, Cable/Satellite, Phone, Internet/SiriusxM/Netflix/Amazon Prime, Cell Phone/iPhone/iPad, Security System/Storage/Window Cleaning/House Cleaning, Paper/Magazines/Kindle/Audible/Babbel,/Job Expense/Professional Dues/Lawn/Landscaping/Pool/Pest Control/Hot Tub/Snow Removal, Home Maintenance/Repairs/Furnishings, Donations/Church/Temple/Charity/Political, IRA/Savings/Deferred Comp/HSA/FSA, 401(k)/403(b), Personal Spending/ATM/Gaming/Computers/Music Lessons, Hobby/Golf/Gym/Boat/Dock/Snow Skiing/Biking/Gardening/Hunting, Pets/Food/Vets/Sitting/Grooming/Prescriptions/ Insurance, Christmas/Hanukkah/Holidays/Weddings/Birthdays/Gifts, Miscellaneous.

Finally, in the bottom left-hand corner is the desired fruits of your labor. Your monthly Surplus or Deficit. This is calculated by subtracting your "Fixed Outflows" and "Variable Outflows" from your "Total Inflows."

As you can see…being accurate and building a great plan along with the resulting peace of mind takes time, effort, and knowledge or working with a Wealth

Management Firm who specializes in creating, maintaining, and providing ongoing guidance in these key building blocks of Personal Finance expertise.

The DiNuzzo Money Bucket Stack Analysis™ (dmbsa™): Organizing Your Investments into Understandable "DiNuzzo Money Buckets™"

Because of my background as a CPA, I look at every household as "the Smiths, Inc.," "the Jones Organization," or "Team Robinson." You simply cannot make valued personal finance decisions without knowing your Net Worth, assets, liabilities, incomes, expenses, and their various unique "flavors." These are the mission-critical levers and switches you will manage throughout your life and retirement. Every dollar of your household savings needs to be identified and have a purpose...a strategy. After a lifetime of hard work, you owe it to yourself to make sure you have a strategy for every dollar regarding its investment purpose, Asset Allocation, emotions management, tax management, accumulation management, withdrawal management, and estate goal maximization. Leaving your hard-earned money on the table for "Mr. Market" or "the tax man" should be unacceptable. I would rather it go to heirs and charities.

—P.J. DiNuzzo

Not only is there but one way of doing things rightly, there is but one way of seeing them, and that is seeing the whole of them.
—John Ruskin, *The Two Paths*, 1885

Everything should be made as simple as possible, but not simpler.
—Albert Einstein (1879–1955)

Separate your assets into the four "DiNuzzo Money Buckets™" of the "DiNuzzo Money Bucket Stack Analysis™" (DMBSA™), and your "DiNuzzo Financial Wellness LifePlan™" for financial independence and retirement success will begin to become crystal clear.

In this chapter, as I introduce the concept of the DiNuzzo Money Bucket Stack Analysis™ (DMBSA™), you will see *your* unique personal finance picture develop and come into focus. This is where the whole process starts to make sense, and all of the hard work you put into your personal financial checkup, Personal Balance Sheet (PBS), and Retirement Cash Flow Statement (RCFS) begins to come to fruition. As I said earlier, my goal is to take Nobel Prize-winning empirical research and make it practical and beneficial for everyone, and I've found my "Bucket" metaphor has worked exceptionally well over the decades to illustrate this process. The Bucket Stack analogy clarifies the importance of separating your money into different categories for different purposes, which then determines the proper Asset Allocations, time horizons, risk solutions, cash flow *and* withdrawal strategies.

The key benefit of the DMBSA™ is that it completes and brings into focus your "personal finance triangle for success."

In your personal finance triangle for success, you will see a symbiotic relationship between your PBS, RCFS, and DMBSA™. None of them, individually, provides all or even *most* of the answers. Even two of them together do not provide all of the answers. However, when you have three of them working together, you have a clear picture. This is when you can start to get excited about the process and your pathway to success, relaxation, peace of mind, and living your most meaningful and Best-Life! It is important to recognize that your personal financial plan is *fluid and requires ongoing guidance.* However, once you have gathered the data that you worked on earlier, you can start to move forward in planning with tremendous confidence—even as a novice.

Your "Wheelbarrows" of Investments

FIGURE 2.2. **Your "Wheelbarrows" of Investments**

The Discovery Meeting – "We Need a Second Opinion. Can You Help?"

Source: DiNuzzo Private Wealth, Inc. (DPW)/DiNuzzo Wealth Management (DWM)

The first step is to discover and identify what assets you currently have, and this is where many people experience a sense of overwhelm or uncertainty. If you're like most individuals, you don't give your financial independence/ retirement plan a lot of thought when you're in your 20s, 30s, 40s, or maybe even your 50s. You're working, you might have a family, and you've got multiple responsibilities and challenges before you: your job, your boss, your bills, your spouse/partner, your children, your health, your parents, your brothers and sisters, your friends. All these challenges seem to constantly demand your immediate attention, so you just "throw this money over your shoulder" into a big pile. You know you'll eventually need it for retirement, and you tell yourself you will organize it later.

All of a sudden retirement is starting to come around the bend, and you've got this unwieldy pile of various assets and investments that you haven't really thought much about. Suddenly you think or even panic, "I need to get organized."

So let's pretend you've made an appointment with us to discuss creating and collaborating with you to develop your one-of-a-kind "DiNuzzo Financial Wellness LifePlan™." You come into our office, bringing all of your assets in a large metaphorical "wheelbarrow"—your IRAs, CDs, money market funds, checking accounts, bonds, mutual funds, 401(k)s, 403(b)s, and annuities all in varying amounts. You know you need help organizing and assessing these assets to develop a Financial LifePlan and retirement income plan, but you're not sure what to do next.

Examining Your Investments, in Search of a Second Opinion

FIGURE 2.3. **Let Our Wealth Planning Team Analyze Your Buckets**

Source: *DiNuzzo Private Wealth, Inc. (DPW)/DiNuzzo Wealth Management (DWM)*

Now let's say you've pushed your metaphorical wheelbarrow of assets into one of our conference rooms and dumped it on the floor. If it wasn't clear to you before, it is now: you need help understanding not only what you've got, but formulating a clear plan to get what you still need. Fortunately, that's when things begin to make sense for us. Once I can see your entire financial picture spread out on our conference room floor, so to speak, we can start to build a plan for the rest of your life with the "DiNuzzo Money Bucket Stack Analysis™"

(DMBSA™). We advise that all pre-retirees would benefit from the same value-added fundamental procedure. Our recommendation is that you can never start planning too soon but ideally 10 years before your targeted retirement date. The ideal *minimum* period to start planning would be approximately 5 years. But even if you have less than 5 years there is still material value to getting started sooner rather than later.

Organizing Your Investments into Money Buckets

FIGURE 2.4. DPW/DWM Will Work with You to Start Getting Organized

Source: DiNuzzo Private Wealth, Inc. (DPW)/DiNuzzo Wealth Management (DWM)

At this point, as you can see from Figure 2.4, *DPW/DWM Will Work with You to Start Getting Organized*, we're starting to make some sense of your entire "pile" of investments. We've pulled out our Buckets, rolled up our sleeves, and started to organize the pile into four distinct categories: "Cash Reserves," "Needs" (Risk Capacity), "Wants" (Risk Tolerance), and "Dreams/Wishes" (Quality of Life/Legacy).

"**Cash Reserves**" form the foundation of everyone's DiNuzzo Financial Wellness LifePlan™, pre-retirement plan, and retirement income plan. The Cash Reserves Bucket has a *dual* purpose as do *all* of our other Buckets. Managing our *two* omnipresent planning "macro" challenges; "Art and Science." Art in our world is "Emotions Management" and Science is "numbers and quantitative management." Our LifePlan is contemporarily and constantly advising, guiding, and solving for Planning AND Emotions Management. Regarding financial planning we are solving ideally for a minimum (floor) of 12 months' cash related to total household monthly living expenses and a maximum (ceiling) of 36 months' cash. Relative to the other dual challenge, "Emotions Management," we want to identify your "sleep at night" number and do everything possible to ensure it is achieved. In case of an emergency, you don't need to worry about what's happening in the stock market, the bond market, or what the Federal Reserve "is up to.." This Bucket contains cash and cash equivalent investments, such as checking accounts, savings accounts, money market funds, certificates of deposit (CDs), ultra short-term bonds, and short-term fixed annuities. It should contain *no stock or stock mutual fund investments*. Additionally, in retirement, Cash Reserves must be fully funded *before* moving on to invest in stock and bond portfolios.

Again, while you're working, the *minimum* goal for your Cash Reserve Bucket should be six times (6x) your monthly living expenses. In retirement, the minimum balance should be 12 times (12x) your monthly living expenses or your "sleep at night" number, whichever is higher. *Ideally*, your Cash Reserve bucket in retirement would have a maximum of three years' worth of expenses. Occasionally individuals require a balance higher than 36 months. If that is your "sleep at night" threshold then that goal is what we will solve and plan for.

The next, most crucial section of the DMBSA™ can be compared to the mid-section, or "core," of a human body…the "Needs Bucket." But, before I explain the value and function of the next two buckets, "Needs" (Risk Capacity) and "Wants" (Risk Tolerance), I need to identify and have you understand the importance of the *four types of risk* humans are exposed to in their investment portfolios, as defined by behavioral science. The four aspects of risk and their level of importance in The DiNuzzo Financial Wellness LifePlan™ are:

1. Risk Capacity ("Needs")   (high importance, essential, mission critical)
2. Risk Tolerance ("Wants")   (high importance, nonessential, mission critical)
3. Risk Perceived   (low importance)
4. Risk Required   (very low importance)

Risk Capacity ("Needs") is the very minimal margin of error and risk that an individual investor *literally* can afford to take regarding their "Essential" expenses. It is purely a *financial calculation* that determines an investor's "Needs" expenses. Risk Capacity has to do with whether, for a given level of risk, the investor's financial situation can withstand the impact of a worst-case outcome. It has *nothing* to do with how much risk you can tolerate psychologically. Again, Risk Capacity is an absolute financial calculation, based on your most important expenses: "Needs" (food, clothing, shelter, healthcare, and transportation), which, again, are separate from the amount of risk you can tolerate psychologically.

The next risk level, *Risk Tolerance* ("Wants"), is more subjective because it is more directly related to and affected by the individual investor's "comfort level" with volatility. As such, Risk Tolerance is more of a *personality characteristic* and addresses your "nonessential"/"discretionary" expenses. A proper understanding of your Risk Tolerance will strike a balance between "growth and defense" in your Asset Allocation, and utilize index investing which has the inherent benefit of an approximately 90-year track record. This gives us more confidence to manage potential downside volatility through future market "corrections" and "bear markets." While Risk Tolerance is technically a stable attribute, it is not set in concrete. My experience suggests that it may decrease with age, albeit slowly. My research indicates that technically risk tolerance neither evaporates in bear (down) markets nor escalates in bull (upward) markets. Of course, we will witness cyclical behavior patterns where individuals will viscerally gravitate toward more risk in bull markets and less risk in bear markets. However, Risk Tolerance is more deeply ingrained and innate for each individual investor. However, overall, the variable we are analyzing here is behavior, and long-term behavior generally does not change significantly.

Although *Risk Perceived* has a low importance in my list above, it is important to internalize other comments from the numerous Dalbar research studies. Perceived Risk is one of the top causes of severe underperformance for the average individual investor. The other top two are lack of investment knowledge, followed by lack of self-control and discipline. Perceived risk can certainly be viewed as an element in one or both of these.

If an individual purchases an investment assuming that the worst-case scenario is a 10% drop in value (Perceived Risk), but it drops 20% or more, this might emotionally dislodge them and cause them to make subpar decisions such as liquidating some, most, or all of their holdings. Generally, what someone does in a risky situation (financially or otherwise) will be determined by their risk perception (this also includes how they have addressed their Risk Tolerance and Risk Capacity). What someone chooses to do depends upon the risk they perceive, their emotional risk preference, and the worst outcome they think they could survive. Individual investors should not give their "Good Housekeeping Seal of Approval" to any investment strategies where risks are not clear, as is often the case with improper risk perceptions. I attempt to educate individual investors about their downside risk perspective in terms that they can easily understand, so that they can more readily understand the risks they are facing.

Risk Required is the last type of risk, and it carries a *very low* level of importance. Risk Required is not actually a risk that is required, *but rather* a rate of return that is required. It has a low level of importance because I would never base any financial decision, such as your Asset Allocation, upon the level of return necessary to be generated by your portfolio in order to try to make your plan successful. When I analyze an individual investor's circumstances, resources, and goals, I use my expertise, spreadsheets, proprietary formulas, and collective wisdom of the "DiNuzzo Financial Wellness LifePlan™" to determine the rate required to achieve your goals—e.g., your own unique "household index" target rate of return for success. There will be a risk level associated with that return. Upon initial analysis, for example, the return required might be impossibly high—such as 20% per year. In that case we need to perform a reality check by reviewing your goals and objectives (along with all of our other financial planning tools) in order to bring this required return down over time to a plausible level. Generally, given any fall in investment portfolio values, the Risk Required will have increased unless goals have been reduced, delayed, or abandoned.

Risk Capacity ("Needs"). Now that I have defined the four kinds of investment risk, we can return to discuss the roles of the next two Buckets. Again, we *only* need to be concerned with two aspects of risk, *Risk Capacity* and *Risk Tolerance*, because together they both comprise over 99% of your relative risk exposure. Your Risk Capacity Bucket is funded after your Cash Reserve Bucket has been fully funded. In other words, if you don't have enough money to fund your Cash Reserves Bucket, even if your other Buckets are fully funded, you're not ready to retire. The primary reason Financial LifePlans and retirement plans blow up is because individuals withdraw too much money. Pragmatically, it means that the individual doesn't have enough money saved. Out of the Risk Capacity Bucket you will pay for all of your "Essential Expenses"–"Needs" in retirement, such as food, clothing, shelter, healthcare, and transportation. Your Risk Capacity Bucket should be invested very Conservatively/Moderately in a portfolio including stocks, bonds, mutual funds, and potentially guaranteed income that ideally won't drop by materially more than 10% in any one calendar year.

If as a retiree you have a "guaranteed income gap" on your Retirement Cash Flow Statement (RCFS), this bucket will provide the withdrawals to cover it.

For example, if your Social Security income is not enough to cover your food, clothing, shelter, healthcare, and transportation, this bucket will cover the monthly cash flow withdrawal shortfall for these expenses.

Risk Tolerance ("Wants"). Your Risk Tolerance Bucket is funded *after* your Risk Capacity Bucket has been fully funded. Out of this bucket you will pay for all of your discretionary "Wants" in retirement, such as vacation, travel, gifting, dining out, hobbies, and holidays. This portfolio should be invested typically in a "Balanced" portfolio strategy that ideally won't drop by materially more than 20% in any one calendar year.

My Risk Tolerance Bucket recommendation at age 70½ for IRA Required Minimum Distributions (RMDs) would typically have a *maximum* Asset Allocation of 60/40 (60% stock index mutual funds, 40% bond index mutual funds). Our most common Asset Allocation for clients when initiating RMDs at age 70½ is 50/50. If you observe the long-term data of over 90 years in most of our US Asset Classes, and approximately 50 years in International Developed Market Asset Classes you can observe the reason why I settle on approximately 50/50. In retirement, once you start to take withdrawals from your portfolio you always need to follow my #1 rule for this challenge…"Play Defense First." The downside risk of these portfolios (50/50) would be generally the maximum that you would want to subject volatility for monthly living expenses in your portfolio during retirement. You simply *cannot* ordinarily sustain a portfolio that could drop by considerably *more than* 20% in any one calendar year for these mission-critical "Want" expenses. The basic math of ever getting back to your previous portfolio "high's" if this occurs is daunting.

Legacy/Quality of Life ("Dreams/Wishes"). This bucket contains any "extra" assets in your overall aggregate portfolio—after all of your mission-critical and lifestyle withdrawals are satisfied and your first three Buckets have been funded. This Bucket ideally would serve as your long-term "cushion." While you're living, you would draw from this bucket for "quality of life" expenditures, such as extra travel, donations, gifting, vacations, or a second home.

After you're deceased, it becomes your "legacy," becoming the strategic Bucket exclusively dedicated to funding your beneficiaries, heirs, and charity.

Structuring Your Buckets in an Orderly Manner

FIGURE 2.5. **Structuring Your Buckets in an Orderly Clarifying Manner**

Source: DiNuzzo Private Wealth, Inc. (DPW)/DiNuzzo Wealth Management (DWM)

Now that you've put each asset into its proper bucket, you can begin to stack them in their proper order.

"Cash Reserves" (The Footer/Foundation Bucket)

Starting at the base of my DMBSA™ illustration in Figure 2.5, *Structuring Your Buckets in an Orderly Clarifying Manner*, which shows an example of an individual's money Bucket stack, you'll see the "Cash Reserves" Bucket—the most important part of this blueprint for success. Like any architectural endeavor, your structure is only going to be as solid as your base, and I want to be extraordinarily certain that your Cash Reserve Bucket is rock solid. Again, you want to maintain six times (6x) the value of your monthly expenses in your bank accounts, checking, savings, short-term bond funds, etc., while you are working. So, for example, if your monthly expenses are $8,000 per month while you are working, you want to maintain $48,000 in these combined accounts. More importantly, as the focus of my book is on investing for financial independence and enjoying a successful DiNuzzo Financial Wellness LifePlan™ and retirement, you want to maintain at least 12 times your monthly expenses in your Cash Reserves Bucket during retirement. If your monthly expenses in retirement are $8,000, for example, then you want to maintain $96,000 as a minimum in your Cash Reserve Bucket.

That will cover your basic expenses. But some people are more comfortable with establishing an additional "second level" of Cash Reserves. The most common example is when individuals' "sleep-at-night number" is higher than their 12x monthly number. I will provide cash management analysis and recommendations for those additional assets, often placing them in fixed income securities, such as bonds with a very short maturity. We may be comfortable holding bonds or bond mutual funds with one-, two-, or three-year maturities in that second level to achieve a higher level of income in the Cash Reserve Bucket. Also, a fixed annuity with a top-rated insurance company, which provides a higher yield, may be a good solution for many individuals as well. If you are short on your Cash Reserve target, especially while you are working, I would refer back to your Personal Balance Sheet, at the Taxable Assets listed directly below your Cash Reserve total. We would mentally flag some of these taxable accounts, whether joint or individual, to cover your Cash Reserve/emergency fund balance, in order to build the safest and strongest base for your Financial Wellness LifePlan.

Risk Capacity ("Needs")

The next Bucket, after we have established the foundation of your investment plan, is the *Risk Capacity* bucket. As I mentioned earlier, the Risk Capacity bucket is the first "core" area of your personal finances and its purpose is to satisfy any "Guaranteed Income Gap" identified in the Retirement Cash Flow Statement. In a minority of cases there is no income gap, such as when one or both spouses/partners have a defined benefit (pension plan) that covers all critical monthly expenses, then no Risk Capacity bucket is necessary. In these instances, I simply adjust the overall investment strategies accordingly. In the majority of cases, however, you will have a Risk Capacity need, and this will clearly show up as an income gap on your RCFS. In Figure 2.5, this is $500,000.

Risk Tolerance ("Wants")

Moving up the DMBSA™, we come to the *Risk Tolerance* Bucket, the second core strength area of your personal finances. After we have satisfied the needs of your Cash Reserve and Risk Capacity Buckets, additional assets would then start to accumulate in your Risk Tolerance Bucket—in this case $1,000,000.

Legacy/Quality of Life ("Dreams/Wishes")

Finally, we have $300,000 of additional assets in your top Bucket. This Bucket has maximum flexibility and is typically invested in a 70/30 Asset Allocation and often has additional investments allocated at 100/0.

In general, the higher the stack of money the better, but it's important to understand that a $100 bill from the bottom bucket is going to be very different than a $100 bill taken from the top. Each Bucket will have different time horizons, risk solutions, cash flow management strategies, Asset Allocations, growth targets, and withdrawal strategies.

Ideally the question marks hovering over your head have now turned to something more pleasant such as palm trees, now that you're starting to see visible progress and your customized plan is really starting to take shape.

Surveying the Stack

FIGURE 2.6. **Beginning to Bring Your Entire Investment Plan Together**

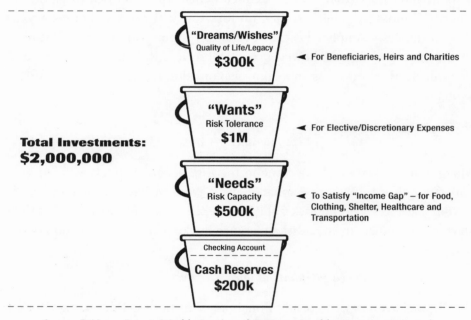

Source: *DiNuzzo Private Wealth, Inc. (DPW)/DiNuzzo Wealth Management (DWM)*

Now that your assets are all in the right buckets, and the buckets are stacked in the right order, we can take a moment to sit back and admire our work. In this scenario, you would probably be experiencing some relief: you would know every Bucket was funded, and that you even had extra money for your Legacy ("Dreams/Wishes") bucket. For example, one of my new clients discovered that he had $1.5 million in his Legacy Bucket, and he was still working at age 65 for $30,000 a year. How relieved would he have been to know this earlier? He was continuing to work simply because he just didn't know how exceptionally strong his plan was.

Developing a Detailed Cash Flow Plan

FIGURE 2.7. **Developing a Detailed Cash Flow Plan**

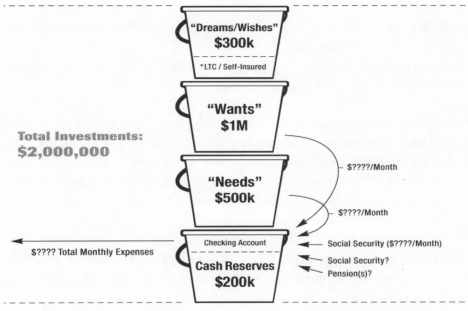

Source: DiNuzzo Private Wealth, Inc. (DPW)/DiNuzzo Wealth Management (DWM)

After we know what we have, we can now create a detailed cash flow plan for your pre-retirement and retirement, based on the amount and location of your assets, and see the DMBSA™ in action. In Figure 2.7, on the left-hand side of the bottom Bucket, based on your Personal Balance Sheet (PBS), we would list your expected total monthly expenses. Practically speaking, your detailed cash flow plan is going to answer the question, "Where is that money going to come from to pay for these monthly expenses in retirement after I am no longer receiving a paycheck?"

Notice at the top of the Cash Reserve Bucket the thin band titled *checking account*. In retirement, all of your monthly *income* will flow into your checking account (from the right on the illustration), and your total monthly expenses will flow out of your checking account (to the left, on the illustration), ideally like clockwork, to pay for the total expenses per month. For this example, the income coming into your checking account could include Social Security for one or both spouses/partners, and any defined benefit "pension" if applicable.

The Risk Capacity ("Needs") bucket on the right side of the illustration shows an arc of income flowing into the top section of your Cash Reserves (your checking account). That money is earmarked for paying your core fixed monthly "Needs" and Essential Expenses.

As I previously stressed, the most highly correlated element for a positive retirement experience and success is ensuring you have zero debt, which includes paying off your mortgage on any residences. Typically the only acceptable debt in retirement would be a short-term auto loan. Satisfying any debt requirements would also come from your Risk Capacity Bucket.

My Risk Tolerance Money Bucket, as noted earlier, is for covering all of your additional "*Discretionary*"/"*Non-Essential*" monthly expenses or "Wants." We would normally draw a predetermined amount from this bucket into your checking account to fund discretionary spending.

In the Legacy/Quality of Life Bucket, note the "LTC/Self-Insured" label at the bottom. This refers to any expenses you may have related to Long-Term Care Insurance (LTC); if you're "self-insured"[e.g. don't own an LTC policy(s)], that would be paid out of this bucket.

Before you begin to accumulate investments for your "Legacy/Quality of Life," you must earmark an adequate amount for any self-insured *healthcare* expenses. The longest gap and area of exposure regarding this expense is prior to age 65. If an individual retires prior to 65 and they do not have health coverage, then have to pay out of pocket for healthcare or hospitalization until they reach the "Medicare Life Raft." That expense, in many cases, can exceed the total of their mortgage payments over the course of their life on their primary residence.

After healthcare and hospitalization, the next critical element to address is Long-Term Care (LTC). Although only a minority of retirees ever require extended Long-Term Care (LTC), it is an extraordinary expense if they do. This is definitely an area where the ostrich approach does not work!

For instance, typical assisted living facility expenses exceed $8,000 per month, and in some cases can be over $10,000 per month. The average Long-Term Care (LTC) stay for an individual who needs an assisted living or skilled nursing facility is approximately between three to three-and-a-half years. In dollars and cents, this exposure per individual can approach $300,000 per spouse/partner *or more*. Individuals who have between $250,000 and $1 million of Investments have the greatest risk exposure and thus possess the most likely need for Long-Term Care (LTC) insurance, especially if they have strong Legacy aspirations. If an individual has less than $250,000 in investment assets, they typically will not be able to afford Long-Term Care (LTC) Premiums through retirement, although they should attempt to acquire the insurance. Starting approximately when an individual's investment assets are over $1 million, and especially when they are over $2 or $3 million, many decide to simply "self-insure" with their Legacy/Quality of Life ("Dreams/Wishes") portfolio.

Customizing Your Unique Asset Allocation

Probability is the very guide of life.

—Cicero

Now we can bring everything together. I've clarified each Bucket's purpose, milestones, goals, and objectives. I've identified, tagged, and organized every one of your hard-earned dollars into its unique "Bucket." I've placed the Buckets into their proper order. I've clearly illustrated the cash flow coming in from your funding sources for all of your monthly income needs (on the right side of Figure 2.8, *Customizing Your Unique Asset Allocations*). Finally, we can add the most important aspect and the final missing ingredient: the Asset Allocations (investment strategies), as shown on the left side of Figure 2.8.

FIGURE 2.8. **Customizing Your Unique Asset Allocations**

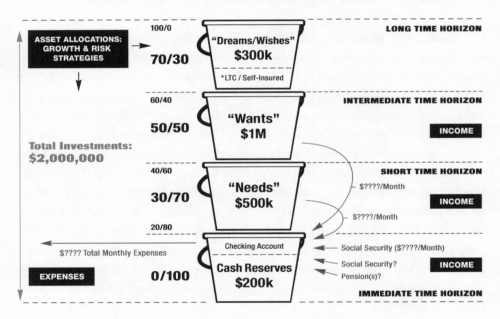

Source: DiNuzzo Private Wealth, Inc. (DPW)/DiNuzzo Wealth Management (DWM)

Asset Allocation (Asset Mix) is financial jargon for how much you hold in stocks versus bonds in your portfolio. As you look at all the activity coming in and out of that Cash Reserves Bucket at the bottom of the DMBSA™, you might notice that the money in the Legacy ("Dreams/Wishes") Bucket has no systematic or immediate expected withdrawals. When I point out to clients the long term or even extremely long-time horizon of these assets and investments the entire picture comes into focus. In fact, you may have a 99% probability that you're never going to touch that money at the very top.

As I'll discuss in more detail below, the Risk Capacity and Risk Tolerance Buckets will typically be placed on a DiNuzzo Descending *Glidepath*™ (with the allocation becoming consistently more moderate/conservative) for the rest of your life, since these are the Buckets that will provide monthly living expenses. To extend my metaphor, the Legacy Bucket will stay on a 30,000-foot cruising altitude, in most cases, for the remainder of your life.

That's why at the *very* top of the Legacy Bucket, you will see 100/0 (100% stocks, 0% bonds). As an example, that could be 100% in a stock portfolio for Roth IRAs, which is actually very common for the Legacy Bucket. Why a Roth IRA? Because it's currently arguably the best "account type" available to individual investors. It literally grows tax-free and the withdrawals are tax-free. If you had any money to leave to your children or grandchildren, you would want them to inherit a Roth IRA. Your children are likely to survive you by 30 years or more, and your grandchildren are likely to survive you by 60 years or more. Thus an aggressive growth strategy (up to 100% in stocks) in many cases, makes all the sense in the world as it can provide 10's or even 100's of thousands of dollars in additional growth over your loved one's life expectancies.

I can only find one quote from Albert Einstein in which he stated that he was "amazed" by anything, when observing the significance of "compound interest" as one of the greatest marvels of the universe. Heed Mr. Einstein's observation by keeping your Legacy money invested for aggressive growth—the extra 2% or 3% per year will be dramatic over time, and your beneficiaries' appreciation will be beyond words.

The most common Asset Allocation I recommend for the Legacy Bucket is 70/30. Seventy percent in stocks is the maximum amount that you would place in a portfolio in stocks and still maintain any noticeable downside benefit *vis-à-vis* risk/volatility. Thirty percent in bonds can provide palpable downside protection in a bad stock market period. But if you have just 10% or 20% in bonds, you're *not* going to notice much benefit in a bad market from a risk-adjusted basis. My minimum in this Bucket is 60/40 and my maximum, of course, is 100/0: 100% stocks and 0% bonds.

Concerning the *Risk Tolerance* ("Wants") Bucket, our most common Asset Allocation for this bucket is 50/50. As I will describe later in more detail, this is the average Asset Allocation for my typical client retiring in their 60s and taking withdrawals from their portfolio, especially when clients reach age 70½ and are taking RMDs (Required Minimum Distributions). Recommended ideal Asset Allocation ranges for this challenge should be 40/60 minimum and 60/40 maximum. The goal of this withdrawal portfolio is for the underlying investments to *never drop more than 20%* or more in any single calendar year.

As mentioned above, I recommend that this strategy, along with any other strategy from which you take monthly withdrawals for living expenses, typically be placed on a Glidepath throughout your retirement years. The Glidepath will lower the equity/stock exposure by approximately either 1% per year, 5% over a five-year period of time, or 10% over a 10-year period of time. Thus, for example, a typical retiree would have a 50/50 portfolio at age 65 for their Risk Tolerance bucket. To maintain their unique Glidepath, their portfolio would be at a 40/60 level (40% in stocks and 60% in bonds) at age 75, and 30/70 (30% stocks and 70% bonds) at age 85.

As a reminder, our DiNuzzo Financial Wellness LifePlan™ and retirement income plans are always based on the age of the *youngest* spouse, because one of our mantras is that we never want to run out of money before we run out of breath. It is not satisfactory just to have sufficient assets for the older spouse, but we must always plan on the younger spouse's age as well. I am commonly planning on a 30-year block of time (or until approximately your early- to mid-90s) for your retirement plan. I may, due to family data and demographics, actually plan for even longer, but I generally never want to plan for less than this.

Concerning your *Risk Capacity* Bucket, my historic preference is a *minimum* 25% in stock indexes, and 75% in bond indexes and a *maximum* Asset Allocation of 40/60 (40% in stock indexes, 60% in bond indexes). Our most common Asset Allocation for this Bucket is 35/65. If there is an "Income Gap" identified in your cash flow statement (RCFS), it is vital to remedy that with a "very low risk" or "guaranteed income" portfolio. The reason is that the Risk Capacity Bucket is paying for your *essential* expenses—food, clothing, shelter, healthcare, transportation, and education. This number will vary in every single analysis because it is completely unique to *every* individual investor and household.

I am able to evaluate Risk Capacity by analyzing the individual investor's financial statements and evaluating his or her particular financial life situation. I recommend that a client's "core expenses" for retirement income planning be covered by "guaranteed income," such as US Treasuries, FDIC insured investments such as CDs, or a 35/65 All-Indexed investment portfolio. In some cases "guaranteed income" may also include Single Premium Immediate Annuities (SPIA) or other previously purchased annuities, which have guaranteed lifetime withdrawal "living" benefit riders. Again, if an All-Indexed investment portfolio is utilized, the allocation would range from a minimum of 25/75 to a maximum of 40/60. Again, if you go this route, your target is to build a portfolio that will not drop by 10%, or much more, during any single calendar year.

And of course, for the *Cash Reserves* Bucket at the bottom (base), your Asset Allocation should always be 0/100. Again, the Cash Reserves Bucket is the *foundation* of your entire DiNuzzo Financial Wellness LifePlan™. It should have no equity/stock exposure. In fact, you want all, or at least most, of this bucket to be in FDIC insured assets (such as checking accounts, savings accounts, CDs, and money market funds) and/or government bonds. Again, in some cases, in the second level of this Bucket, you will have ultra-short-term bonds and/or fixed annuities. This is, after all, your "sleep-at-night" Bucket, and your investments must reflect that financial and emotional goal.

I want clients to have a minimum of 12 times their monthly living expenses in that Cash Reserve Bucket when they go into retirement. Again, ideally, we'd like to have up to three years in the Cash Reserve bucket for maximum peace of mind.

In conclusion, with the DiNuzzo Money Bucket Stack Analysis™, you now have a clear set of milestones, goals, and objectives, and a roadmap. You have a clear plan identifying your assets, liabilities, income, expenses, and Net Worth. My plan also identifies your "income gap" (if applicable), which is addressed by guaranteed income or an appropriate conservative/moderate solution from your Risk Capacity Bucket. Your Cash Reserves give you peace of mind, knowing that you have between one and three years' expenses on hand. You have a "Balanced" strategy for your Risk Tolerance Bucket, being able to take reasonable withdrawals out of your portfolio and have your portfolio projected to grow on a risk-adjusted basis to maintain your purchasing power through the future.

Additionally, if you do have Legacy ("Dreams/Wishes") assets, you will easily be able to identify them and have a specific long-term strategy related to those assets. Oftentimes, after our customization, my average client will have three or even four different Asset Allocation strategies in their DiNuzzo Financial Wellness LifePlan™. I will specify a conservative/moderate strategy for their Risk Capacity assets of approximately 35% in stocks. I will have a balanced growth strategy for their Risk Tolerance assets of approximately 50% in stocks and an aggressive growth strategy for their Legacy/Quality of Life assets anywhere from 70% to 100% in stocks. This is always a *very specific and customized solution* for you and your family or household.

"TAX BUCKETS"

FIGURE 2.9. **Tax Buckets (By Most Common Accounts)**

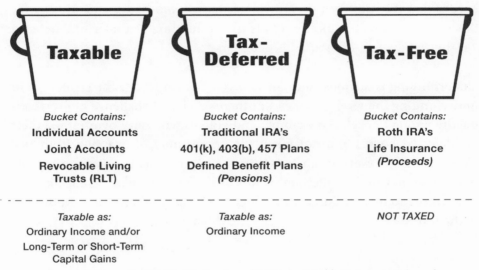

Taxable	Tax-Deferred	Tax-Free
Bucket Contains:	**Bucket Contains:**	**Bucket Contains:**
Individual Accounts	**Traditional IRA's**	**Roth IRA's**
Joint Accounts	**401(k), 403(b), 457 Plans**	**Life Insurance (Proceeds)**
Revocable Living Trusts (RLT)	**Defined Benefit Plans (Pensions)**	
Taxable as:	*Taxable as:*	*NOT TAXED*
Ordinary Income and/or Long-Term or Short-Term Capital Gains	Ordinary Income	

Source: DiNuzzo Private Wealth, Inc. (DPW)/DiNuzzo Wealth Management (DWM)

When you develop your investment portfolio(s), you also need to consider their target values *vis-à-vis* the three primary "Tax Buckets."

Your "taxable bucket" might be an individual, joint investment account, and/or bank accounts.

Your "tax-deferred bucket" might include an IRA, SEP-IRA, 401(k), 403(b), or other investments where the taxes you pay on the money in those investments are *deferred*. Your money grows in tax-deferred accounts for a period of time, and once you reach the age of 70½, as long as you're not working for the same organization, you have to take a Required Minimum Distribution (RMD) out of that portfolio per year and pay the taxes on it.

The third, final bucket is the "tax-free bucket," which might include a Roth IRA or taxable account, for example.

It's imperative that you diversify your investments across the three tax buckets, and equally important that you properly fund each of them. My experience is that rarely, if ever, do individuals have a knowledge and strategy for this challenge which typically results in overfunding or underfunding each Tax-Bucket by 100's of thousands of dollars.

Underfunding is obvious, and I'm sure you can appreciate the challenges in underfunding the wrong bucket, but there's an equal challenge of *overfunding* the wrong bucket. For example, individuals who have overfunded their tax-deferred bucket and not taken the opportunity of enacting Roth IRA Conversions to lower that amount miss the opportunity to enjoy the benefits of more money in their lifetime, as well as the benefits of being able to leave much more to their children and/or heirs, who may inherit those Roth IRAs in the future.

"WITHDRAWAL BUCKETS"

As illustrated in Figure 2.10, *Withdrawal Buckets*, careful thought needs to be applied to funding levels and targets along with withdrawal amounts and timing regarding your various "account types." While you are working, any possible withdrawals would ideally be limited to "taxable" account types. You do not want to corrode your long-term plan by taking withdrawals from your "tax-deferred" or "tax-free" Buckets.

Your strategy will change materially when you reach age 70½ due to IRS RMD requirements. At this point of inflection the "taxable" Bucket will move up and *initial* withdrawals for monthly living expenses etc. will come from your "tax-deferred" (IRA) Bucket.

FIGURE 2.10. **Withdrawal Buckets: Typical Withdrawal Sequence**

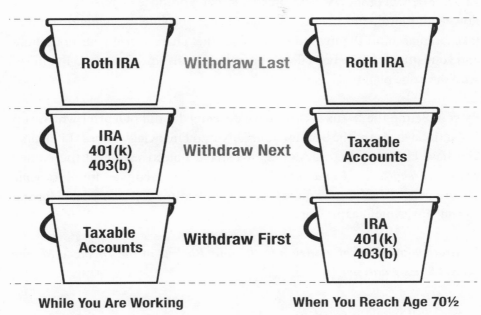

Source: *DiNuzzo Private Wealth, Inc. (DPW)/DiNuzzo Wealth Management (DWM)*

Again, there are numerous funding and withdrawal strategies applicable to these Buckets both while you are working and after you are retired that should be well thought in advance. We incorporate this process and challenge into your customized financial statements, DiNuzzo Money Bucket Stack Analysis™, and DiNuzzo Financial Wellness LifePlan™.

YOUR UNIQUE MONEY BUCKET STACK ANALYSIS™
FORMS THE BASIS FOR YOUR CUSTOMIZED
DINUZZO FINANCIAL WELLNESS LIFEPLAN™

As your Family CIO, you need the best planning tools possible. You can only build a strong foundation for your DiNuzzo Money Bucket Stack Analysis™ if you take the time to develop a solid blueprint and roadmap. Perhaps the most valuable benefit of the DMBSA™ process is that it produces a personalized cash flow, withdrawal, and investment plan that is absolutely *unique* to you and takes into account the myriad of variables that characterize your household and your situation. I've been developing these plans since 1989, and I've never seen the same plan twice.

By completing the DMBSA™, you have developed a full blueprint which you will ultimately use as the base for your DiNuzzo Financial Wellness LifePlan™. You have clear targets, milestones, goals, and objectives for all the money you've *worked so hard to accumulate*, and a customized plan for all of your investments in the future. You're well on your way toward your goal of having a great "investment experience," and *relaxing*.

Separate your "pile" of money into the four Buckets of the DiNuzzo Money Bucket Stack Analysis™ (DMBSA™):

1. *"Cash Reserves"*
2. *"Needs" (Risk Capacity)*
3. *"Wants" (Risk Tolerance)*
4. *"Dreams/Wishes" (Legacy/Quality of Life)*

Create a customized "right-fit" Asset Allocation for the money in each Bucket and set your withdrawal portfolios on your plan specific Glidepath to target your best risk/reward trade-offs over time.

STRATEGIC ("BUY AND HOLD") VS. TACTICAL ("MARKET TIMING") ASSET ALLOCATION

PLACING THE ODDS IN YOUR FAVOR

Strategic Asset Allocation, proper diversification, and utilizing low expense index funds are the Holy Grail of investing.

—P.J. DiNuzzo

Investment Policy (Asset Allocation) is the foundation upon which portfolios should be constructed and managed.

—Charles D. Ellis, *Investment Policy*

Asset Allocation is a strategy, advocated by Modern Portfolio Theory, for maximizing gains while minimizing risks in your investment portfolio.

—Roger Ibbotson, Yale University Professor of Finance, Chairman and Founder, Ibbotson Associates

Investing in the absence of an Investment Policy Statement [Asset Allocation] reduces decision making to an individual event-driven process of chasing short-term results, eliminating the expectation of achieving the long-term returns of capitalism.
— Mark T. Hebner, *Index Funds: The 12-Step Program for Active Investors*

ASSET ALLOCATION = RISK AND RETURN ALLOCATION

The *most* important investment decision you will make in your financial lifetime is how you decide to allocate your assets (e.g., stocks vs. bonds), both in aggregate and within your individual portfolios. Before I begin, it is important you have a full, firm, and comfortable understanding of the definition of *Asset Allocation*. Asset Allocation is simply the percentage of stocks (equities) versus the percentage of bonds and cash (fixed income) that you are going to maintain in your portfolio(s).

Your Asset Allocation will determine the success of your portfolio over time for two reasons: first, it is the primary driver for *returns*, and second, it largely determines the future *risk* (downside) of your portfolio as well. In the quote above, Roger Ibbotson summed it up quite well when he said, "Asset Allocation is a strategy, advocated by Modern Portfolio Theory (MPT), for maximizing gains while minimizing risks in your investment portfolio." This applies to individual investors as well as to the largest of portfolios managed by major institutions.

As my title of this chapter suggests, you need to ask yourself if you are going to approach your Asset Allocation decision *strategically* or *tactically*. Put simply, Strategic Asset Allocation is a "buy and hold" approach, and Tactical

Asset Allocation involves "market timing," "style drift," "manager selection," and "performance chasing." As I have illustrated in the data presented throughout my book, the supermajority of active mutual fund managers are using some form of a tactical, market timing strategy. Often, they have not established an absolute, fixed Asset Allocation—i.e., 60/40 (60% in stocks and 40% in bonds). They may start there, but as they *feel* the market view is improving, they may increase their exposure to stocks and go to 65% or 70% in stocks or more. Of course, if they feel the market "appears" worse, looking into the near and intermediate future, they may go down to 55% or 50% in stocks *or less*.

I advocate the exact opposite approach. My recommendation is a strategic, "buy and hold" approach with a firm, fixed Asset Allocation based upon your unique goals and objectives. My goal is to stay 99% invested in your customized portfolio(s) with 1% or less in cash. I do *not* want to time the market and take the risk that you have 5%, 10%, 15%, or more in cash when the market makes a move. Again, I will set your Strategic Asset Allocation—such as 60/40—and we will maintain that by staying 99% invested in your stock and bond positions within the portfolio. I want your entire portfolio of assets working for you 24/7/365.

The rest of my chapter will present the data that shows in detail why a proper Asset Allocation is so important to your financial future, and why a "buy and hold," strategic approach is so powerful. I will start by broadly looking at stocks and bonds respectively as a single Asset Classes. Then later I will add further detail within those Asset Classes. Although a 60/40 portfolio with 60% placed in a Total Stock Market Index and 40% placed in a Total Bond Market Index will perform quite well, you can further diversify within each asset classification. Such techniques have historically and going forward are expected to provide a higher rate of return while maintaining or even lowering your expected level of risk.

THE BEDROCK OF YOUR INVESTMENT STRATEGY: ASSET ALLOCATION DRIVES RISK AND RETURN

Approximately 94% of variability of a fund's investment return is due to Asset Allocation. (Study of 91 large pension funds over a 10-year period.)

> —Gary P. Brinson, L. Randolph Hood, and Gilbert L. Beebower "Revisiting Determinance of Portfolio Performance: An Update," 1990 working paper completed as a follow-up to "Determinants of Portfolio Performance," Financial Analysts Journal, July–August 1986.

FIGURE 3.1. **Asset Allocation Drives Risk and Return**

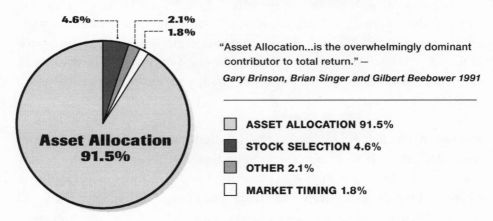

"Asset Allocation...is the overwhelmingly dominant contributor to total return." —
Gary Brinson, Brian Singer and Gilbert Beebower 1991

- ☐ ASSET ALLOCATION 91.5%
- ■ STOCK SELECTION 4.6%
- ☐ OTHER 2.1%
- ☐ MARKET TIMING 1.8%

The landmark Asset Allocation research in the 1980s and early 1990s culminated with the 1991 research by Gary Brinson, Brian Singer, and Gilbert Beebower. They determined that Asset Allocation is the *overwhelmingly dominant contributor* to portfolio volatility and total return. This research regarding Asset Allocation is ongoing. However, looking at a 10-, 20-, or 30-year time horizon or longer, the greater the exposure to stocks in the portfolio, the greater the expected rate of return (over full market cycles and periods with statistically significant data). In order to *begin* to anticipate a statistically significant expectation for the returns, based on the 90-year historic data, stock market exposure data should have a *minimum* 10-year holding period. Valid *statistically significant* expectations actually begin with 20-year-plus holding periods. As you can see in the Asset Allocation pie chart, Asset Allocation is by far the strongest determinant of your portfolio performance and risk. Surprising to many, individual stock selection, mutual fund selection, and market timing only account for a slight percentage of the overall risk and return, despite the fact that these are the variables most investors focus on. This research is not to be underestimated. It forms the bedrock foundation of your investment belief system and strategy.

FIGURE 3.2. **The Dynamics of the Asset Allocation Decision**

Hypothetical Returns: July 1, 1999 – June 30, 2019

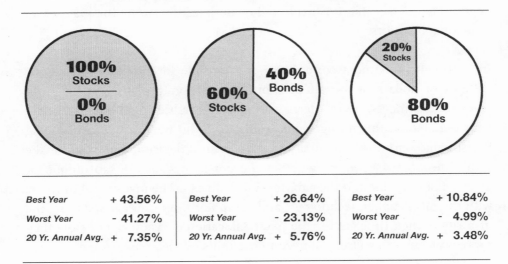

Best Year	+ 43.56%	*Best Year*	+ 26.64%	*Best Year*	+ 10.84%
Worst Year	- 41.27%	*Worst Year*	- 23.13%	*Worst Year*	- 4.99%
20 Yr. Annual Avg.	+ 7.35%	*20 Yr. Annual Avg.*	+ 5.76%	*20 Yr. Annual Avg.*	+ 3.48%

Source: Morningstar, Inc.

We can extrapolate from the study that for the long-term individual investor who maintains a consistent asset allocation and leans toward index funds, asset allocation determines about 100% of performance.
—Roger Ibbotson, Ibbotson Associates, *The True Impact of Asset Allocation on Returns*

My graphs in Figure 3.2, *The Dynamics of the Asset Allocation Decision*, show how the power of Asset Allocation drives portfolio performance over your lifetime. You can see the clear connection and correlation between how much money you have in stocks and the performance of your portfolio in both up and down markets. Simply stated, over the course of your life, a 100% stock portfolio has provided a greater rate of return than a 60% stock portfolio. Likewise, a 60% stock portfolio has provided a greater return than a 20% stock portfolio. The inverse is true during down markets. Again, the Asset Allocation decision is the most important decision you will make and directly correlates to the upside and downside "capture" rates in your portfolio, despite the fact that it is neglected or underestimated by the majority of individual investors.

Institutional investment committees—responsible for profitably managing trillions of dollars on behalf of enormous corporate plans, not-for-profit plans, endowments, TAFT-Hartley funds, universities, and foundations—have understood this for ages. For example, if you were on an institutional investment committee, the first and most critical decision you would make would be *Asset Allocation*—whether the portfolio sizes are $50 million or greater than $1 billion. If the smartest individuals in the investment universe with the most capital, technology, and computer firepower are spending the majority of their time getting the Asset Allocation decision right before they move on to anything else, you need to heed this learned observation.

Also, you may find it interesting to note that the average *institutional* Asset Allocation is approximately 65% in stocks and 35% in bonds. Most will have an Asset Allocation *minimum* of 60/40 and *maximum* of 70/30. Roughly speaking, their historic approach is approximately 2/3 in stocks and 1/3 in bonds. Similarly, my ideal recommended long-term growth strategy for ideal risk/reward trade-off is a 70/30 portfolio, with 70% in stocks and 30% in bonds.

My professional opinion is that a 70/30 allocation is the last optimal stop along the "stock exposure highway" before you get up to 100% in stocks. Anything less than 30% in bonds doesn't offer much in downside protection. Based upon the historic data for the last 90 years in the capital markets, I have come to the following conclusion: If invested properly, a 70/30 allocation is likely to give you a return approximately *equal to* the s&p 500, with 1/4 to 1/3 the risk of the s&p 500! At this point, for an aggressive growth strategy, you have basically reached a maximum point regarding *risk vs. reward*. For extraordinarily long time horizons, such as Legacy Bequests, Roth IRAs, and individuals in their 20s or 30s, a 100% stock, 0% bond portfolio may be ideal. But again, 100/0 is a pure and absolute growth portfolio; it is *not* a risk-adjusted strategy.

Everything else being equal, *time* (Time Diversification) is your best ally regarding your long-term expected returns (and risk mitigation), and also the most important investment variable in the balance of risk versus reward. I will go into greater detail later about my recommended portfolio Asset Allocations for various goals and time horizons.

In the meantime, to calculate your approximate Asset Allocation of stocks versus bonds, a classic common rule of thumb is to subtract your age from the number 100 (or 110 if slightly more growth oriented). This gives you a "ballpark" idea regarding the percentage of stocks you might have in your portfolio at your particular age. For example, if you are 40 years of age, then 100 minus 40 equals 60. Therefore 60% of your portfolio would be invested in stocks. Or, more simply, you could use the reciprocal of the rule and simply hold the percentage of bonds in your portfolio that is equal to your age. A 40-year-old investor would hold 40% in bonds. In my experience, although the time-honored rules have fluctuated in popularity over many decades, if an investor is more than 10% *above or below* these *rules of thumb*, they generally are incorrectly allocated. For instance, if you arrive at the 60/40 calculation identified above, and you are more than 70% or less than 50% in stocks, very likely your portfolio(s) are incorrectly allocated and not properly aligned with your unique risk profile and return goals and objectives.

THE WRONG ASSET ALLOCATION MIX CAN COST YOU YEARS OF RETIREMENT: PHILIP AND SARAH

Philip and Sarah came to see me in 2009. Philip was a professor and his wife, Sarah, was the family homemaker, staying home to raise the couple's four children while taking care of the household. Philip had enjoyed a long career and the couple did not have an extravagant life-style; as a result, they had amassed a healthy nest egg.

Philip had a 403(b), a Roth IRA, and a traditional IRA, and he and Sarah shared a joint taxable account. Their investments had been doing well through the mid-2000s, despite a dip in the stock market at the end of 2007. The couple had begun 2008 with Philip expecting to retire that spring. He and Sarah planned to celebrate his retirement with a trip to the Grand Canyon followed by visits to Nevada and California to see their children and grandchildren. Then they would return to Pittsburgh, where they looked forward to relaxing, entertaining friends in their home, spending time on hobbies and volunteering, and playing tennis.

Unfortunately, Philip had been following an 80/20 investment strategy. On his financial advisor's recommendation, he had invested 80% of his portfolio in stocks and 20% in bonds, and the couple had, in fact, put 82% in stocks and just 18% in bonds. This strategy might have made sense for Philip and Sarah when they were young newlyweds, but as Philip approached the final years of his career, an 80/20 Asset Allocation had put his retirement goals at risk.

In 2008, the Great Recession hit, and the couple's investments were devastated. The drawdown drop in their portfolio value was so egregious, Philip was forced to cancel his retirement.

When they came to see me the following year, Philip was still working. He had decided that he would not retire until his portfolio had regained all the value it had lost in 2007, 2008, and 2009. I worked with the couple to put them on a path to retirement as expeditiously as possible, but their situation could have been avoided if they had had a plan and aligned their Asset Allocation mix with Philip's age, his years to retirement, and their retirement goals. They could have been relaxing, traveling, and spending time with their children and grandchildren, but the wrong strategy cost them those precious years because Philip had to delay his retirement and continue working.

Remember the Pollyannaish *emotional flaw* embedded in the typical individual investor who always wants to be all in stocks when the market is going up versus all in cash when the market is going down.

Previously, Figure 3.2 gave you the "bird's-eye view" regarding the *power of Asset Allocation* and the importance of your Asset Allocation decisions. In Figure 3.3, *Hypothetical Portfolio Returns*, we are taking a deep dive and looking at the "granular view" *vis-à-vis* the significance of Asset Allocations and how they affect expected portfolio returns and risk. As you move from left to right, you are looking at six index portfolios with *hypothetical* returns from 1973–2018. The direct correlation between a higher percentage of stocks and a higher expected return is blindingly obvious from this data. As you add more stocks to your allocation, your expected rate of return increases, and your annualized standard deviation (risk) percentage rises accordingly.

FIGURE 3.3. **Hypothetical Portfolio Returns**

	Fixed	Defensive Growth	Moderate Growth	Normal Growth	Very Aggressive Growth	Maximum Aggressive Growth
EQUITY *(Stocks)*	0%	20%	40%	60%	80%	100%
FIXED INCOME *(Bonds)*	100%	80%	60%	40%	20%	0%
Annualized Return (1973-2018)	6.0%	7.5%	9.0%	10.6%	11.7%	12.9%
Annualized Standard Deviation (1973-2018)	2.4%	3.7%	6.3%	9.2%	12.2%	15.2%
Lowest One-Year Return (Worst 12 Consecutive Months)	0.2%	-9.7%	-21.9%	-32.8%	-42.6%	-51.3%
Highest One-Year Return (Best 12 Consecutive Months)	22.6%	25.5%	33.7%	46.1%	63.0%	82.9%

Assumes all strategies have been balanced monthly. Annualized standard deviation is calculated from monthly data.

All performance results of the balanced strategies are based on the performance of indicies with model/back-tested asset allocations; the performance was achieved with the benefit of hindsight; it does not represent actual investment strategies. The model's performance does not reflect advisory fees or other expenses associated with the management of an actual portfolio. There are limitations inherent in model allocations. In particular, model performance may not reflect the impact that economic and market factors may have had on the advisor's decision-making if the advisor were actually manging client money.

Past performance is no guarantee of future results.

Source: Morningstar, Inc.*

Moving on, it is even easier to see the variation between the lowest and highest one-year return. The lowest one-year (consecutive 12 month) return rate for the defensive growth portfolio (20/80) is a -9.7%, whereas, on the far right, the lowest return for the maximum aggressive portfolio (100/0) is a -51.3%. Now that you have looked at the downside, you need to see how the same allocations fared on the upside. The highest consecutive 12-month, one-year return for the 20/80 allocation is +22.6%, while the 100% stock portfolio is +82.9%. This is a deeper look at the power of Asset Allocation. It should be obvious after looking at this data, the direct relationship in your mind and the importance of your stock-to-bond ratio(s).

FIGURE 3.4. **Typical Asset Allocation Diversification**

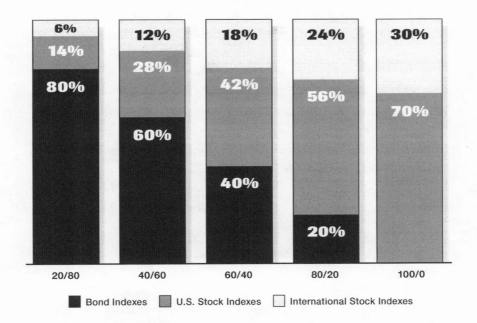

Overview of Portfolios

■ Bond Indexes   ■ U.S. Stock Indexes   □ International Stock Indexes

Once we have identified your broad Asset Allocation between stocks and bonds, we can begin to diversify within these broad Asset Classes. Gary Binson, Ron Surz, and Roger Ibbotson have made tremendous contributions to the field with their research on diversification allocation, which has focused on the importance of identifying which mix of indexes is best for individual investors. This image helps you to understand the broadest level of Asset Classes that I utilize in portfolio construction, identifying just the three largest broad Asset Classes: Bond indexes, US Stock indexes, and International Stock indexes. Obviously, as I mentioned previously, all investors, and their portfolios, have a "unique DNA" characteristic and there is a continuum of risk exposures (customized Asset Allocations) necessary to meet your unique "Needs" (Risk Capacity) and "Wants" (Risk Tolerance) milestones, goals, and objectives.

The allocations in Figure 3.4, *Typical Asset Allocation Diversification*, illustrate variations within 20/80 (20% stock and 80% bond), 40/60, 60/40, 80/20, and 100/0 portfolios. You can see the relative percentages in each portfolio and the ratios as we increase from 20% in stocks, to 40%, and so forth. If you look at the most aggressive portfolio, which would be 100% in stocks and zero in bonds, listed as 100/0, my recommended stock allocation is 70% to *Domestic (US) Stock* indexes and 30% to *International Stock* indexes.

> *To reduce risk it is necessary to avoid a portfolio whose securities are all highly correlated with each other. One hundred securities whose returns rise and fall in near unison afford little protection than the uncertain return of a single security.*
>
> —Harry Markowitz, Nobel Laureate,
> *Efficient Diversification of Investments*

FIGURE 3.5. **Benefits of Asset Allocations**

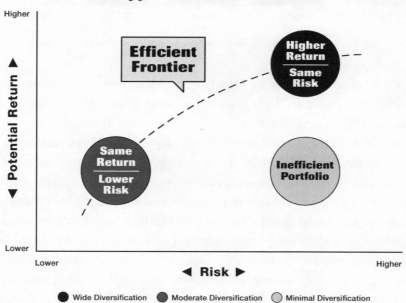

Source: Ibbotson Associates.

Here in Figure 3.5 you can observe what academic research has identified as "The Efficient Frontier." I will be delving into this topic more thoroughly in later chapters, but for this chapter I will simply focus on the power of proper Asset Allocation. In plain English, most portfolios individuals have can be *reconstructed* to have the same expected rate of return with materially less risk, *or* have a significantly higher expected rate of return with the same risk level. The supermajority of portfolios constructed by individuals fall well below the Efficient Frontier based on available long-term capital market data.

In observing that the Efficient Frontier is curved, a key finding of the concept was the benefit of proper diversification. Optimal portfolios that fall along or in close proximity to the Efficient Frontier tend to have a higher degree of diversification than the portfolios that fall below. Portfolios that fall below the Efficient Frontier have a *lower* expected risk-adjusted return than is available. The Efficient Frontier concept was introduced by Nobel Laureate Harry Markowitz in 1952 and remains the cornerstone of Modern Portfolio Theory (MPT).

> *The only new thing in the world is the history you don't know.*
> —Harry S. Truman

TOO LITTLE IN GROWTH (STOCKS): LARRY AND THERESA

Larry is an actuary and his wife, Theresa, is a schoolteacher. They have a commensurably high risk for tolerance that's common in dual-income couples, but they are also what I refer to as Family Stewards, so their risk tolerance is tempered by their priority of ensuring they are covered financially for their lifetime without negatively affecting their legacy. As Family Stewards, they have an *equal* (perhaps even greater) sensitivity to the needs of their children and grandchildren. Larry and Theresa want to leave them a decent inheritance.

When I met the couple, they had close to $350,000 in Roth IRAs. Their retirement plan was extraordinarily solid, with money for all their "Needs" Bucket including food, clothing, shelter, healthcare, and transportation. Each of them had a small pension, and this along with the Required Minimum Distributions (RMDs) and income from Social Security were more than sufficient to support their plan. In fact, they had a comfortable monthly *surplus*.

Their Roth IRAs were essentially what I refer to as a "Dreams and Wishes" Bucket that they could spend however they liked—vacations, travel, gifts, and so on. The DiNuzzo Way™ entails always putting our client's Best-Life first, and at first glance, this seemed like the obvious logical outcome for the couple, based on their investment portfolios. Whatever money was left in this bucket after the last spouse had passed would be distributed to their children and grandchildren.

I created a customized DiNuzzo Financial Wellness LifePlan™ for the couple and it was clear that they had high scores in all their planning buckets: "Cash Reserves," "Needs" (Risk Capacity), "Wants" (Risk Tolerance), and "Dreams/Wishes" (Quality of Life/Legacy). This may sound like a perfect situation for a retired couple, but there was an egregious flaw in Larry and Theresa's investment strategy: only 30% of their IRAs were in stocks.

Since their Wants and Needs were solidly funded, their Roth IRA portfolios were queued up to allow for much more growth, as they would not be touched during their lifetimes. They should have had *at least* 70% in stocks, if not 100%. Assuming a 32-year life expectancy for the couple after retirement, that money would have decades to grow before it was distributed to the children and grandchildren. It's also likely that the beneficiaries would not simply spend it all as soon as they received it, but that they would allow it (or at least part of it) to continue to grow throughout their lifetimes. In essence, the money in Larry and Theresa's Roth IRAs still had 50 to 60 years, or greater, of growth.

To put this in perspective, historically, $350,000 invested 30% in stock indexes and 70% in bond indexes (a 30/70 strategy) would have grown to modestly over $2 million over the past 30 years. Compare that to investing 100% of the same amount in a globally diversified stock index portfolio. Over the past 30 years, that portfolio would have grown to materially over $7 million. By ignoring the probable longevity of their Roth IRA portfolio and instead choosing to invest their "Dreams and Wishes" Bucket too conservatively, Larry and Theresa had positioned themselves to potentially miss out on earning an additional *$5 million* on their investment that could have been passed on to their beneficiaries.

Again, this is not the strategy to follow for money that you will need during your lifetime. But if you have money set aside for your children and/or grandchildren, like Larry and Theresa do, you need to stop looking at it as a short-term investment and instead treat it like the long-term time horizon investment it is, with many years of growth (and the risk tolerance that comes with those years) ahead of it. Otherwise, you could fall far short of your opportunity *and* your goals as a Family Steward, and leave a much smaller inheritance behind for your children and your children's children—in Larry and Theresa's case, $5 million less.

Figure 3.6, *Portfolio Risk and Return* provides a continued illustration of the Efficient Frontier. You will notice that a 20% stock portfolio with 80% bonds (20/80) has historically contained a surprisingly *lower risk level* than a 100% bond portfolio. This is because even though bonds have a lower risk level than stocks, they do have periods over the average five-year business cycle where on average they are losing money as well due to market induced reduction to their face value. Historically, during this period when bonds are losing money, stocks typically grow and more than make up for the bonds' slide in value. Notice the change after you pass the 40% mark in stocks. You begin to see a balance between the risk of placing more stocks in your portfolio and the reward of a higher return. If you think of investing relative to the "financial scales of justice," then if you put "one pound of return" in your portfolio, you never want to put any more than "one pound of risk" in your portfolio at the same time. The image previous to this one, Figure 3.5 *Benefits of Asset Allocations*, shows how most investors invest below the Efficient Frontier and ineffectively place 2 pounds or more of *risk* in their portfolio for only 1 pound of expected *return*.

FIGURE 3.6. **Portfolio Risk and Return**

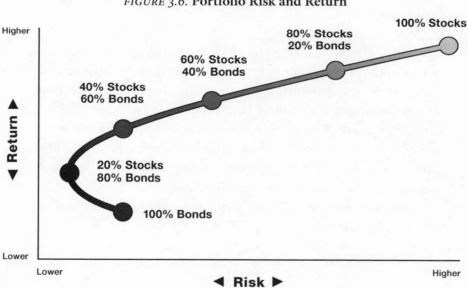

Still, I figure we shouldn't discourage fans of actively managed funds. With all their buying and selling, active investors ensure the market is reasonably efficient. That makes it possible for the rest of us to do

the sensible thing, which is to index. Want to join me in this parasitic behavior? To build a well-diversified portfolio, you might stash 70 percent of your stock portfolio into a Wilshire 5000-index fund and the remaining 30 percent in an international-index fund.

—Paul Samuelson, Nobel Laureate, from John C.
Bogle's *The Little Book of Common Sense Investing*

FIGURE 3.7. **Typical Efficient Frontier for US and International Stocks**

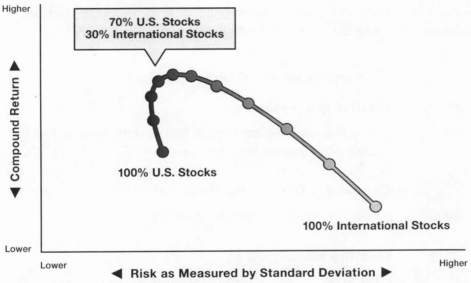

In Figure 3.7, *Typical Efficient Frontier for US and International Stocks,* I delineate the *equity* Efficient Frontier as I compare portfolios with a blend of US and International stocks. The top of the curve is the location of the optimal blend of these two Asset Classes. This image relates back to the 100% stock portfolio (100/0). Whereas I have an excellent database for the US capital markets, going back to approximately 1926, the International database does not go back as far and begins in approximately 1970. Nonetheless, a 40+ year history relative to this image provides very valuable insight in constructing your portfolios. Historically the ideal long-term mix recommendation has been approximately 70% US stocks and 30% International stocks. I would never overreact to a short-term vacillation based on my expectations (such as US underperformance *or* overperformance), but instead monitor it on a long-term, rolling period basis. Remember my mantra of always managing your portfolios based on a philosophy, strategy, implementation, and discipline. This understanding of the Efficient Frontier gives you the confidence to keep a steady hand through periods of volatility. Note: Vanguard Investments has historically recommended 30% of stock exposure dedicated to International. Vanguard recently *increased* their International stock exposure guidance to approximately *40%* of the overall stock allocation per portfolio.

FIGURE 3.8. **Investor Goals for Fixed Income**

Capital Preservation

- Ongoing capital preservation and liquidity management
- Long-term capital preservation

Customize Overall Portfolio Volatility

- Adjust asset mix to match volatility preferences

Liability Management

- Uncertainty with respect to liabilities allows for trading-off risk (funding gap ratio) with unexpected returns

Total Return

- Trading-off risks with expected returns

With Figure 3.8, *Investor Goals for Fixed Income*, I introduce the concept of *fixed income/bonds*, which will serve as the "anchor," "ballast," and "volatility mollifier" for your portfolio. The investor goals for Fixed Income serve first and foremost to *mitigate risk* in your investment portfolio. The fixed income in your portfolio, based on my recommendation, will be approximately that of high-quality short-term and intermediate term bond indexes. On a risk-adjusted basis, the incremental returns in your portfolio will be better seized on the equity/stock side of your investments rather than chasing low quality, hybrid, or long-term bond interest rates. There are only two "Premiums" available in the bond market; "Term" (Length) and "Credit" (Quality) Bonds, again, are for capital preservation, to reduce overall portfolio volatility, and for liability management. When you look at your portfolios throughout the remainder of my book, you will be looking at everything through the lens of *Total Return*. This means that you will be looking at the expected rates of return and the associated volatility and risk in the portfolio not just for the individual underlying index at the Asset Class level, but for the *entire portfolio as a whole*.

THE IMMENSE VALUE OF BONDS IN YOUR ASSET ALLOCATION

If you were to look at the bond market over a reasonable period of time, for example over a recent approximate 50-year period, you would begin to appreciate the value of bonds from a big-picture perspective. Figure 3.9, *Evaluating Fixed Income (Bonds) Typical Maturity Risk/Return Trade-Off*, illustrates the benefit of having this robust of a database. As you progress from One-Month US Treasury Bills, you see the annualized compound returns move up in proportion to the annualized standard deviation (risk). However, around the one-year mark, the standard deviation (risk) increases sharply and then intersects with the compound return around the five- to seven-year mark. Because I include bonds in my clients' Asset Allocation, primarily as a risk mitigation position, I do not want to overextend their bond term average maturity typically beyond this five- to seven-year risk/return "sweet spot."

Again, the key points to remember regarding bonds in your Asset Allocation are lowering the risk in your portfolio, maintaining a high credit quality,

staying in "investment grade" bonds, and keeping the bonds short to intermediate term. My portfolios have historically and consistently included primarily government bonds, AAA, AA, A, and BBB+ graded bonds.

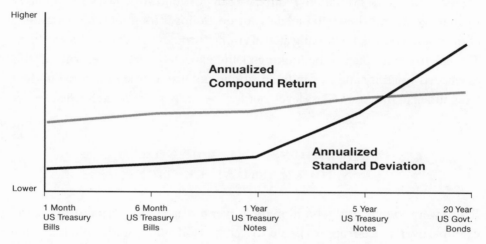

FIGURE 3.9. Evaluating Fixed Income (Bonds)
Typical Maturity Risk/Return Trade-Off

1964 – 2018

Not all investors define risk as standard deviation. Some investors may seek to hedge long-term liabilities using long-term
bonds. Historically, longer-maturity instruments have higher standard deviations than shorter maturity instruments.

THE DANGERS OF HAVING A
HIGH-RISK TOLERANCE AND BASING
YOUR PLAN ON IT: ABE AND ANNA

Abe is the CEO of a manufacturing company and Anna is an accountant. They have three children, all grown and on their own. Abe and
Anna aren't only a couple, they're a team when it comes to saving
money and managing their finances. Over the years, they've jointly

weighed every expenditure and have made sacrifices for the benefit of their nest egg. After forty years of steady employment, they have a lot to show for it in their portfolios.

The stability provided by their dual-income status accentuated Abe and Anna's higher-than-normal tolerance for risk.

When I met them, they were invested 100% in stocks. Even though they'd taken some serious financial hits over the years, they had recovered each time and were comfortable continuing with this strategy—basically what I refer to as "going 85 mph in a 55-mph speed zone" with no reasonably safe retirement "off-ramp" in sight. Any typical bear market (with stocks down 20% or more) would have effectively derailed or at *least* put a *significant dent* in their retirement plans.

Neglecting to control that which you *can* control in your portfolios thereby exposing your retirement to unnecessary risks in this manner is *never* a good strategy, not at twenty-one years old and certainly not when you're nearing the end of your professional career. A future bear market in retirement could flip your plan upside down and you would not have sufficient time to recover.

As I listened to Abe and Anna explain their investments to me, I thought about all the other couples I'd met who had followed the same strategy but had come to me much too late. They'd been in the same financial danger zone—"going 85 in a 55"—and when we hit a bear market, they had crashed *hard*. After decades of work, sacrifices, and methodical savings, this *one* non-strategic and toxic Asset Allocation choice had crashed their retirement plans.

While you're working, the optimal concept is "save and grow," whereas after you're retired, it morphs into "play defense first." Playing defense first in retirement *mandates* understanding that portfolios from which you're taking withdrawals can only afford to go down a certain percentage limit in a bear market and still be expected to grow back to the previous levels. Driving too fast can cut some muscle from your portfolio but if it cuts into the bone, there is *permanent damage.*

For some people I spoke with, the implosion had been catastrophic. This draconian result could cause your retirement plans, plans for your children, and your legacy goals to never be met.

The stress around these situations cannot be emphasized enough. Couples who suffer through an event like this, caused by basing their plans solely on their high-risk tolerance, are not only financially but often *emotionally* and even *physically* devastated, not only due to the permanent loss in value of their portfolios but also by the fact that *their situation could have easily been avoided—knowledge they acquired after the fact, unfortunately.* By the time it happens, it's too late and they can't turn back the clock to fix everything. They will never recover their portfolios' value that they lost by choosing to invest 100% in stocks in a portfolio that is targeted for providing withdrawals to live off of the rest of their lives.

These circumstances are more common than you would imagine. The "masking effect" that occurs in dual-income households is like a protective shell that allows couples to endure volatility in the market while they're working, but that all changes when they are nearing retirement and have limited time to recover the lost value in their portfolios, or when they stop working and are unable to generate any more income. The paycheck that's been filling their "retirement silo" stops, and if the silo has suddenly been depleted by a bear market, they are going to have to live out the rest of their lives on a scarce amount of "corn."

If you're "driving this dangerously fast," you *can* do something about it, but time, as they say, is of the essence. Don't risk your retirement plans by going 85 mph when you could enjoy a long, well-funded retirement by simply slowing down to 55. Otherwise, your retirement could be derailed and all your plans could be sent headlong into the ditch.

FIGURE 3.10. **Typical Credit Premiums in Investment Grade Bond Returns**

1973 – 2018

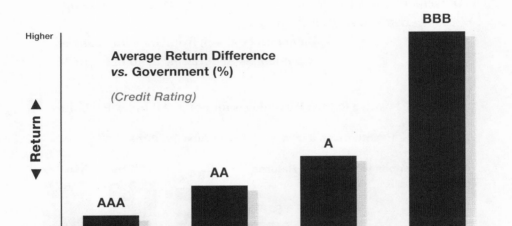

Figure 3.10, *Typical Credit Premiums in Investment Grade Bond Returns* illustrates the bond market's "Credit Premiums." I remind investors that these are the only two identifiable premiums in the bond market that are available, Term and Credit. In other words, these are the fundamental two "factors" to take into consideration when investing in bond indexes. Specifically, for your portfolio of blended bond indexes, the terms should be "short to intermediate" and the credit "Investment Grade."

Again, most of your positions will be US Government, AAA, AA, A, or BBB+ quality. Figure 3.10, *Credit Premiums in Investment Grade Bond Returns* illustrates the premiums across the various Investment Grades available in the market over an approximately 40-year period. To reiterate, I do not believe in investing in "junk bonds," because I believe that you can achieve a better risk-adjusted rate of return on the stock side of the portfolio instead of going lower on the credit quality on the bond side of the portfolio.

> *The investor with a portfolio of sound stocks should expect their prices to fluctuate and should neither be concerned by sizeable declines nor become excited by sizeable advances.*
>
> —Benjamin Graham, from *The Little Book of Common Sense Investing* by John C. Bogle

FIGURE 3.11. **Positive Return Percentages for 60/40 All Index Portfolios**

Hypothetical: January 1, 1969 – June 30, 2019

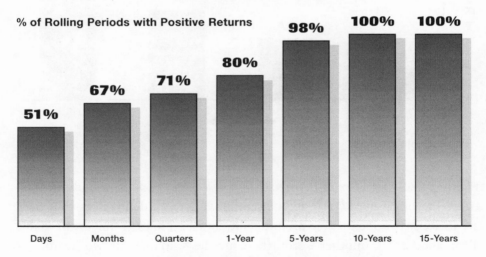

Source: Morningstar, Inc.*

An important and significant part of our job as Wealth Managers is "managing expectations." The portfolio that I have illustrated in Figure 3.11, *Positive Return Percentages for 60/40 All Index Portfolios* shows 60% DFA stock positions and/or benchmarks, along with 40% DFA bond positions and/or benchmarks. This illustration covers the 50-year period starting on January 1, 1969. The "expectations to manage" are that over these 50 years, you could see that, on any given day, the percentage of days with positive returns versus negative is virtually a "coin flip." Moving on to rolling monthly returns, you see positive returns approaching approximately two out of three monthly returns. For quarterly returns, you see positive returns for approximately three out of four quarters. For annual returns over these recent 50 years, the 60/40 portfolio had positive returns for approximately 78% of those 50 years. The most significant portion of the illustration is the negative percentage in the one-year data: approximately 22% of the time, a 60/40 portfolio registered a negative rate of return over the course of one year. You need to commit to memory that any typically allocated stock and bond portfolio will experience *negative* returns, on average, once every 4–5 years. The key is to look at the 5-year rolling average, with 60/40 being positive 95% of the time, and over the course of 10 years being positive 100% of the time. When building portfolios for our clients, we need to always manage the downside first, or "play defense first," in our portfolios. If you can handle the downside, the upside will always take care of itself. I have always reiterated to clients that we are implementing a portfolio strategy for the "rest of your life," not just some short-term "noise filled" period of time.

> *Yes. First, get diversified. Come up with a portfolio that covers a lot of asset classes. Second, you want to keep your fees low. That means avoiding the most hyped but expensive funds, in favor of low-cost index funds. And finally, invest for the long term. [Investors] should simply have index funds to keep their fees low and their taxes down. No doubt about it.*
>
> —Jack R. Myer, from *The Little Book of Common Sense Investing* by John C. Bogle

Hypothetical Diversified All Index Portfolios vs. S&P 500 Index

Thinking about diversified All-Index portfolios versus the S&P 500 only exposes you to the bigger picture that will continue to unfold throughout the remainder of my book. The S&P 500 is a basket of 500 of the, generally speaking, largest "Blue Chip" stocks available in the US stock market, and I will refer to it as a common benchmark when thinking about a *globally diversified* basket of indexes invested in DFA (Dimensional Fund Advisors) funds. The S&P 500 has had an approximately 10% annualized rate of return per year over the recent 50-year period (January 1968 through December 2018). The S&P 500 has typically underperformed a 100% stock portfolio by 1% or 2% but has approximately the same amount of risk. On the flip side, a 60/40 portfolio has slightly underperformed the S&P return over these 50 years, but with much less risk. I will be referring back to this concept a number of times throughout the remainder of my book, but I wanted to introduce it here to discuss the benefits of building the *globally diversified* indexed portfolio and of curating optimal risk-adjusted portfolios.

As you may remember from earlier, individuals consistently make investment mistakes because they cannot properly manage their emotions. Individuals' investment mettle is consistently challenged by the "yin" (bear) and "yang" (bull) of the capital markets. By building proper Asset Allocations according to the unique variables in your life, I want to build all-weather portfolios that can work throughout all seasons and allow you to maintain your positions through bull (up) and bear (down) markets. The average duration of bull and bear markets varies significantly. The average bull market since 1926 has lasted approximately 30 months, while the average bear market has lasted only approximately 11 months (although it often feels like 111). The average return for the upward bull market is usually an eye-opener for individuals: 110% versus the average bear market draw down of minus 26%. When the market is dropping, individual investors mentally overweigh the negative by two or three times, i.e., a 1% reduction in the value of the market in your portfolio is viewed by the average investor as much more painful, and they react and internalize that much more than a commensurate 1% capital appreciation in their portfolio. Beware, this emotional bias can prove to be very costly.

Figures 3.12a–3.12e show the Asset Allocation of five significant portfolio "mile markers," beginning with Maximum Aggressive Growth 100% in stocks going down to the most conservative ("Defensive") growth portfolio with 20% in stocks. All 16 mutual funds are DFA institutional funds and have a five-letter symbol which can be accessed through any financial source regarding pricing. For each portfolio, all of the Asset Classes from the DFA US Large Company down to the Emerging Markets Small Cap would be included in the equity/stock Asset Class I have referred to in this chapter. The bottom four positions list the fixed income/bond positions in the portfolio.

FIGURE 3.12A. **100% Stocks/0% Bonds: Maximum Aggressive Growth**

Typical Portfolio Allocation

GENERAL ASSET CLASS		SPECIFIC INDEX	
40.0%	**U.S. Large**	20.0%	DFA U.S. Large Company Index
		20.0%	DFA U.S. Large Cap Value Index
20.0%	**U.S. Small**	10.0%	DFA U.S. Small Cap Index
		10.0%	DFA U.S. Small Cap Value Index
10.0%	**Real Estate**	10.0%	DFA Real Estate Index
20.0%	**International**	5.0%	DFA International Large Company Index
		5.0%	DFA International Large Value Index
		5.0%	DFA International Small Company Index
		5.0%	DFA International Small Cap Value Index
10.0%	**Emerging Markets**	3.0%	DFA Emerging Markets Index
		3.0%	DFA Emerging Markets Value Index
		4.0%	DFA Emerging Markets Small Cap Index
0.0%	**Fixed Income**	0.0%	DFA 5-Year Targeted Credit Bond Index
		0.0%	DFA 5-Year Global Bond Index
		0.0%	DFA Intermediate U.S. Investment Grade Bond Index
		0.0%	DFA Intermediate World ex.U.S. Bond Index

FIGURE 3.12B. **80% Stocks/20% Bonds: Very Aggressive Growth**

Typical Portfolio Allocation

GENERAL ASSET CLASS		SPECIFIC INDEX	
32.0%	U.S. Large	16.0%	DFA U.S. Large Company Index
		16.0%	DFA U.S. Large Cap Value Index
16.0%	U.S. Small	8.0%	DFA U.S. Small Cap Index
		8.0%	DFA U.S. Small Cap Value Index
8.0%	Real Estate	8.0%	DFA Real Estate Index
16.0%	International	4.0%	DFA International Large Company Index
		4.0%	DFA International Large Value Index
		4.0%	DFA International Small Company Index
		4.0%	DFA International Small Cap Value Index
8.0%	Emerging Markets	2.4%	DFA Emerging Markets Index
		2.4%	DFA Emerging Markets Value Index
		3.2%	DFA Emerging Markets Small Cap Index
20.0%	Fixed Income	5.0%	DFA 5-Year Targeted Credit Bond Index
		5.0%	DFA 5-Year Global Bond Index
		5.0%	DFA Intermediate U.S. Investment Grade Bond Index
		5.0%	DFA Intermediate World ex.U.S. Bond Index

FIGURE 3.12C. **60% Stocks/40% Bonds: Traditional Growth**

Typical Portfolio Allocation

GENERAL ASSET CLASS		SPECIFIC INDEX	
40.0%	U.S. Large	20.0%	DFA U.S. Large Company Index
		20.0%	DFA U.S. Large Cap Value Index
20.0%	U.S. Small	10.0%	DFA U.S. Small Cap Index
		10.0%	DFA U.S. Small Cap Value Index
10.0%	Real Estate	10.0%	DFA Real Estate Index
20.0%	International	5.0%	DFA International Large Company Index
		5.0%	DFA International Large Value Index
		5.0%	DFA International Small Company Index
		5.0%	DFA International Small Cap Value Index
10.0%	Emerging Markets	3.0%	DFA Emerging Markets Index
		3.0%	DFA Emerging Markets Value Index
		4.0%	DFA Emerging Markets Small Cap Index
0.0%	Fixed Income	0.0%	DFA 5-Year Targeted Credit Bond Index
		0.0%	DFA 5-Year Global Bond Index
		0.0%	DFA Intermediate U.S. Investment Grade Bond Index
		0.0%	DFA Intermediate World ex.U.S. Bond Index

FIGURE 3.12D. **40% Stocks/60% Bonds: Moderate Growth**

Typical Portfolio Allocation

GENERAL ASSET CLASS		SPECIFIC INDEX	
16.0%	**U.S. Large**	8.0%	DFA U.S. Large Company Index
		8.0%	DFA U.S. Large Cap Value Index
8.0%	**U.S. Small**	4.0%	DFA U.S. Small Cap Index
		4.0%	DFA U.S. Small Cap Value Index
4.0%	**Real Estate**	4.0%	DFA Real Estate Index
8.0%	**International**	3.0%	DFA International Large Company Index
		2.0%	DFA International Large Value Index
		2.0%	DFA International Small Company Index
		2.0%	DFA International Small Cap Value Index
4.0%	**Emerging Markets**	1.2%	DFA Emerging Markets Index
		1.2%	DFA Emerging Markets Value Index
		1.6%	DFA Emerging Markets Small Cap Index
60.0%	**Fixed Income**	15.0%	DFA 5-Year Targeted Credit Bond Index
		15.0%	DFA 5-Year Global Bond Index
		15.0%	DFA Intermediate U.S. Investment Grade Bond Index
		15.0%	DFA Intermediate World ex.U.S. Bond Index

FIGURE 3.12E. **20% Stocks/80% Bonds: Defensive Growth**

Typical Portfolio Allocation

GENERAL ASSET CLASS		SPECIFIC INDEX	
8.0%	**U.S. Large**	4.0%	DFA U.S. Large Company Index
		4.0%	DFA U.S. Large Cap Value Index
4.0%	**U.S. Small**	2.0%	DFA U.S. Small Cap Index
		2.0%	DFA U.S. Small Cap Value Index
2.0%	**Real Estate**	2.0%	DFA Real Estate Index
4.0%	**International**	1.0%	DFA International Large Company Index
		1.0%	DFA International Large Value Index
		1.0%	DFA International Small Company Index
		1.0%	DFA International Small Cap Value Index
2.0%	**Emerging Markets**	0.6%	DFA Emerging Markets Index
		0.6%	DFA Emerging Markets Value Index
		0.8%	DFA Emerging Markets Small Cap Index
80.0%	**Fixed Income**	20.0%	DFA 5-Year Targeted Credit Bond Index
		20.0%	DFA 5-Year Global Bond Index
		20.0%	DFA Intermediate U.S. Investment Grade Bond Index
		20.0%	DFA Intermediate World ex.U.S. Bond Index

We maintain the Asset Class positions regarding the mutual funds in each portfolio listed in these Figures and other similar diversifications. In the next chapter, we'll continue our discussion about Asset Allocation in more precise terms and learn how to optimize risk and return in your allocations for the stock and bond portions of your portfolios in particular.

Asset Allocation can make you or break you. A strategic "buy and hold" Asset Allocation strategy can safeguard you and your investments from your emotions sabotaging your portfolio returns. As a starting point, your exposure to stocks should be approximately 100 (or 110) minus your age, but Asset Allocation goes much deeper than simply stocks vs. bonds and needs to be customized for every household based on a DiNuzzo Financial Wellness LifePlan™. Your allocation across subcategories of Asset Classes (i.e., International, Emerging Markets, US Large Cap, US Small Cap, US Bonds, Corporate Bonds, Municipal Bonds, etc.) further affects your risk vs. return. Many investors accept a greater risk and/or lower return than necessary because their allocation in these Asset Classes is below anything even materially close to the available Efficient Frontier.

DIVERSIFICATION TO MAXIMIZE REWARD VS. RISK

A Fiduciary investment process curated under a Fiduciary Standard will instinctively mandate a globally diversified portfolio strategy which embraces statistically significant known empirical research that is sensible, persistent over time, pervasive across markets, and cost-effective to capture.

—P.J. DiNuzzo

Five different growth and income funds at five different mutual fund families is not full and proper diversification.

—P.J. DiNuzzo

It is better to mistake a rock for a bear than it is to mistake a bear for a rock.

—Anonymous

A Copernican Revolution...the most fundamental thing that has happened to the investment process – the development of Modern Portfolio Theory, the Theory of Efficient Markets, the scientific understanding of risk/return relationships, and the importance of diversification in portfolios.

—John H. Langbein, Chancellor Kent Professor
of Law and Legal History at Yale Law School,
Reporter, "The Uniform Prudent Investor Act"

A rising tide may lift all boats, but every year some vessels in the stock market spring a leak. Broad diversification ensures they won't sink the whole portfolio.

—Weston Wellington, Dimensional Fund
Advisors (DFA), "From the Research Desk"

My ninth-grade history teacher, Mr. Michael Hornick, had a sign on each of the four walls in his classroom. They all had the same message:

"Those who choose to ignore the past are doomed to repeat it."

True diversification means exposure to the entire universe of stocks and bonds, with exposure to every appropriate Asset Class in order to access all known premiums.

After we have identified the ideal Asset Allocation(s) across your portfolio(s), our attention shifts to what on one hand is painfully obvious, and yet on the other is often underestimated and even dismissed: full and proper diversification. Most individuals *overestimate* how diversified their portfolios are. With "true" diversification, you want to access the available worldwide capital markets and "Premiums." By premiums, I mean "factors" or "dimensions" that would allow you to expect a rate of return greater than a "safe" investment like treasury bonds or other standard indexes. Also, you want the available cost/

benefit trade-offs, with the goal being to add value to your portfolio construction, investment by investment. As I begin to add more precise Asset Classes to your portfolio—i.e., US Large Value stocks, US Small Cap stocks, etc.—each addition should accomplish *at least* one of the following two objectives: it should either *increase expected return* or *decrease expected risk*. Ideally it will accomplish *both* goals. There is *no reason* to add any additional investment(s) to your portfolio if *at least* one of these two objectives is not met.

Let's start with the theoretical portfolio I have discussed throughout my book—60% in stocks and 40% in bonds—beginning with two Asset Classes: the S&P 500 for our 60% stock (equity) position, and the Total Bond Market Index for our 40% bond (fixed income) position. Let's begin with the stock side. First, we need to ask the ultimate questions for full and proper diversification: Can we improve our expected rate of return and/or lower our projected risk in the portfolio by adding an Asset Class?

The answer is yes. You can access available worldwide market premiums such as Equity Premiums, Value Premiums, Small Cap Stock Premiums, Direct Profitability Premiums, and possibly, Capital Investment Premiums, along with the powers of diversification through International Developed Markets, Real Estate, and Emerging Markets. As you will see, we can build a multi-asset portfolio with approximately five US Asset Classes: US Large Stocks, US Large Value, US Small, US Small Value, and Real Estate. Internationally, there are seven Asset Classes: International Large Core, International Large Value, International Small Cap Core, International Small Value, Emerging Markets Core, Emerging Markets Value, and Emerging Markets Small Cap. Diversifying in this way over time can materially increase your expected rate of return while decreasing the expected risk in your portfolio. I strongly recommend studying the model allocations discussed in the previous chapter, and consider researching the pros and cons of those strategies for your own investments—for example, your 401(k) or 403(b)—and identifying if you have any major Asset Class imbalances or "holes." Oftentimes, individuals will be missing a multitude of the above-mentioned Asset Class exposures.

DIVERSIFICATION AND ASSET ALLOCATION

As I proffered, Asset Allocation (stock allocation vs. bond allocation) is the "granddaddy" of diversification. In this chapter, we're going to take a deeper dive into the data by looking at various desirable Asset Classes to gain a greater appreciation for the diversification benefits of Asset Allocation.

Nobel Prize winner Harry Markowitz analyzed the then-current investment belief that if you took one risky Asset Class and combined it with one or two other risky Asset Classes, you would fundamentally manifest a riskier cumulative effect in your portfolio. Markowitz identified that if the "risky assets" had a *low correlation* (movement in relationship to each other), you may well be able to lower the overall risk and standard deviation, or volatility, in the portfolio, by combining the proper investments/ Asset Classes during your portfolio construction. Taught in virtually every graduate level finance class in America, Modern Portfolio Theory (MPT), based on Markowitz's research, is one of the basic philosophies behind the Uniform Prudent Investor Act, which describes the mandate for major institutions and institutional fiduciaries to diversify, and that these trustees or fiduciaries who fail to diversify do so at the risk of violating the law and being held accountable.

According to Modern Portfolio Theory (MPT), the ideal correlation for two Asset Class investments would be two Asset Classes which were *inversely* correlated to each other at a "minus 1" correlation. Regarding correlations, the continuum would start at a +1, which means that two Asset Classes move in *exactly* the same direction at the same rate as each other versus the midpoint of a correlation of zero (0), meaning that if there was a *zero correlation* between two Asset Classes when they were measured relative to each other, there is *absolutely no correlation*. To clarify, they would be *completely random* and possess no predictive value regarding the movement of Asset Class B after and when observing Asset Class A. The final most extreme point on the continuum would be a -1 correlation in which, as I mentioned earlier, Asset Class A and Asset Class B move in *exactly the opposite direction* at the same rates.

Modern Portfolio Theory (MPT) is so widely accepted that it is used as the foundation for portfolio construction not only by Strategic Asset Allocation index advisors (such as myself), but even by market timers, stock pickers, and contrarians. The expansive benefit you receive from MPT is the lower *correlation over time* between US Developed Markets vs. International Developed Markets, Real Estate Markets, Bond Markets, and the Emerging Markets.

When constructing your portfolio(s) for proper diversification, after you make the initial and most important diversification decision regarding Asset Allocation (e.g., 60% in stocks and 40% in bonds), the next broad decision you need to make for the portfolio is how much of your stock portfolio you will place in Domestic (US) vs. International Asset Classes. Based on four decades of examining the market, my rule of thumb is approximately two-thirds exposure to US Asset Classes and one-third in International Asset Classes (specifically, 70% US and 30% International—with international including Emerging Markets). This second level of diversification gives us a higher probability for success *vis-à-vis* risk/reward and a solid second step as you progress through the various asset categories and related "premiums" for your diversification strategy.

The next major areas of diversification to add to your portfolio, in order to position yourself as well as possible for risk/return adjusted success, includes the seven following Asset Classes/"factors" (both Domestically and Internationally) to a portfolio which already holds the S&P 500 index/US Large Blend/Core as its starting point.

1. Small Cap Stocks
2. Value Stocks
3. International Stocks
4. Emerging Market Stocks

5. Real Estate Stocks
6. Direct/Expected Profitability "Premium/Dimension/Factor" Stocks
7. Capital Investment "Premium/Dimension/Factor" Stocks
    (currently under research)

Finally, *time* is an immensely valuable ally in your diversification strategy. "Time Diversification" of risk relates to the concept that a risky portfolio becomes less risky when held over a long investment period. This is another mission-critical concept to internalize for success. My professional opinion is that a higher allocation to equities (stocks) is optimal and desirable for investors with longer holding periods. As the data in the next image, Figure 4.1 *World Market Capitalization* indicates, you want to have *at least* a five-year time horizon to have any exposure into the equity/stock market. My *ideal minimum* holding period is *10 years* for exposure to equity (stocks) in a portfolio. I consider 10 years as the ideal *minimum* because it is at that point you *begin* to have statistical level of confidence that Asset Classes in your portfolio(s) are going to least approach your long-term desired outcomes. The remainder of the chapter will present a granular view of the data behind the diversification strategy broadly outlined above.

WORLD MARKET CAPITALIZATION

In Figure 4.1, *World Market Capitalization*, I am sharing with you the lens through which I view the investment universe. When you consider what it means to be fully diversified, you need to analyze the entire world capital markets.

As you take a look at the available capital markets worldwide, which totaled $37.5 trillion as of December 31, 2018, it is quite interesting to note the size and scope of these global markets. The above graph represents the Developed Markets, the Emerging Markets, and the Frontier Markets. Frontier Markets are economies and countries that, if they continue to progress, could ultimately become Emerging Markets. As Emerging Markets continue to grow and progress, they could one day be labeled as Developed Markets, which represents fuller maturation. Although the United States capital markets have been occasionally maligned, they still represent close to one-half of the total World Market Capitalization: in the investment universe, they are the 800-pound gorilla.

FIGURE 4.1. **World Market Capitalization (Percentage as of December 31, 2018)**

DEVELOPED MARKETS				EMERGING MARKETS	
1. United States	54%	8. Australia	2%	14. China	3%
2. Japan	8%	9. Italy	1%	15. Korea	2%
3. United Kingdom	5%	10. Spain	1%	16. India	1%
4. Canada	3%	11. Sweden	1%	17. Taiwan	1%
5. France	3%	12. Netherlands	1%	18. Brazil	1%
6. Germany	2%	13. Hong Kong	1%	19. South Africa	1%
7. Switzerland	2%				

When you examine the capitalization of the world markets, it is clear that you want access to all of them and potentially desire exposure appropriate to the size of the market. For example, you would want a small percent of your portfolio, approximately 10% of your total stock target, to be in the Emerging Markets. If you have a 100% stock portfolio, you want 10% in Emerging Markets. If you have a 60% stock allocation in your portfolio, you want 6% in the Emerging Markets. I want to "index the entire planet Earth," *and* index it properly.

In my typical portfolio recommendation, I hold over 14,000 stocks within institutional index funds in over 40 countries around the planet accessing fundamental market "premiums." With these 14,000+ stocks, I am tilting toward value in my portfolios to access the Value Premium that has been exhibited in the US Domestic Markets for over 90 years. I access the Value Premium in International Developed, as well as Emerging Markets.

Then, I incorporate the newly identified premium, Direct Profitability, into my portfolios. This premium can be incorporated into existing funds and is available with a more dedicated *tilt* in stand-alone funds.

Additionally, our Portfolio Management Team is in the process of ongoing research to develop strategies to include the newest identified Premium/Factor/Dimension, Capital Investment, into our equity positions when it comes to fruition.

Lastly, I include a Small Cap tilt in my portfolios, including US Small Cap stocks, International Developed Market Small Cap stocks, and finally Emerging Market Small Cap stocks.

EQUITY UNIVERSE

In Figure 4.2, *Equity Universe*, you are witnessing the entire equity universe of global stocks represented by the large square, and the average holdings for the traditional Wall Street mutual fund located in the bottom right-hand corner. It is startling to see just how little diversification is typically available through the typical active stock mutual fund. Even worse, I have noticed over the decades that the average self-directed investor who has a bias toward purchasing individual stocks owns even fewer stocks in their portfolio than the typical Wall Street stock mutual fund!

Imagine if you were observing an additional square approximately one-quarter of the size of the average holdings of Wall Street mutual funds. This tiny hypothetical square would represent the average number of individual stocks held in self-directed individuals' stock portfolios. In contrast, you want to be proactive and strategic, placing the odds in your favor with every decision you make in building your portfolio(s). We want to index over 10,000 individual companies through diversified Asset Classes across the globe, which historically have produced the most desirable risk-adjusted results.

FIGURE 4.2. **Equity Universe**

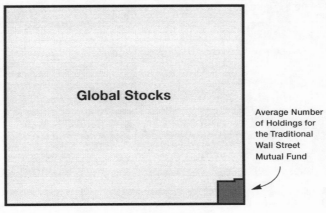

Source: Morningstar, Inc.

THE NECESSITY OF DIVERSIFICATION

If you knew what was going to happen in the economy, you still wouldn't necessarily know what was going to happen in the stock market.
> —Warren Buffett, *Fortune*, April 14, 2008,
> "What Warren Thinks..."

Diversification is an integral element of successful portfolio management. You simply cannot be a successful *risk-adjusted* long-term investor without proper diversification. As is illustrated in Figure 4.3, *The Necessity of Diversification*, many investors are familiar with the randomly shaded matrix of worldwide

Asset Classes regarding their volatility and annual performance. I can think of a no more instructive tool than a thorough study and knowledge regarding the randomness of Asset Class returns.

FIGURE 4.3. The Necessity of Diversification: Annual Return (%)

	1999	2000	2001	2002	2003	2004	2005	2006	2007	2008	2009	2010	2011	2012	2013	2014	2015	2016	2017	2018
High	EM 72%	RE 28%	SV 18%	ISV 6%	ISV 66%	ISV 35%	EM 30%	RE 35%	EM 36%	1F 4%	EM 72%	SC 31%	LC 2%	RE 23%	SV 43%	RE 23%	ISV 4%	SV 27%	EM 37%	1F 2%
	SC 25%	SV 21%	RE 13%	RE 4%	EM 60%	RE 32%	ISV 23%	IV 34%	IV 10%	SV -34%	ISV 40%	SV 29%	RE 2%	ISV 22%	SC 42%	LC 14%	LC 1%	SC 24%	ISV 28%	RE -4%
	LC 21%	LV 10%	SC 13%	1F 4%	SV 54%	EM 30%	IV 15%	EM 29%	LC 5%	SC -36%	IV 39%	RE 24%	1F 1%	LV 22%	LV 40%	LV 10%	RE 1%	LV 19%	IV 26%	LC -4%
▲ Return ▼	ISV 19%	1F 7%	1F 6%	IV -9%	SC 51%	IV 29%	RE 13%	ISV 28%	1F 5%	LC -37%	SC 36%	EM 22%	LV -3%	SV 19%	ISV 32%	SC 4%	1F 0%	EM 12%	LC 22%	LV -12%
	IV 16%	SC 2%	LV 4%	EM -9%	IV 50%	SV 25%	LV 10%	LV 20%	ISV 3%	RE -40%	RE 33%	LV 20%	SC -3%	EM 19%	LC 32%	SV 3%	SC -3%	LC 12%	LV 19%	SC -13%
	SV 10%	0%	ISV -5%	SV -10%	RE 36%	LV 18%	SV 9%	SV 20%	IV -3%	LV -41%	SV 32%	IV 18%	IV -6%	SC 18%	IV 23%	1F 0%	IV -3%	IV 8%	SC 12%	EM -14%
	LV 5%	ISV -3%	EM -7%	LV -15%	LV 34%	SC 18%	SC 6%	SC 17%	ISV -3%	LV -42%	LV 30%	LC 15%	IV -17%	IV 17%	RE 2%	EM -2%	SV -6%	ISV 8%	SV 10%	SV -16%
	1F 5%	LC -9%	LC -12%	SC -19%	LC 28%	LC 11%	LC 5%	LC 16%	SV -8%	IV -46%	LC 27%	IV 11%	EM -17%	LC 16%	1F 0%	LV -5%	LV -6%	RE 7%	RE 9%	IV -17%
Low	RE -2%	EM -29%	IV -15%	LC -22%	1F 2%	1F 1%	1F 2%	1F 5%	RE -19%	EM -49%	1F 2%	1F 1%	ISV -17%	1F 1%	EM -3%	IV -7%	EM -16%	1F 1%	1F 1%	ISV -23%

■ LC - US Large Cap	■ SV - US Small Cap Value	■ EM - Emerging Markets
■ LV - US Large Cap Value	□ RE - US Real Estate	□ ISV - Intl. Small Cap Value
□ SC - US Small Cap	■ IV - Intl. Large Cap Value	■ 1F - 1 Year US Fixed

Source: Morningstar, Inc.®

The chart shown in Figure 4.3, *The Necessity of Diversification* demonstrates the annual performance, from top to bottom, over a recent 20-year period of worldwide Asset Classes from 1999 to 2018. Let's focus for a moment on US Large Cap stocks, as represented by the S&P 500. In 1999, it experienced a very good year with a +21% return. However, in 2000, this Asset Class had a subpar year and was down -9%, followed by another bad year in 2001 down -12%. Finally, it was down -22% in 2002.

Just from a simple point of observation when viewing this image it should be obvious to even a casual observer that trying to predict in advance which Asset Class is going to perform the best in an upcoming year is a fool's errand.

Individual investors often evaluate the performance of mutual fund managers without taking into consideration the Asset Class they are tracking. If an individual mutual fund manager does well, it is most likely because the Asset Class he or she was targeting did well. If the manager is managing a US Small Stock fund, and US Small Stocks did 10% better than the S&P 500 that year, the manager's superior performance is typically due to the Asset Class they are managing, not their own genius. Individual investors flock to these managers, as they continually chase performance, like a moth to a flame.

TOO MUCH MONEY IN A
SINGLE STOCK: TONY AND GEORGE

Tony was a single guy who worked in the automotive industry. He lived in Michigan, worked for General Motors, and had a high percentage of his investment portfolio in company stock.

It's natural for investors to have a bias for investments they're familiar with. For example, people in the United States invest in a higher percentage of US stocks, while people in Germany own a higher percentage of German stocks. Likewise, people who work for a company tend to have a higher percentage of their portfolio in that stock than is prudent. They believe they know more about the company than they do about other companies they could invest in, and that gives them a sense of comfort—but it is a false sense of security.

Tony retired from GM with 70% of his portfolios in their stock. Within a few years' time, during the meltdown that lasted from around 2007 to 2009, the value of that stock went to zero. As a result, Tony's quality of life was permanently reduced for the rest of his life. He was able to get by without having to return to work, but his retirement plans suffered a dramatic impact.

When Tony came to see me, he thought all was lost, but per The DiNuzzo Way™ of passionately pursuing positive improvement, I was able to develop a customized DiNuzzo Financial Wellness LifePlan™ that put him in a better situation to live out his retirement. I couldn't turn back the clock and recover his lost investment, but I could help him plan a better future.

Another gentleman, George, is an entrepreneur who had his own drywall business. Like Tony, George wasn't diversified—he had all his money in tech stocks. George sold his business and retired in 1999, when he was in his 50s. Soon after, we experienced the dot-com bubble burst or the "tech wreck" as it was also known. George's retirement savings lost 80% of its value and he had to go back to work, this time, working for someone else.

These are just two examples of what can happen when you are not properly diversified. They may appear extreme, but they're more common than you might think and ones that I continue to see to this day. People can also make the mistake of not diversifying properly between large and small cap stocks, and between US and International stocks. Again, they tend to invest in what's most familiar. Finally, there's a tendency for some people to invest in whatever they deem is "hot" at the moment—industries they believe will experience the most growth.

Here's something to think about: a few decades ago, during the second half of the 1990s, I met with hundreds of investors who were 100% in US growth and tech stocks, represented by the NASDAQ composite. In March 2000, the NASDAQ composite hit its all-time high. Then, it fell—and it did not recover its value until *2016*.

Being under-diversified can cost you a lot of money and years off your retirement, not to mention undue stress as you watch your hard-earned money dwindle away to a small percentage of what you worked for. The good news is, this mistake is avoidable with a properly diversi-fied portfolio of investments.

DiNuzzo Private Wealth, Inc. (DPW)/DiNuzzo Wealth Management (DWM) approaches every opportunity and every challenge "IN Gratitude," regardless of the circumstances. If you're hesitating to reach out for help from a Fiduciary-based advisor because you're embarrassed or ashamed that you've made a huge mistake, you should know that investment mistakes are extremely common, and our cli-ents' errors are not ours to judge.

If you recall the Dalbar research I cited earlier, one of the key points was that the average individual investor only holds on to their stock and bond posi-tions for 3 to 4 years. If we follow the US Small Cap Value Asset Class from year to year in Figure 4.3, it will remind you of my "Emotional Investment Roller Coaster™" graphic from earlier, and you can easily imagine someone jumping off at some point during that ride. And, of course, many people did, resulting in the underperformance seen in the typical portfolio. Many individuals bailed out of this Asset Class in 1998 or 1999, and then had the ultimate financial come-uppance in 2001, when the Asset Class rose back up to 21%, and was back at the top for the performance period versus the S&P 500 losing -12%. This is classic Asset Class volatility and rotation during a market cycle.

Figures 4.4–4.6 present the data from Figure 4.3 in more detail. Here you are observing the vacillation of returns on a year-to-year basis for US Large Cap (S&P 500) "Blue Chip" stocks. We can see the movement from the best performing Asset Class, to the middle of the pack, to above average, to below average—back and forth. Although US Large Cap would be the first Asset Class investment, we would include on the stock side when building our portfolio, there were many years when it was in the bottom 25% or even the worst performing Asset Class. As I mentioned earlier, let's look at 1999, when this Asset Class was one of the top performing investments (+21%), after also performing well in 1995, 1996, 1997, and 1998. Unfortunately, as a result of this winning streak, most individual investors started to *overweight* this Asset Class in the *late* 1990s. Then, again, they ran into a period in 2000 where it was down -9%, followed by 2001, when it was down -12%, and then 2002, when it was down -22%. As we'll see in the next two Figures, other major worldwide Asset Classes have shown even greater volatility.

FIGURE 4.4. **The Necessity of Diversification**

Annual Return (%) for U.S. Large Cap (LC)

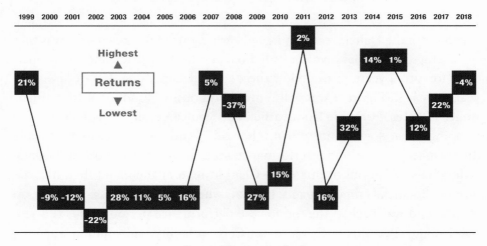

Source: Morningstar, Inc. *

Figure 4.5, *The Necessity of Diversification: Annual Return for International Large Cap (IV)* elucidates the volatility of International Large Cap Value stocks' performance on an annual basis. Here we see even more volatility than the US Large Cap, going from top Asset Class performance, to the middle of the pack, to the worst performing, and back up again. As we learned earlier from Dalbar's research data, the average individual only holds their investments for approximately 3 to 4 years, and with these cycles within cycles, you can begin to see why individuals consistently underperform. Lacking a *strategy* that takes into account the regular subcycles within Asset Classes, individuals are unable to ride out these periods. They simply lose confidence in the mutual fund, mutual fund manager, or individual stock and sell unnecessarily. Remember, the stock market is *always* surprising in the short term, but it is *never* surprising in the long term.

FIGURE 4.5. **The Necessity of Diversification**

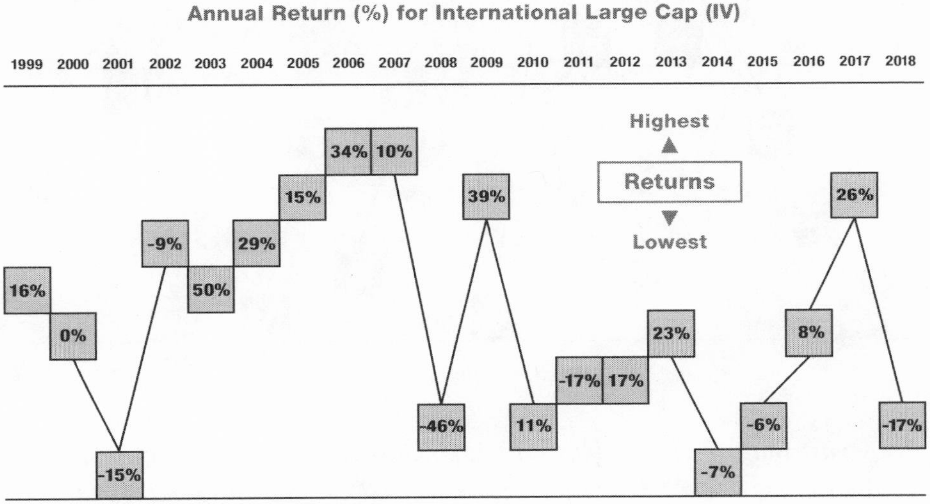

Annual Return (%) for International Large Cap (IV)

Source: Morningstar, Inc.*

In the last of my series, Figure 4.6 illustrates some of the most mercurial volatility available in worldwide Asset Classes: the Emerging Markets index. It jumps from last place to first place and back with almost typical regularity. As I often remind clients, the highest expected rate of return in the equity markets in our future lifetime should be in the Emerging Markets. However, we want to have just a small exposure to this Asset Class, due to the fact that when the Developed Markets worldwide "catch a cold," the Emerging Markets often "catch pneumonia." Again, we can see, with the wild volatility of the Emerging Markets, an investor who does not have the proper investment philosophy and strategy will likely bail out of these positions even more quickly than the International Large Cap Funds (Figure 4.5).

FIGURE 4.6. **The Necessity of Diversification**

Annual Return (%) for Emerging Markets (EM)

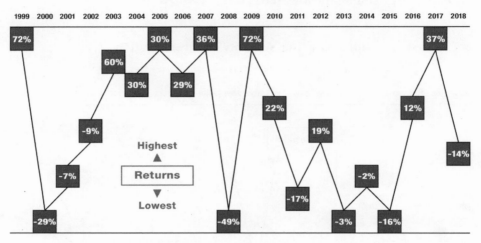

Source: *Morningstar, Inc.*®

A vast industry of stockbrokers, financial planners, and investment advisers skims a fortune for themselves off the top in exchange for passing their clients' money on to people who, as a whole, cannot possibly outperform the market.

—Michael Lewis, "The Evolution of an Investor,"
Conde Nast Portfolio, December 2007

In Figure 4.7, I am analyzing the "Style Drift vs. Style Purity" of the S&P 500 index over a recent 36-year period from January 1, 1982 through December 31, 2017. The S&P 500 US Large Cap index is referred to as a "blend" or "core" because it averages approximately 50% Russell 1000 US Large *Growth* and 50% Russell 1000 Large *Value* Asset Class type stocks. This and other indexes' "style purity" benefits and adds value to us in building our portfolios because we don't have to concern ourselves with loathsome performance deteriorating "style drift."

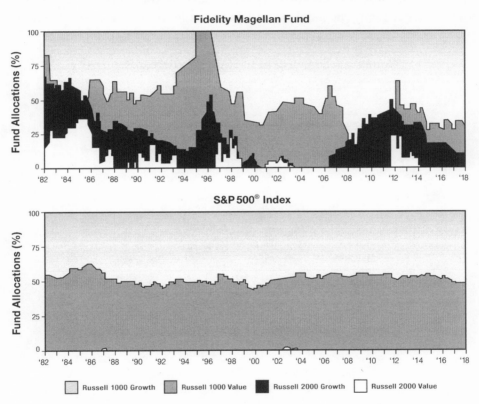

FIGURE 4.7. **Style Drift vs. Style Purity**

36 Years: January 1, 1982 – December 31, 2017

Sources: Mark T. Hebner, author, Morningstar, Inc.

Additionally, in Figure 4.7 I have chosen the Fidelity Magellan Fund to contrast and illustrate style drift and Asset Class vacillation within an actively managed stock mutual fund. The Fidelity Magellan Stock Fund was the largest mutual fund available in the market for years and was once managed by the famous stock picker, Mr. Peter Lynch. Back in 1982, the fund would have been classified as a Small Growth Fund since most of the stocks in the fund were in the Russell 2000 Small Growth category. A few years later, in the mid- to late-1980s, this fund would have been viewed as a Large Growth stock mutual fund. A few years later in 1995, it would have been classified primarily as a Large Value stock mutual fund. Moving forward to the early- to mid-2000s, the fund has shifted back to being classified primarily as a Large Growth stock mutual fund.

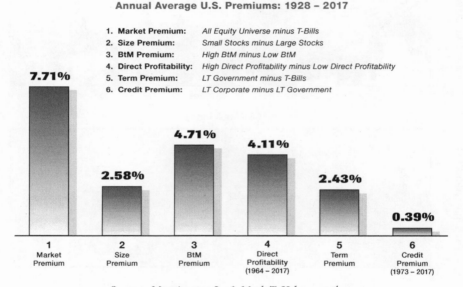

FIGURE 4.8. **Dimensions of Higher Expected Returns**

Sources: Morningstar, Inc.*, Mark T. Hebner, author.

When individual investors are first exposed to this type of analysis, they are generally shocked to see the fluctuations within a fund that they are holding in their portfolio. This "style drift" illustrates one of the premier challenges in using an active mutual fund manager to handle a particular Asset Class within your portfolio. If you had hired this manager to be a large growth manager, numerous times this manager would have moved out of the large growth range and transitioned into value or small growth. You also will notice, from 1998 through 2009, there were times when the portfolio held significant amounts of cash in the portfolio (the one-year US Treasury) in an attempt to "time the market." Additionally, most individuals assume that their stock fund is fully invested in stocks at all times, but may be surprised to discover there are times when they are only 80% or 90% invested in stocks, due to holding significant positions in cash.

There are fundamentally six known Premiums/Dimensions/Factors available in the global capital markets, and by this, I mean there are only six reasons to expect a higher return rate than a "risk-free" rate such as a treasury bond and/ or a premium over a benchmark index. There are four equity (stock) premiums and two fixed income (bond) premiums, and in strategically developing your Asset Allocation, my goal is to access all six available premiums. The four Equity Premiums (that is to say, the four empirically identified, statistically significant reasons to invest in the stock market) are as follows:

1. The Equity Risk Premium, or "market factor." This simply means that stocks have provided a higher level of return than bonds (due to their inherently higher level of risk) over appropriate holding periods, as indicated by the stock market's rate of return over and above short-term US Treasury Bills (T-Bills). As you can see in Figure 4.8, *Dimensions of Higher Expected Returns: Average Annual US Premiums* this premium was 7.71% per year from 1928 through the end of 2017. This includes the *entire* equity universe of stocks and is the *largest and most significant premium available*. In other words, this is the number one reason why you would want to invest in stocks, especially if you have the proper time horizon. (As a reminder, to place any money in the stock market, your time horizon needs to be at least five years, and ideally ten years or longer.)

2. The Small Cap Premium, or the "size factor." This means that small stocks historically outperform large stocks. As my 90-year

THE SEVEN KEYS TO INVESTING SUCCESS

database indicates above, the size factor has produced an additional premium of 2.58%.

3. The Value Premium, also known as the "book-to-market factor" or the "value factor." This means that value stocks tend to outperform growth stocks. One characteristic of value stocks is that they have a high book-to-market ratio, meaning that the book value divided by the market value is greater than 1. The Value Premium (value over growth) has been 4.71% over the last 90 years.

4. The newly identified Direct/Expected Profitability Premium. This is indicated by the difference between the returns of a stock with high expected profitability and the returns of a stock with low expected profitability. The Expected/Direct Profitability Premium has been estimated at approximately 4.11% a year *since 1964*.

Recently, the academic community has identified (and Dimensional Fund Advisors has opened new funds for) a new equity/stock market premium called Direct Profitability. New research has identified a robust proxy for a new investable dimension of higher expected return through "expected profitability." The finding that companies with high direct profitability have higher stock returns appears pragmatic to most market participants. The research additionally indicates that a higher expected return carries with it, greater risk. There have been three "breakthroughs" that have enabled the identification of this newfound premium:

a. Nobel Prize winner Eugene Fama and Ken French's research in 2006 regarding profitability

b. Robert Novy-Marx's research that has seized and stabilized gross profitability into consistently identifiable pervasive and persistent observations

c. Recently concluded "out of sample" research that confirmed the Direct Profitability Premium in Non-US Developed Markets and in the worldwide Emerging Markets

Stay tuned for even more exciting developments regarding this research that has produced the newest identified premium *since 1992*, when the Fama/ French research identified the Value Premium and created the Three-Factor (Market, Value, and Size) and the Five-Factor models, as it usually takes a number of years to fully diagnose and incorporate investment research breakthroughs of this magnitude.

On the bond side, there are *only two* premiums and thus two reasons to invest in the bond market.

5. The "Maturity Factor" Premium (or "Term" Premium), which is the rate of return of long-term government bonds minus T-bills. This premium has been 2.43% over a recent 90-year period.

6. The "Credit Factor" Premium, which is the rate of return of long-term corporate bonds minus long-term government bonds. Higher risk organizations, such as corporations, must pay a higher rate of interest relative to government bonds because of their lower (riskier) credit rating, in order to attract capital from the investment capital market to purchase their bonds. This premium has produced an additional 0.39% per year.

My firm includes these six "factors" as the basis of every analysis when compiling our broad Asset Allocation and specific Asset Allocations across all of our portfolios, and I recommend the same approach in my book.

In Figure 4.9, we see the three (3) additional premiums available in the stock market, after the initial building block "Equity/Stock Risk Premium." This Figure especially focuses on one of the newest premiums, "Direct Profitability." The Direct

Profitability Premium is represented in Figure 4.9 in column three and is the academic community's most recent discovery as it has just contemporarily come to fruition for me to begin including it in my portfolios over the past few years.

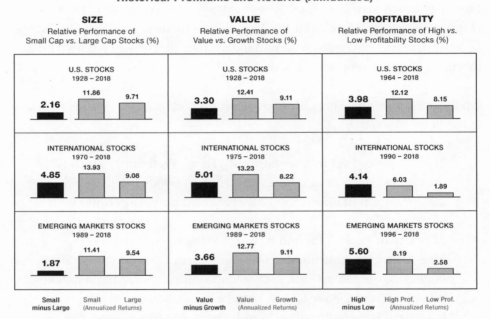

FIGURE 4.9. **Dimensions of Expected Returns**

Historical Premiums and Returns (Annualized)

Dimensions of Returns Up to 91 Years* (1/1/1928 - 12/31/2018) Information provided by Dimensional Fund Advisors LP. All returns are in USD. Premiums are calculated as the difference in annualized returns between the two indices described over the period shown. MSCI indices are gross div. For US stocks, indices are used as follows. Small Cap minus Large Cap: Dimensional US Small Cap Index minus the S&P 500 Index. Value minus Growth: Fama/French US Value Research Index minus the Fama/French US Growth Research Index. High Prof minus Low Prof: Dimensional US High Profitability Index minus the Dimensional US Low Profitability Index. For developed ex US stocks, indices are used as follows. Small Cap minus Large Cap: Dimensional International Small Cap Index minus the MSCI World ex USA Index (gross div.). Value minus Growth: Fama/French International Value Index minus the Fama/French International Growth Index. High Prof minus Low Prof: Dimensional International High Profitability Index minus the Dimensional International Low Profitability Index. For Emerging Markets stocks, indices are used as follows. Small Cap minus Large Cap: Dimensional Emerging Markets Small Cap Index minus MSCI Emerging Markets Index (gross div.). Value minus Growth: Fama/French Emerging Markets Value Index minus Fama/French Emerging Markets Growth Index. High Prof minus Low Prof: Dimensional Emerging Markets High Profitability Index minus the Dimensional Emerging Markets Low Profitability Index. Profitability is measured as operating income before depreciation and amortization minus interest expense, scaled by book. Indexes are not available for direct investment and performance does not reflect expenses of an actual portfolio. Unless indicated otherwise, the performance includes reinvestment of dividends and capital gains but do not include the deduction of IFA's advisory fees, transaction costs or taxes. Past performance is no guarantee of future results. Actual returns may be lower.

For detailed information on the hypothetical backtested performance data in this chart, including sources, updates and important disclosures, see ifabt.com. See "Index Descriptions" at ifaindexes.com for descriptions of Dimensional and Fama/French index data.

In the first column on the left, the Size Premium of small stocks outperform-ing large stocks is evident in US stocks, Non-US Developed Markets, and Emerging Markets. In the middle column, we see the relative price, or Value Premium manifesting itself in the US, Non-US Developed, and Emerging Markets as well. In the last column, on the right, we see our hypothetical hold-ings of the Direct Profitability Premium, again in the US, Non-US Developed, and Emerging Markets. I expect that Direct Profitability will actually be more rigorous than the Size Premium and may even approach the statistical signif-icance of the Value Premium in the future (which, for students of the capital markets and investment geeks, is exciting stuff!).

FIGURE 4.10. **Risk and Return Are Related**
Dimensions of Stock Returns Around the World

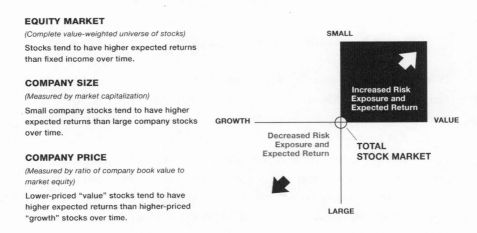

As you can see from Figure 4.10, *Risk and Return Are Related*, I am incorpo-rating a portfolio strategy sensitive to the Value Premium and the Small Cap Premium advantages. I am tilting the portfolio from a market-centric posi-tion, such as the S&P 500 or the total stock market, toward the upper right quadrant of the chart. When diversified properly, adding Small stocks and Value stocks to your Asset Allocation mix can provide you with materially higher long-term return expectations.

THE OVERFUNDED TAX-DEFERRED BUCKET: PETE AND MARY

Pete is a retired engineer. He and his wife, Mary, have a million-dollar-plus investment portfolio of total investments. They thought they were properly allocated between taxable, individual, joint tax-deferred (traditional IRAS), and tax-free (Roth IRAS) investments. To their chagrin, at the DiNuzzo Financial Wellness LifePlan™ meeting, they discovered they were not.

Following The DiNuzzo Way™ of relentlessly striving to exceed our customer's expectations, I created a customized DiNuzzo Financial Wellness LifePlan™ for Pete and Mary that exposed a costly error in their strategy but revealed tremendous opportunity for improvement.

Pete, who is the Family Chief Investment Officer (FCIO), had dramatically overfunded his tax-deferred IRA. When he turns age 70 next year, he will be making a monthly over-withdrawal, beyond his needs, of more than $3,000 a month due to the IRS's Required Minimum Distribution (RMD) rules. Generating approximately $40,000 in excess annual withdrawals, the couple will be pushed into a higher tax bracket and be forced to pay much more in federal, and potentially state taxes than they had anticipated. In Wealth Management parlance, I refer to situations such as this as "golden handcuffs."

Putting a lot of money into a tax-free account sounds like a great strategy, but you have to examine every investment as part of your overall "basket" of investments, and everyone's situation is different. If you have to pay an additional $8,000 in taxes every year and your life expectancy is an additional 32 years—well, do the math. That's *more than a quarter of a million dollars* to Uncle Sam, without even figuring in the growth of that money if it had been properly invested. Overfunding a tax-deferred bucket may seem like a good problem to have, when it can in fact be an enormously expensive mistake.

SIZE AND VALUE EFFECTS ARE STRONG AROUND THE WORLD

One of the many benefits of diversifying properly is the benefit of utilizing index investing. One of the key characteristics you want to consider when building an optimal portfolio is a *track record*—more specifically, a *long track record*, and ultimately, a *very successful long track record*. One of the magnet-like insights that drew me to indexing and Efficient Market Theory over four decades ago was the graph shown in Figure 4.11 illustrating how "size and value effects are strong around the world."

This data informs the strategy regarding how I typically diversify portfolios for clients at our firm. Although we've mentioned this before, I want to draw particular attention to the date range of the database cited under the bar graphs for US Large and US Small. This database is maintained at the University of Chicago Booth Graduate School of Business, which is also where the official stock prices are kept, and covers an unmatched 90 years in length. We have a 90-year database regarding returns and standard deviation (volatility) for US Asset Classes ranging from US Large Blend and US Large Growth, all the way down to the bottom tier in market capitalization to US Small Value, US Small Blend, and US Small Growth—which is a significant building block for the diversification of a portfolio.

History doesn't repeat itself, but it rhymes.

—Mark Twain

FIGURE 4.11. **Size and Value Effects are Strong Around the World**

(Annual Index Data)

US Stocks 1928 – 2017

1. US Small Value   4. S&P 500
2. US Small Cap   5. US Large Growth
3. US Large Value   6. US Small Growth

**Non-US Developed
Market Stocks 1970 – 2017**

7. International Small
8. International Value
9. MSCI EAFE
10. International Growth

**Emerging Markets
Stocks 1989 – 2017**

11. Emerging Value
12. Emerging Small
13. MSCI Emerging Market
14. Emerging Growth

Source: Morningstar, Inc.

Premier index benchmark fund manager Dimensional Fund Advisors (DFA) is figuratively synonymous with the University of Chicago Booth Graduate School of Business. Out of the 74 Nobel Laureates in economics, 28 of them have either taught at or graduated from the Booth Graduate School of Business. With my direct access to DFA since the early 1990s, and countless seminars, workshops, headquarters meetings, face to face and phone meetings, I have enjoyed the benefit of standing on the shoulders of giants, building our strategies based on massive volumes of Nobel Prize-winning research along with their exemplary investment committee and research team.

If we look at Non-US Developed countries, we're getting close to a 50-year track record. For Emerging Markets, we're approaching 30 years.

Here's my point: you're *lucky* if the average *active manager or team* has been kept intact long enough to have a five- or 10-year track record, let alone a

15-year track record. Once you start getting up to a 20-year track record or longer, the few remaining average active managers are typically preparing for retirement.

The column #3 bar graph on the far left, showing the US Large Value annualized compounded return of +10.41% over this recent 90-year period, illustrates the historic performance of the Value Premium in the market, thus I would "tilt" the portfolio by adding US Large Value to your Asset Class mix. To the left of it in column #2, you will see the US Small Capitalization Stocks with the same 90-year track record and core position. Comparing the Small Cap annualized compounded return of +11.76% against the return of the S&P 500 (US Large Cap Core) to the right in column #4 illustrates the long-term US Small Cap Premium in the capital markets. Thus I would also place the US Small Cap index Asset Class exposure in every portfolio. Finally, on the US equity (stock) diversification front, the US Small Value (column #1) equity total return of +13.36% over the last 90 years, for my US Small Value "tilt," would be added to your portfolio.

As I have previously mentioned, I have experienced the same premiums worldwide in Non-US Developed Market stocks, with the MSCI EAFE (column #9) of +9.62% over a shorter period of time, as the full database for International Developed Markets is only available from January 1, 1970. Nonetheless, I have an approximate 50-year database for International Developed Markets, and we can see the premiums that we would want to add to your portfolio with International Small and International Value clearly illustrated.

Our final area for full and proper equity diversification is Emerging Market stocks. Emerging Markets are the most recent newcomers to the global markets, with their database beginning on January 1, 1989. However, even though this is the shortest database we have regarding global index Asset Classes, it still represents an approximate 30-year database of returns and standard deviation (volatility)—which, again, significantly exceeds the tenure of the typical active mutual fund manager.

Looking at the Emerging Market Small and Emerging Market Value positions, you see evidence of the Value and Small Cap Premiums worldwide, as well as the obvious outperformance of Emerging Markets Small over the Emerging Markets Large Cap Blend. Even more clearly distinguished is the Emerging Market Value Premium relative to the Emerging Markets Large Cap Index Asset Class.

Because there is also a monumental database available that clearly illustrates the palpable premium of equities/stocks over fixed income/bonds over the last 100 years, it is easy to wonder why the average individual investor underperforms so consistently and dramatically. I utilize this massive body of knowledge to increase your probability for success at every "fork in the road" along your DiNuzzo Financial Wellness LifePlan™ highway to success.

THE UNDERFUNDED TAXABLE BUCKET: JACK AND CAROL

Jack and Carol are lawyers who came to see me a year prior to their retirement. During our DiNuzzo Financial Wellness LifePlan™ process, I discovered they were moderately overfunded in their traditional, tax-deferred IRAs. This would impact their taxable liability in retirement, so I analyzed strategies to improve their situation. At first, a Roth IRA Conversion appeared to be just the ticket to ease their future tax burden.

With a Roth IRA Conversion, they would transition money from their tax-deferred IRA bucket into their tax-free Roth IRA bucket. I had worked out the numbers and presented a number of scenarios showing how this conversion would save them a lot of money over time. The final phase was figuring how much money they needed to pay the US Treasury every year in taxes on that money they were going to move into their Roth IRAs.

Per The DiNuzzo Way™ of helping clients make smart money and Best-Life choices, I created a customized DiNuzzo Financial Wellness LifePlan™ to help them sort out the details of this strategy. I presented the plan to the couple, and this is when I discovered the major stumbling block in the plan: Jack and Carol had less than $10,000 in the bank and no other taxable cash or investments. They simply did not have the cash on hand to make the annual tax payments required to make the conversion.

This error could have been prevented if they would have engaged in a planning process years sooner. Because they had waited until a year before their retirement, the mistake ended up costing Jack and Carol more than $100,000. They could have had that money to use in their retirement or to leave to their children, but it was never to be, simply because of a false assumption that they would not need a properly funded taxable account after they quit working. Like many investors, Jack and Carol had faithfully poured money into their tax-deferred IRA accounts to the detriment of underfunding their taxable funds, which they would later need for an instance exactly such as this.

THE RISK DIMENSIONS DELIVERED

Figure 4.12, *Risk Dimensions Delivered*, covers 1926 through 2017. There may be "no free lunch," but this Figure illustrates that lunch is available for a significant discount relative to what most other individual investors are paying for it.

I consistently remind investors that their *time horizon is mission critical* for proper portfolio management. Consider this: if someone received a windfall of $300,000 and decided they were going to take that $300,000 and purchase a new house within the next two or three years, I would *never* recommend any exposure to the equity capital markets. No one should have stock exposure to the capital markets if their time horizon *is less than five years*.

As I've repeatedly stated over the past four decades, if these Premiums/ Dimensions/Factors were available every day, every week, and every year, everybody's grandmother and great-grandmother would be investing in them.

You need to have the proper time horizon in order to position the probability for success on your side. As you can see from Figure 4.12, these probabilities have been compelling.

As I mentioned before, there are three other stock premiums after the "Equity Risk Premium" which are recognized as "statistically significant" over our epic databases: the Value Premium, Size Premium, and Profitability Premium. This Figure shows the historical track record of these premiums over various and lengthening periods of time. For example, the horizontal bar shows US Value vs. Growth over one-, five-, and 10-year periods of time. Notice the starting point is July of 1926. This means that for any five-year period—1926 to 1931, 1927 to 1932, 1928 to 1933, etc.—value has beaten growth 75% of the time. Over the average 10-year period of time, value has beaten growth 84% of the time. Now again, this is just one element in our "recipe" or "formula" for diversification. I'm not going overboard; I'm just adding a reasonable portion of value to your portfolio instead of growth after we have established our core positions, which again remember, are half growth and half value.

As we analyze these returns from shorter holding periods vs. longer holding periods, you will notice the probability of success increases over longer periods of time. As mentioned previously, when we build a DiNuzzo Financial Wellness LifePlan™ for someone from their initial point of retirement, we always like to build *at least* a 30-year plan. Again, your primary objective is "to never run out of money before you run out of breath."

FIGURE 4.12. **Risk Dimensions Delivered**

Historical Performance of Premiums Over Rolling Periods

MARKET *BEAT* T-BILLS
Overlapping Periods: July 1926 – December 2018

10-Year	**85%** of the time
5-Year	**78%** of the time
1-Year	**70%** of the time

Market is Fama/French Total US Market Research Index.
T-Bills is One-Month US Treasury Bills.
There are 991 overlapping 10-year periods, 1,051 overlapping 5-year periods, and 1,099 overlapping 1-year periods.

VALUE *BEAT* GROWTH
Overlapping Periods: July 1926 – December 2018

10-Year	**83%** of the time
5-Year	**74%** of the time
1-Year	**60%** of the time

Value is Fama/French US Value Research Index.
Growth is Fama/French US Growth Research Index.
There are 991 overlapping 10-year periods, 1,051 overlapping 5-year periods, and 1,099 overlapping 1-year periods.

SMALL *BEAT* LARGE
Overlapping Periods: July 1926 – December 2018

10-Year	**73%** of the time
5-Year	**63%** of the time
1-Year	**57%** of the time

Small is Dimensional US Small Cap Index.
Large is S&P 500 Index.
There are 980 overlapping 10-year periods, 1,040 overlapping 5-year periods, and 1,088 overlapping 1-year periods.

HIGH PROFITABILITY *BEAT* LOW PROFITABILITY
Overlapping Periods: July 1926 – December 2018

10-Year	**99%** of the time
5-Year	**85%** of the time
1-Year	**67%** of the time

High is Dimensional US High Profitability Index.
Low is Dimensional US Low Profitability Index.
There are 547 overlapping 10-year periods, 607 overlapping 5-year periods, and 655 overlapping 1-year periods.

Source: Dimensional Fund Advisors LP. MSCI data ©MSCI 2019, all rights reserved. S&P data ©2019 S&P Dow Jones Indices LLC, a division of S&P Global. All rights reserved. ©2019 Index Fund Advisors, Inc. (IFA.com)

Looking lower on the graph, the Small Cap Premium of US Small vs. Large is not as large as the Value Premium, but it is still statistically significant. Looking at longer holding periods, Small Cap beat Large 57% of the time in one-year periods, 64% of the time in five-year periods, and 72% of the time in 10-year periods.

If I am investing for an individual in their 20s, I would expose their portfolio to the same Asset Classes—US Large, US Large Value, US Small, US Small Value, Real Estate, etc.—all the way up through their 90s (if their portfolio risk/reward still included equities). We are typically going to own these Asset Classes for our entire lives; we're just going to reduce the percentage of those positions in our portfolios (with the exception of our "Dreams/Wishes," or Legacy/Quality of Life, bucket). For example, a typical individual's stock portfolio will go from 100% in stocks when he or she is right out of college to 20% or even 10% in stocks when he or she is in their 90s, but the stock portion would always have exposure to these same Asset Classes.

Here's how I pragmatically take advantage of the Equity Premiums in a portfolio. As you recall, there are only four current reasons for investing in stocks, and the first and most significant is the Equity/Stock Risk Premium. In other words, the total stock market returned approximately +8% over and above short-term US T-Bills over the last 90 years. The key word in this premium is *risk*; investing in stocks carries additional risk. Thus, again, you need to have the *proper time horizon* of at least five years (preferably ten or more) if you're putting any money into the stock market.

Then, when we come to an investment "fork in the road" and need to choose between value and growth, to take advantage of the premiums defined above, we will "tilt" toward value: the probabilities of success are distinctly on our side. Then we ask, should we just have all large stocks, or does it make sense to have any small? Well, again, the probability over a projected holding period is that small will allow us the potential opportunity to make *more* money with less risk. So we'll choose the path that has a higher probability of success by adding Small Caps to our portfolios. Ditto for Direct/Expected Profitability.

WHY DIVERSIFY? STOCKS VS. INDEXES

I have shown the benefits of indexed investing over active management both in this chapter and throughout my book. The illustration below should be an eye-opener for anyone who has invested in individual stocks.

FIGURE 4.13. **Individual Stocks vs. Index Portfolios**

40 Years: January 1, 1976 – December 31, 2015

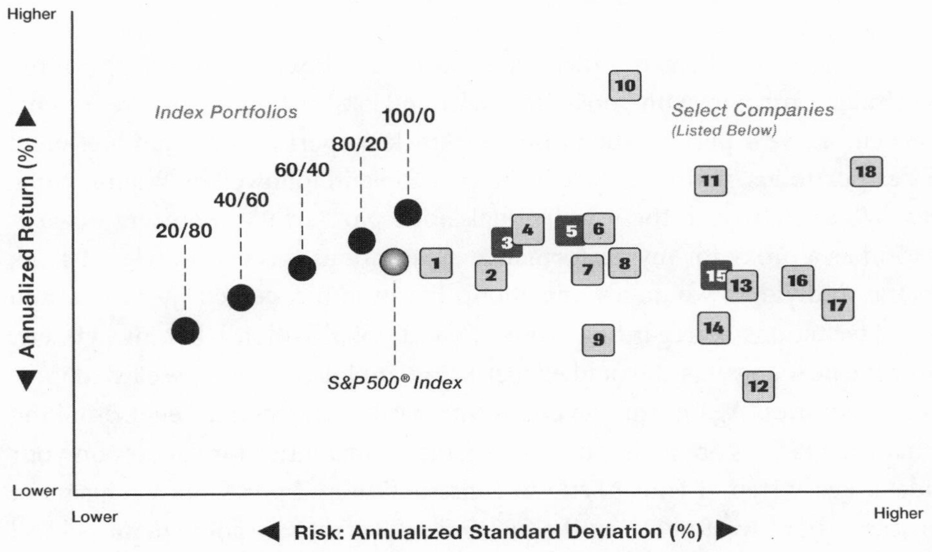

1. Exxon Mobil	4. McDonald's	7. Merck	10. Wal-Mart	13. JPMorgan Chase	16. Hewitt-Packard
2. Proctor & Gamble	5. Pfizer	8. Travelers	11. Boeing	14. Caterpillar	17. Bank of America
3. Johnson & Johnson	6. United Technologies	9. IBM	12. Alcoa	15. Am. Express	18. Intel

Source: Morningstar, Inc.*

In this illustration of stocks vs. indexes, Figure 4.13 *Individual Stocks vs. Index Portfolios*, once again I have another extensive period of time (40 years), from January 1, 1976 through December 31, 2015. This shows the Asset Allocation models going from 20% in stocks up through 100%. Return your attention to the typical 100% stock/0% bond portfolio, and let's compare this to individual equities. Risk is measured on the horizontal axis in annualized standard deviation.

Looking at the individual equity positions, you will see that all the individual equities listed are to the right of the 100/0 portfolio, meaning they are more volatile (riskier) individual investments. This means that when our 100/0 portfolio is in negative territory, the individual stock positions will likely be down a materially greater percentage.

You can also see there is a distinct *minority* of individual stocks above the All-Index portfolio with 100% in stocks and 0% in bonds. This represents a recent 40-year period when only one stock outperformed my represented index portfolios, with Walmart at the very top and followed by Boeing, Intel, etc. We can also use these individual stock plots over this recent 40-year period as a proxy for my performance expectations for any individual stock that an individual would ask me about. For example, currently, what would my expectations be regarding Google, Facebook, Twitter, Uber, or Lyft, etc. over the next 40 years? I would expect a similar plot *vis-à-vis* these listed individual equities. Again, this reverts to my basic fundamental tenet of taking what the markets are giving us and placing probabilities for success on your side at every step of your portfolio construction and portfolio management process. Your investments are the fuel and energy that are going to propel and drive your DiNuzzo Financial Wellness LifePlan™ forward over your entire life expectancy and you want the best fuel possible.

The portfolios are set up on a risk continuum. If you look at the 100% stock portfolio and look toward the left, it has averaged approximately +12.5% per year after expenses over this recent 40-year period. Also of equal interest, pay attention to standard deviation. Standard deviation is around 15 if you look at it on the bottom of the chart. That's the benefit of the recipe that we discussed earlier.

Look at all the squares to the right of the 100/0 portfolio in this Figure. Note that all these squares have exhibited materially higher risk than that portfolio over the last 40 years.

The problem with owning individual stocks is that investors are generally underdiversified. Individual investors usually have "highly concentrated" positions in 1, 2, or 3 stocks. You just need to get your ruler out, lay it horizontally at the 100/0 portfolio, and ask yourself, are more of these individual stocks below or above that line? The supermajority are below that line—meaning that they have exhibited higher risk *and* lower annualized rate of return than the All-Indexed portfolio of 14,000+ stocks diversified over 40+ countries.

This brings me back to Efficient Market Theory and all of the challenges of timing the market. Yes, there are stocks that have done better than the market. I always expect that. There will always be a minority percentage of individual stocks and active mutual fund managers who will do better. The problem is that we just don't know what or who they are ahead of time. And additionally, if we currently identify the active mutual fund managers and the stocks that have done better than average the last 10 years, *very infrequently* will they outperform during the next 10-year period of time. So even once you identify them, they typically don't repeat in the subsequent period. Successful investing just isn't that easy. Chasing returns is quite simply *not* the way to go.

So yes, Walmart did better than the market and better than the 100% stock portfolio. But take a look down below at Alcoa, IBM, and Caterpillar.

One stock that has fallen off of this list is GM. Up until their bankruptcy a few years ago they were the worst long-term performer on this list. This is particularly poignant to me because growing up in a steel mill town outside Pittsburgh, Pennsylvania, from the time I could walk, all I heard was that GM was the greatest company in the United States of America. Both of my grandfathers worked in steel mills—one for 49 years, the other one for over

40 years—and my father worked in a steel mill for 25 years. My entire life I heard things like, "As GM goes, so goes the country," and "a company like GM would never go out of business."

Well, we know that they went out of business. On their deathbed the government put them on life support, but there were billions of dollars that were lost and will never be repaid. So, if you would have invested in that company, which was considered to be the bluest of the blue chips over most of this 40-year period, you would have been wiped out. The only thing that I know for certain about individual stocks is that they all will *eventually* go out of business. It's not a question of if; it's only a question of when.

No stock is going to live on ad infinitum. Eventually, bad financial decisions are made, and the market changes and moves against you faster than your adjustments. Think about the hottest stocks when you were growing up. When I was growing up, Bethlehem Steel was one of the top 20 companies in the United States. If you would have suggested to anyone when I was growing up that Bethlehem Steel would ever go out of business, they would have literally hauled you away somewhere in a white jacket with your arms behind your back. Think about something like that, Bethlehem Steel going out of business, and at the same time Microsoft had not even been introduced to an idea in any garage in the Seattle, Washington area. The market constantly evolves, and constantly generates "creative destruction." In most cases, management doesn't change very well. So why gamble and accept the daunting risk of owning just 1 or 2, or even 5 or 10, individual stocks?

Also, I recognize that a lot of individuals who work for a company own that company's individual stock, both inside and outside their 401(k) plan. For example, Alcoa is a Pittsburgh, Pennsylvania-based Fortune 500 company, and I have worked with a lot of Alcoa employees as clients. You can see how poorly Alcoa has done over these 40 years, yet there are still individuals who will swear up and down that they "bleed Alcoa blue," they're so devoted to the company. A fundamental emotional tenet that Behavioral Scientist and

Professor Terrence Thomas Odean references is that individuals are a lot more comfortable with what they know. So, if you're working for a company such as Alcoa—and Alcoa is a good company; they've done well over the years— but just from a pure return perspective, take a look at what they've earned: a below average return of approximately 5% per year over these 40 years.

Hypothetical Diversified All Index Portfolios vs. US Total Market Index

When he was alive, if you ever had the good fortune to listen to Mr. Jack Bogle ("Uncle Jack") from Vanguard Investments, one of the fathers of index-ing, he often referred to the Total Stock Market Index Fund as the only stock fund necessary to own in your portfolio. Again, I have not and would not in any way impugn the Total Stock Market Index, as over an average 10-year period of time it is outperforming three out of four (approximately 75%) of all "active" stock managers. At the risk of overstating the obvious, it has not nor would it ever "go out of business," as thousands and thousands of active mutual funds do and have done over time.

The total stock market rate of return over this recent 50-year period is slightly more than +10%. However, a globally diversified DFA hypothetical index benchmark portfolio "generated" an approximate +12% rate of return, with slightly less risk as the Total Stock Market Index. This illustrates the benefits of the diversification formula for success: (1) the foundation of International, Emerging Market, and Real Estate diversification mentioned at the begin-ning of the chapter, and (2) taking advantage of the premiums available in the market by tilting to value and small and most recently Direct/Expected Profitability. This helps you meet your ultimate goal of optimizing your port-folio(s) on a risk-adjusted basis. When comparing the DFA index benchmark portfolios to the Total Stock Market Index, it certainly is not a case of good versus bad, but rather one of good versus better. The Total Stock Market Index is an excellent equity index for your portfolio. I simply believe that with the tools we have available, I can better construct client long-term portfolios at a higher level.

FIGURE 4.14. **70% Stocks/30% Bonds: Aggressive Growth**

Typical Portfolio Allocation

GENERAL ASSET CLASS		SPECIFIC INDEX	
28.0%	**U.S. Large**	14.0%	DFA U.S. Large Company Index
		14.0%	DFA U.S. Large Cap Value Index
14.0%	**U.S. Small**	7.0%	DFA U.S. Small Cap Index
		7.0%	DFA U.S. Small Cap Value Index
7.0%	**Real Estate**	7.0%	DFA Real Estate Index
14.0%	**International**	3.5%	DFA International Large Company Index
		3.5%	DFA International Large Value Index
		3.5%	DFA International Small Company Index
		3.5%	DFA International Small Cap Value Index
7.0%	**Emerging Markets**	2.1%	DFA Emerging Markets Index
		2.1%	DFA Emerging Markets Value Index
		2.8%	DFA Emerging Markets Small Cap Index
30.0%	**Fixed Income**	7.5%	DFA 5-Year Targeted Credit Bond Index
		7.5%	DFA 5-Year Global Bond Index
		7.5%	DFA Intermediate U.S. Investment Grade Bond Index
		7.5%	DFA Intermediate World ex.U.S. Bond Index

Now let's begin putting together the Asset Allocation strategy discussed earlier with the diversification strategies illustrated in this chapter so far. In Figure 4.14, we can see the specific Asset Class allocations of a typical 70/30 (70% stock, 30% bond) portfolio, which I refer to as an "Aggressive Growth" portfolio. In this portfolio, 28% of our holdings are in US Large Stocks, divided evenly between US Large Cap (14%) and US Large Cap Value (14%) index benchmarks with DFA. Next, we have 14% in US Small, again divided evenly between US Small Cap (7%) and US Small Cap Value (7%) DFA institutional Asset Classes. Then for diversification purposes, we have 7% in Real Estate (REIT) Indexes; and Internationally 3.5% in International Large Company, 3.5% in International Large Value, 3.5% in International Small Company, and 3.5% in International Small Value. Finally, the stock portion of my allocation is rounded off with a 7% exposure to Emerging Markets, ideally with 2.1% in DFA Emerging Market Large Cap, 2.1% in Emerging Market Value, and 2.8%

in Emerging Market Small Cap. On the bond side of the portfolio (30% exposure), I produce a weighted average, which would represent an intermediate term bond indexed portfolio utilizing four DFA Bond Index benchmark positions, *to provide you with the best projected risk-adjusted total return* in your portfolios at every level.

DIVERSIFICATION PHILOSOPHY: STANDING ON THE SHOULDERS OF GIANTS

To reiterate a basic point I made earlier: building a portfolio begins at the very top with your *Investment Philosophy*. Once you've identified your Investment Philosophy, then you develop your *Strategy* based on the philosophy. Then once you've developed your strategy, you *implement* it. After you implement it you need to maintain your *discipline*. Unfortunately, most people invest in stocks without a philosophy or a strategy which typically results in a poor investment experience. Philosophy > Strategy > Implementation > Discipline is the winning formula.

I realize I've presented a lot of data and have taken a very granular view to substantiate my investment philosophy behind diversification. But if you are going to be successful in the investment portion of your Financial Wellness LifePlan, you really need to understand the terrain and the history in order to establish a strong philosophy, which will in turn generate a strong strategy, which will in turn yield a strong plan for implementation, which can allow you to relax and maintain a successful discipline.

One of my goals in this book is *financial education*. Out of all of the continuing education consultations I have done with prospective and existing clients, most can easily adapt to and agree with the positions that I'm making. Most people in the Pittsburgh, Pennsylvania area, like most people around the nation, do not have a PhD in Investments or a PhD in Personal Finance, but they do have a PhD in common sense. Most people appreciate being educated and not being "sold to." They appreciate someone who wants to enter into a partnership and collaborate, consult, and provide advice and guidance to them working in a relationship of equals.

I'm standing on the shoulders of giants, utilizing Nobel Prize-winning research to build your portfolio. None of us want to be investors who were "sold" something. We want to be "buyers." We want to invest from a position of strength, from a position of knowledge, from a position of being educated. The supermajority of individuals' portfolios were "sold" to them. If they were at a full-service brokerage firm, or if they purchased an annuity, or if something in the media grabbed their attention, typically these investments were *not a Fiduciary-based proactive part of a plan*. They were not evaluated on the basis of whether they either increased the return or decreased the risk for the overall portfolio.

The only two reasons to add any investment to your portfolio are to increase return or decrease risk, and the good news is that you can do both with a properly diversified portfolio. This means exposure to the entire universe of companies, appropriately weighted toward the known market Premiums and Asset Classes with offsetting risk correlations. After you determine your basic stock/bond Asset Allocation, taking into account your milestones, goals, "Needs," "Wants," "Dreams/Wishes," and investment time horizon, your next step in your "recipe/formula" is to diversify your equity (stock) allocation (for example, with a 70% Domestic and 30% International split), followed by your bond positions. Finally, "tilt" your portfolio toward the available Equity Premiums (after core positions are filled…Value, then Small, followed by Direct/Expected Profitability) to maximize returns while minimizing risk.

INDEXING VS. ACTIVE INVESTMENT MANAGEMENT

MAKING EFFICIENT MARKET THEORY WORK FOR YOU

Best-of-breed indexing founded on Efficient Market Theory (EMT) and available Market Premiums/Dimensions provides you with a persistent and pervasive investment strategy metaphorically akin to waves relentlessly hitting the beach...powerfully, methodically, repeatedly, 24/7/365.

—P.J. DiNuzzo

We are only beginning to understand how subtle and efficient is the communication mechanism we call the market. It garners, comprehends, and disseminates widely dispersed information better and faster than any system man has deliberately designed.

—F.A. Hayek, Nobel Laureate, circa 1974

Most investors, both institutional and individual, will find the best way to own common stocks is through an index fund that charges minimal fees.
  —Warren Buffett, Chairman, Berkshire Hathaway, and legendary
    American investor, Berkshire Hathaway 1996 shareholder letter

The best way in my view is to just buy a low-cost index fund and keep buying it regularly over time, because you'll be buying into a wonderful industry, which in effect is all of American industry…people ought to sit back and relax and keep accumulating over time.
  —Warren Buffett, *MarketWatch*, May 7, 2007

All the time and effort that people devote to picking the right (mutual) fund, the hot hand, the great manager, have in most cases led to no advantage.
  —Peter Lynch, *Beating the Street*

[Most investors would] be better off in an index fund.
  —Peter Lynch, *Barron's*, April 2, 1990

Invest in low-turnover, passively managed index funds and stay away from profit-driven investment management organizations…The mutual fund industry is a colossal failure…resulting from its systematic exploitation of individual investors…as funds extract enormous sums from investors, in exchange for providing a shocking disservice…Excessive management fees take their toll, and [manager] profits dominate fiduciary responsibility.
  —David Swensen, Chief Investment Officer, Yale University

On "Mad Money," [Jim] Cramer promotes a mindless short-term approach to markets by encouraging frenetic trading of individual stocks. Such a high-cost, tax-inefficient strategy almost guarantees failure.
  —David Swensen, Chief Investment Officer, Yale University

Q: *"So investors shouldn't delude themselves about beating the market?"*
A: *"They're just not going to do it. It's just not going to happen."*
—Daniel Kahneman, Nobel Laureate in Economics, 2002,
Interview reported in the *Orange County Register*, January 2, 2002

Properly measured, the average actively managed dollar must under-
perform the average passively managed [index] dollar, net of costs.
Empirical analyses that appear to refute this principle are guilty of
improper measurement.
—William F. Sharpe, Nobel Laureate in Economics, 1990,
"The Arithmetic of Active Management," *The Financial*
Analysts' Journal 47, no. 1, January/February 1991, pp. 7-9

Most of my investments are in equity index funds.
—William F. Sharpe, Nobel Laureate in Economics, 1990, "The
Godfather of Index Funds," *BusinessWeek*, July 20, 1998

Why pay people to gamble with your money?
—William F. Sharpe, Nobel Laureate in Economics,
1990, "The Parable of Money Managers," *The Financial*
Analysts' Journal 32, no. 4 (July/August 1976), p. 4

Most investors are pretty smart. Yet most investors also remain heav-
ily invested in actively managed stock funds. This is puzzling. The
temptation, of course, is to dismiss these folks as ignorant fools. But
I suspect these folks know the odds are stacked against them, and yet
they are more than happy to take their chances.
—Jonathan Clements, *The Wall Street Journal*, February 27, 2001

So who still believes markets don't work? Apparently it is only the
North Koreans, the Cubans, and the active managers.
—Rex Sinquefield, Co-Founder, Dimensional Fund Advisors
(DFA), "Active vs. Passive Management," October 1995

While there are active managers who at times 'beat' the market, the success of these outliers is random and not predictive of future success. It is quite simply impossible to predict at what point in time an active manager will be successful...Today, it is a widely acknowledged fact that one person cannot have more information than a market of six billion investors.

—Rex Sinquefield, *Forbes*, September 2013

The results of this study are not good news for investors who purchase actively managed mutual funds. No investment style generates positive abnormal returns over the 1965-1998 sample period. The sample includes 4,686 funds covering 26,564 fund-years.
—James L. Davis, DFA Research, "Mutual Fund Performance and Manager Style," *Financial Analysts Journal* 57 (2001): pp. 19-27

Question: "I wonder if I might ask you...how do you think people should invest for the future...? Should they buy index funds?"
Answer: "Absolutely. I have often said, and I know this will get some of your readers mad, that any pension fund manager who doesn't have the vast majority—and I mean 70% or 80% of his or her portfolio— in passive investments is guilty of malfeasance, nonfeasance or some other kind of bad feasance! There's just no sense for most of them to have anything but a passive investment policy."
—Interview of Merton Miller, Nobel Laureate in Economics, by Peter Tanous, "Investment Gurus," February 1997

Everybody has some information. The function of the market is to aggregate that information, evaluate it, and get it incorporated into prices.
—Merton Miller, Nobel Laureate in Economics

Most of the mutual fund investments I have are index funds, approximately 75%.
—Charles R. Schwab, *Guide to Financial Independence*

Buy Index Funds. It might not seem like much action, but it's the smartest thing to do.

—Interview of Charles Schwab by Jason
Zweig, *Money*, January 2007

At a minimum, index funds and the general focus on cost and diversification are perhaps the most direct practical result of EMH (Efficient Markets Hypothesis) thinking, and we'd argue the most investor-welfare-enhancing financial innovations of the past 50 years.

—Clifford Asness and John Liew

Statisticians will tell you that you need 20 years' worth of data – that's right, two full decades – to draw statistically meaningful conclusions [about mutual funds].* Anything less, they say, and you have little to hang your hat on. But here's the problem for fund investors: After 20 successful years of managing a mutual fund, most managers are ready to retire. In fact, only 22 US stock funds have had the same manager on board for at least two decades – and I wouldn't call all the managers in that bunch skilled.

—Susan Dziubinski, University editor with Morningstar.co
(*Index Funds are the only source of reliable 20-year risk and return data.)

ACTIVELY MANAGED VS. INDEX FUNDS: CHRIS AND PAULA

Chris is a retired chemist and Paula is a retired college professor. They are Family Steward High-Net-Worth Personality Types whose main priorities are to maintain their lifestyle in retirement and have the means to leave a material legacy to their children and grandchildren. The couple had done well for themselves and regularly helped out their siblings with expenses such as medical and dental bills. The DiNuzzo

Way™ includes Core Principles in loyalty and strengthening families—ours and our clients'—so I knew straight off that we were a good fit.

When they came to see me, they had approximately $1 million in a joint, taxable account in addition to their IRAs. The money was in a managed account that was being managed by an active mutual fund manager. The couple believed they had made a smart choice but now, in their retirement, they had questions and they desired a "second opinion."

I don't enjoy being the bearer of bad news but under my Fiduciary Standard, that's often the case when people come to see me who are heavily invested in actively managed stock mutual funds. Over time, the mutual fund in which Chris and Paula had invested nearly a million dollars had *underperformed* the relative benchmark by about 2% per year.

The miracle of compounding can be a beautiful and powerful thing if you use it in your favor. But if you look at the cost of lost opportunity, the results can be alarming. Two percent on a million-dollar portfolio in one year is $20,000. Compound that dollar value over several years or decades, and you can see how dramatic the lost opportunity becomes.

Adding insult to injury, the money was all invested in a taxable account, *and* the active fund was throwing off up to *four times* higher capital gain distributions than a comparable stock index mutual fund strategy, and so they also had to contend with the added tax liability every year.

If you are investing in a taxable account for long-term goals, ideally you would want it to grow "friction-free" with low turnover, commensurately lower realized capital gains, and no negative annual tax consequences. While there's managed turnover in both index and active mutual funds, the actively managed turnover is typically much higher. There's more trading activity, and thus more distributions—and more taxes. Refer to the old saying, "it's not what you make, it's what you keep." If you're paying taxes on 50, 60, 70, or—in some cases I have seen—as much as $80,000 of capital gains distributions a year, you will *not* be taking home as much as you could have by investing in a properly structured index portfolio with less turnover.

Chris and Paula were not aware of this flaw which resulted in a significant detriment to their plan. The lost opportunity and additional tax liability on excessive capital gain distributions, all due to their choice to put their money into an active managed fund, had cost them hundreds of thousands of dollars over time.

Chris and Paula couldn't get back the money they had missed out on or recover the taxes they had paid on their distributions, but I worked with them to develop a customized DiNuzzo Financial Wellness LifePlan™ that eliminated these weaknesses and put them on a better path forward. The plan took advantage of the historically higher expected returns of indexed investments, lowered their tax burden, and ensured they would be able to enjoy their retirement while continuing to help out their family members and leave a lasting legacy for their children and grandchildren.

Efficient Market Theory holds that all the information regarding the value of a security is reflected in its current price, and that over time the best way to take advantage of Efficient Market Theory is through index-based investing.

EFFICIENT MARKET THEORY (EMT)

To design a solid foundation for a winning portfolio, and ultimately a successful DiNuzzo Financial Wellness LifePlan™ and retirement, it is important to understand the history of Modern Finance in general, and Efficient Market

Theory in particular. Efficient Market Theory states that all available information regarding the value of a company is efficiently reflected in its market price (Price Discovery). This theory forms the basis for all of my portfolio investment strategies, including Asset Allocation, Asset Class procurement, diversification, and rebalancing. Taking a moment to appreciate the history of Modern Finance will help you with the emotions management these strategies require. In this chapter, I will look at the benefits of indexing relative to active management. This is a topic of utmost importance to your financial life. How are you going to invest your lifetime savings? Before you can decide that, you must understand how we got to where we are right now.

Innovations in financial markets research over the last fifty years are the nucleus of my belief system that guides DiNuzzo Private Wealth, Inc. (DPW)/DiNuzzo Wealth Management (DWM), and Dimensional Fund Advisors' (DFA) approach to investing. Today, the investment industry takes for granted the calculation of rates of return and the availability of comparative universes for professionally managed funds. But before the mid-1960s, there was neither a generally accepted way to calculate a total return nor a way to compare the returns of different funds. This all changed with the advent of computers and the collection of data for mutual funds as well as for individual stocks and bonds.

Rigorous testing by financial economists of that seminal era led to the development of asset pricing models to evaluate the risk/return characteristics of securities and portfolios, and also led to a theory of market efficiency that suggested excess returns were only achievable by taking on above-market risk. Studies documenting the failure of active managers to outperform market indexes gave rise in the early 1970s to the initial passively managed index funds that relied on capital markets as the source of investment returns.

Further research and data compilation over several decades led to the identification of the multiple Asset Classes and sources of higher expected returns that form the basis of DiNuzzo Private Wealth, Inc. (DPW)/DiNuzzo Wealth Management (DWM), and Dimensional Fund Advisors' (DFA) strategies.

History of Modern Finance and Economics

Conventional Wisdom circa 1950

Once you attain competency, diversification is undesirable. One or two, or at most three or four, securities should be bought. Competent investors will never be satisfied beating the averages by a few small percentage points.

—Gerald M. Loeb, *The Battle for Investment Survival*, 1935

Analyze securities one by one. Focus on picking winners. Concentrate holdings to maximize returns. Broad diversification is considered undesirable.

1952: *Diversification and Portfolio Risk*
Harry Markowitz, Nobel Prize in Economics, 1990

Diversification reduces risk. Assets evaluated not by individual characteristics but by their effect on a portfolio. An optimal portfolio can be constructed to maximize return for a given standard deviation.

1958: *The Role of Stocks*
James Tobin, Nobel Prize in Economics, 1981

Separation Theorem:
1. Form portfolio of risky assets.
2. Temper risk by lending and borrowing.

- Shifts focus from security selection to portfolio structure.
- "Liquidity Preference as Behavior Toward Risk," *Review of Economic Studies*, February 1958.

1961: *Investments and Capital Structure*
Merton Miller and Franco Modigliani, Nobel Prizes in Economics, 1985 and 1990

Theorem relating corporate finance to returns. A firm's value is unrelated to its dividend policy. Dividend policy is an unreliable guide for stock selection.

1964: *Single-Factor Asset Pricing Risk/Return Model*
William Sharpe, Nobel Prize in Economics, 1990

Capital Asset Pricing Model:
- Theoretical model defines risk as volatility relative to market.
- A stock's cost of capital (the investor's expected return) is proportional to the stock's risk relative to the entire stock universe.
- Theoretical model for evaluating the risk and expected return of securities and portfolios.

1965: *Behavior of Securities Prices*
Paul Samuelson, MIT, Nobel Prize in Economics, 1970

Market prices are the best estimates of value. Price changes follow random patterns. Future share prices are unpredictable.

- "Proof that Properly Anticipated Prices Fluctuate Randomly," *Industrial Management Review*, Spring 1965

1966: *Efficient Markets Hypothesis*
Eugene Fama, Nobel Prize in Economics, 2013, University of Chicago

Extensive research on stock price patterns. Develops Efficient Markets Hypothesis, which asserts that prices reflect values and information accurately and quickly. It is difficult if not impossible to capture returns in excess of market returns without taking greater than market levels of risk. Investors cannot identify superior stocks using fundamental information or price patterns.

1968: First Major Study of Manager Performance
Michael Jensen, 1965; A.G. Becker Corporation, 1968

First studies of mutual funds (Jensen) and of institutional plans (A.G. Becker Corp.) indicate active managers underperform indexes. Becker Corp. gives rise to consulting industry with creation of "Green Book" performance tables comparing results to benchmarks.

1971: The Birth of Index Funds
John "Mac" McQuown, Wells Fargo Bank, 1971; Rex Sinquefield, American National Bank, 1973; David Booth

Banks develop the first passive S&P 500 Index funds. Years later, Booth and Sinquefield co-found Dimensional Fund Advisors (DFA), and McQuown sits on its board.

1972: Options Pricing Model
Fischer Black, University of Chicago; Myron Scholes, University of Chicago; Robert Merton, Harvard University; Nobel Prize in Economics, 1997

The development of the Options Pricing Model allows new ways to segment, quantify, and manage risk. The model spurs the development of a market for alternative investments.

1975–1982: Market Efficiency, Interest Rates, and Inflation
Eugene Fama, Nobel Prize in Economics, 2013, University of Chicago

Extends empirical tests to fixed income markets and finds evidence of market efficiency. Finds that nominal interest rates incorporate information on future inflation expectations and that greater inflation uncertainty is positively related to risk premia. Examines the relationship between real interest rates and inflation and shows they are negatively correlated.

1975: A Major Plan First Commits to Indexing

New York Telephone Company invests $40 million in an S&P 500 Index fund. The first major plan to index. Helps launch the era of indexed investing.

> *Fund spokesmen are quick to point out you can't buy the market averages. It's time the public could.*
> —Burton G. Malkiel, *A Random Walk Down Wall Street*, 1973 ed.

1977: Term Structure Models
Oldrich Vasicek, Wells Fargo Bank

Lays the academic groundwork for bond pricing and yield curve models.

1977: Asset Returns and Inflation
Eugene Fama, Nobel Prize in Economics, 2013, University of Chicago; William Schwert, University of Rochester

Study the inflation hedging properties of different assets and finds short-term government fixed income to be an effective inflation hedge.

1977: Database of Securities Prices since 1926
Roger Ibbotson and Rex Sinquefield, Stocks, Bonds, Bills, and Inflation

An extensive returns database for multiple Asset Classes is first developed and will become one of the most widely used investment databases of all time. The first extensive, empirical basis for making Asset Allocation decisions changes the way investors build portfolios.

1981–1984: Interest Rate Parity
Eugene Fama, Nobel Prize in Economics, 2013, University of Chicago; John Bilson, University of Chicago; Richard Meese, University of California at Berkeley; Kenneth Rogoff, Board of Governors of the Federal Reserve System

A forward rate is shown to be the sum of a risk premium and expected future spot rate. Most of the variation in forward rates is due to variations in premiums. Empirical evidence reveals the failure of uncovered interest rate parity, which means that forward rates do not predict short-term currency movements.

1981: *The Size Effect*
Rolf Banz, University of Chicago

Analyzed NYSE stocks, 1926–1975. Finds that, in the long term, small companies have higher expected returns than large companies and behave differently. Dimensional Fund Advisors (DFA) is founded in 1981 and launches the US Micro Cap Portfolio.

1982: *Interest Rates and Inflation*
Eugene Fama, Nobel Prize in Economics, 2013, University of Chicago; Michael Gibbons, Stanford University

Show that real interest rates are negatively correlated with inflation. "Inflation, Real Returns and Capital Investment," *Journal of Monetary Economics* (9): 297-323.

1983: *Variable Maturity Strategy Implemented*
Dimensional Fund Advisors, One-Year Fixed Income Strategy

With no prediction of interest rates, Eugene Fama develops a method of shifting maturities that identifies optimal positions on the fixed income yield curve.

1984: *Information in the Term Structure*
Eugene Fama, Nobel Prize in Economics, 2013, University of Chicago

Finds that risk premiums are an important factor when evaluating forward interest rates. Finds that forward rates implied by the treasury yield curve provide information on the term structure of expected returns.

1985: Term Premiums and Default Premiums in Money Markets
Eugene Fama, Nobel Prize in Economics, 2013, University of Chicago

Presents empirical evidence that the default premium is time varying.

1986: International Size Effect
Dimensional Fund Advisors (DFA), International Small Cap Strategies

DFA Investing vs. Indexing: With no index, DFA creates International Small Cap strategies modeled after the US research. DFA's live returns become the index used in Ibbotson Associates' database. DFA investing is based on a rational return source, and does not slavishly follow indexes or investing conventions.

1989: Business Cycle Patterns in Stock and Bond Returns
Eugene Fama, Nobel Prize in Economics, 2013,
and Kenneth French, University of Chicago

Offer evidence that the expected excess returns on stocks and bonds are typically higher than normal during recessions and lower than normal at business peaks.

1990: Nobel Prize Recognizes Modern Finance

Economists who shaped the way we invest are recognized, emphasizing the role of science in finance: William Sharpe for the Capital Asset Pricing Model, Harry Markowitz for Modern Portfolio Theory (MPT), and Merton Miller for work on the effect of firms' capital structure and dividend policy on their prices.

1992: Multifactor Asset Pricing Model and Value Effect
Eugene Fama, Nobel Prize in Economics, 2013,
and Kenneth French, University of Chicago

Improve on the single-factor asset pricing model (CAPM). Identify "market," "size," and "value" factors/premiums in returns. Develop the three-factor asset pricing model, an invaluable Asset Allocation and portfolio analysis tool. Establish term and default factors for fixed income returns. Dimensional Fund Advisors introduces value strategies based on the research. Lends to similar findings internationally.

1993: *Bond Mutual Fund Performance*
Christopher Blake, Fordham University; Edwin Elton, New York University; Martin Gruber, New York University

Conduct what's believed to be the first comprehensive study of bond mutual fund returns. They conclude that, on average, bond funds underperform relevant indexes after expenses. They also find no evidence of predictability using past performance to predict future performance.

1997: *Inflation-Protected Bonds*

The Treasury conducts the first auction of Treasury Inflation-Protected Securities (TIPS), thus allowing US investors to invest for long periods with minimal default risk and inflation risk.

1999: *Tax Management*

Dimensional Fund Advisors' tax-managed strategies implemented, which seek to maximize after-tax returns by offsetting gains and minimizing dividends. Based on Fama/French research and DFA's "portfolio decision system" trading technology.

2002: *Improved Bond Market Transparency*

National Association of Securities Dealers (NASD) introduces Trade Reporting and Compliance Engine (TRACE), which requires the reporting of US corporate bond trades. This data allows researchers to study trading costs and inequality in the US corporate bond market.

2004: Applied Core Equity

Dimensional Fund Advisors' portfolio construction methodology weights securities by size and value characteristics instead of market capitalization. Total market strategies launched which seek to provide efficient, diversified exposure to the sources of higher expected returns while limiting turnover and transaction costs. Core equity portfolios move beyond traditional, component-based Asset Allocation via vast diversification and cost-efficient market coverage.

2014 Direct/Expected Profitability Premium

There are differences in expected returns across stocks. Variables that tell us what an investor has to pay (market prices) and what they expect to receive (book equity and future profits) contain information about those expected returns. All else equal, the lower the price relative to book value and the higher the expected profitability, the higher the expected return.

Initial work in this area was launched by Nobel Laureate Eugene Fama and Professor Kenneth French, while Professor Robert Novy-Marx receives the lion's share of the credit for his extensive work in identifying this premium.

EFFICIENT MARKETS HYPOTHESIS (EMH)

In 1965, University of Chicago Booth Graduate School of Business professor Eugene Fama, currently viewed as the "father of Modern Finance," focused on the random movement of stocks, which culminated in the publishing of his research paper "The Behavior of Stock Market Prices." It was this groundbreaking paper in which he created the phrase "Efficient Markets." His research intimated that "active management" led to no advantage, and that active stock fund managers performed no better than mere chance alone. In 1970, Professor Fama published his hypothesis, titled: "Efficient Capital

Markets, A Review of Theory and Empirical Work." He found that capital markets continually incorporate all available knowledge and information, which is then reflected in the current market price(s). Although not perfectly efficient, the market remains nearly impossible to "outsmart" and correctly forecast by anyone on a *consistent* basis. The agreement between buyer and seller through the rigors of their independent "Price Discovery" is the *most accurate* assessment of an individual security's value. The only way, on average, an investor may expect to achieve superior performance is to take on additional or excessive risk.

Index management is a "buy and hold" approach based on the "science" of the Efficient Markets Hypothesis. Active investment is the polar opposite of index management and is the "art" of stock picking and market timing based on a market "failure hypothesis"—that the market is supposedly inefficient and will allow them time to purchase securities at a better price, ahead of other investors.

A hypothesis is a speculative guess that has yet to be tested, whereas a theory has been extensively tested and is generally accepted by the academic community. The Efficient Market Theory states that prices are fundamentally fair and information is quickly reflected in market pricing (within five to sixty minutes). Because of this, investors will not be able to systematically "outsmart the market."

In summary, the Efficient Market Theory states:

- Current prices incorporate all available information and expectations.
- Current prices are the best approximation of intrinsic value.
- Price changes are due to unforeseen events and new information.
- "Mispricing" does occur, but not in predictable patterns that can lead to consistent outperformance.

Implications:

- Active management strategies cannot consistently add value through security selection and market timing.
- Passive (index) investments and strategies reward investors with capital market (Asset Class) returns.

One of the more significant and ubiquitous empirical investment research projects was undertaken by James L. Davis of DFA (Dimensional Fund Advisors). Mr. Davis examined 4,686 US (stock) mutual funds from 1965–1998. He found that none of the styles included in the study were able to generate positive abnormal returns when compared to the Fama/French (1993) research benchmark. In 1992, Professors Eugene Fama and Kenneth French published their landmark research paper, "The Cross-Section of Expected Stock Returns," which built upon earlier Nobel Prize-winning research. They identified three key factors that explained as much as 97% of historical returns in a diversified stock portfolio: exposure to Market, Value, and (Small) Size.

> *Hulbert's conclusion: None of the newsletter timers beat the market [over a 10-year period]. The average return was 11.06%. During the same period, Standard and Poor's 500-stock index earned 18.06% annually...*
>
> —Jeffrey M. Laderman, "Market Timing: A Perilous Ploy," *BusinessWeek*, March 9, 1998

> *Professor Wermers says his advice has evolved significantly as a result of this study. Until now, he says, he wouldn't have tried to discourage a sophisticated investor from trying to pick a mutual fund that would outperform the market. Now, he says, "it seems almost hopeless."*
>
> —Mark Hulbert, "The Prescient Are Few," *New York Times*, July 13, 2008

FIGURE 5.1. **Stock-Picking Skill is Statistically Indistinguishable from Zero**

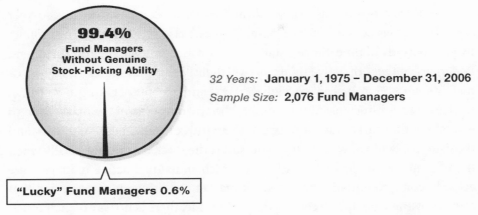

32 Years: **January 1, 1975 – December 31, 2006**

Sample Size: **2,076 Fund Managers**

Source: "False Discoveries in Mutual Performance: Measuring Luck in Estimated Alphas" by Professors Laurent Barras, Olivier Scaillet, and Russell Wermers.

In 2008, Mark Hulbert penned an article in *The New York Times* titled "The Prescient Are Few." His article cited the research of professors Laurent Barras, Olivier Scaillet, and Russell Wermers, which analyzed 2,076 mutual fund managers from 1975 through 2006. During these 32 years, they found that 99.4% of the "active" stock mutual fund managers exhibited no evidence of genuine stock picking skill.

FAILURE OF ACTIVE MANAGEMENT

Figure 5.2, *The Failure of Active Management*, illustrates mutual fund categories of active managers vs. their prospective benchmark index over a recent past decade ending December 31, 2011. Although this graph ends in 2011, I will probably still be showing it to clients 25 years from now. This image covers two (2) uber "bear markets": March 2000–October 2002 and October 2007–February 2009, which both had total losses of 50% or more. Active stock mutual fund managers often opine: "I might not outperform the index on the upside but I do better than the index benchmark on the downside in corrections and bear markets. This chart shows that 95% of active managers of US Large Cap core stock mutual funds *underperformed* the Russell 1000 index over this 10-year period. I see this across all major Asset Classes. I also see this trend over rolling 10-year periods of time. Since I started my practice in 1989, the rolling 10-year *underperformance* of active managers vs. their benchmark index has approximately been 75%. You need to weigh the costs and benefits of taking *at best* a 3 in 10 chance on finding an active manager who will outperform the market versus just taking the market rate of return with an index fund. Once you understand the data, you will *not* want to try to outsmart the stock market, especially when there is no way to predict in advance which individual active managers are actually going to outperform the stock market. Additionally, considering that even knowing who did succeed in the last decade, there is no way of guaranteeing they will have a repeat performance going forward. This seldom happens.

I refer to active investing as "the loser's game." Although the allure and excitement of active management and market timing may be seductive and engaging, it is clearly not the path to take for *long-term* investment success.

> *The deeper one delves, the worse things look for actively managed funds.*
> —Dr. William Bernstein, The Intelligent Asset Allocator

> *It's like giving up a belief in Santa Claus. Even though you know Santa Claus doesn't exist, you kind of cling to that belief. I'm not saying that this is a scam. They generally believe they can do it. The evidence is, however, that they can't.*
> —Professor Burton Malkiel, *20/20*, ABC News, November 1992

> *All such [market beating] strategies have two things in common: First, they won't work. And second, the reason they won't work is that the anonymous investors on the other side of the trade usually have more on the ball than you imagine.*
> —Dr. William Bernstein, *Money*, October 22, 2008

FIGURE 5.2. The Failure of Active Management

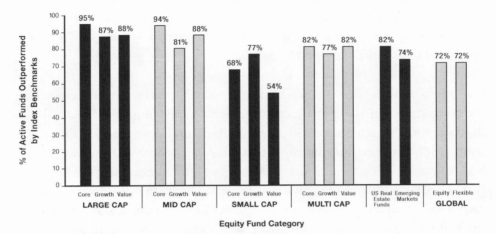

% of Active Public Equity Funds Outperformed by
Index Benchmarks (10 Years as of December 31, 2011)

Source: CRSP* data provided by the Center for Research Prices, University of Chicago.

Back when I got my Master's Degree in Tax Law, the majority of my sixteen classes were taught by professors who were both Attorneys *and* CPAs. Any time I answered a question in class, the professors *always* required me to support my answers. I couldn't get away with a generalization, but had to cite a specific example, e.g., Smith v. the State of Vermont, 1985. This pattern of question, response, and support honed my understanding of tax law. I bring the same passion and rigor to my practice, my clients, and my book. It is not that I am smarter than anyone else, but I won't settle for generalizations. I continually refine my process to fulfill my Fiduciary duty and what I feel is a "sacred responsibility" to my clients.

I take the same pragmatic approach when considering active managers and their performance relative to their benchmark index. The leftmost bar on the chart above shows that 95% of Large Cap active funds were *outperformed* by their benchmark index. Go two more bars over to the right and look at US

Large Value—88% of US Large Value active managers *lost* out to the benchmark index. Go over a few bars more—74% of Emerging Markets stock fund managers lost out to the Emerging Market benchmark index. Finally, on the far right, regarding Global Equity Markets—72% of Global Equity active stock mutual fund managers lost out to the Global Equity benchmark index. So the market is not just efficient in the US, it's efficient worldwide in developed countries and Emerging Markets.

It is dumbfounding how people underestimate the sheer size and quality of the competition in the global capital market's financial arena. Forget about the NFL, NBA, MLB, or NHL with their limited number of teams—you've got tens of millions of extraordinarily highly educated people with almost unlimited resources. They have floors and floors of computers that crunch numbers. They've got teams of analysts and researchers with PhDs in economics, probability, statistics, finance, investing, and behavioral science. It's like the story of the bank robber. When asked, "Why are you robbing these banks?" he answered, "Because that's where the money is." Considering the value of the stock market and the global capital markets, where would you expect all of the smartest minds on earth to be focused? That's where all the money is.

Although it is very alluring to attempt to outperform and outsmart the stock market, in reality, over time, it is a *futile* exercise, as no one possesses a crystal ball. No one has tomorrow's newspaper. Stock prices move based on *new, previously unknown* information. You just *cannot* predict which managers are going to outperform their comparative index over the next five-year or 10-year period. What we do know, though, is that top performers seldom repeat their performance in subsequent periods.

> *In the short run, the stock market is a voting machine but in the long run, it is a weighing machine.*
> —Benjamin Graham, from *The Little Book of Common Sense Investing* by John C. Bogle

FIGURE 5.3. **Failure of Active Management**
15 Years: January 1, 2000 – December 31, 2014

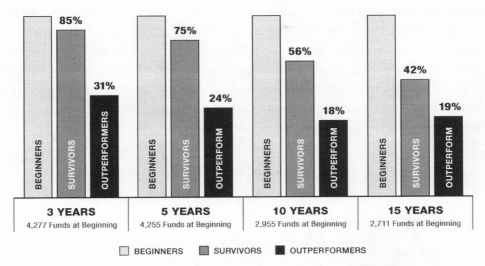

Sources: Center for Research in Security Prices Survivorship/Free US Mutual Fund Database.

Figure 5.3, *Failure of Active Management,* illustrates the failure of active management over this recent period. What we can observe is the same long-term (10 years +) trends beginning to emerge. On average, over extended periods of time, you will witness approximately 75% (3 out of 4) of active mutual fund managers failing to beat their respective benchmarks, and this often begins to take shape within the initial five years.

This is yet another example of trying to "find the needle in the haystack." Investment success is based upon placing the highest long-term probabilities for success on your side, not by structuring outsized "bets" in your portfolio and risking your life's savings.

Many individuals look at indexes as stagnant, monolithic investing, but in reality, nothing could be further from the truth. Examining the largest (company) index, the S&P 500, we can observe dynamic "survival of the fittest" activity. Figure 5.4, *Survivors and Winners of s&p 500 Stocks*, illustrates a number of eye-opening results based on the book *Creative Destruction* by Richard Foster and Sarah Kaplan. Of the original 500 companies that first formed the S&P 500 in 1957, *only* 74 of them still survived 40 years later in 1997. More impressively, *only* twelve individual companies outperformed the aggregate index over a similar period (1957–1998). Success is not attained by guessing, picking, and trading individual stocks but rather by investing in large "baskets" of stocks in the correct areas of the market, maintaining discipline, and letting the market "come to you."

FIGURE 5.4. **Survivors and Winners of s&p 500 Stocks**

A Study of 41 Years (1957 – 1998)

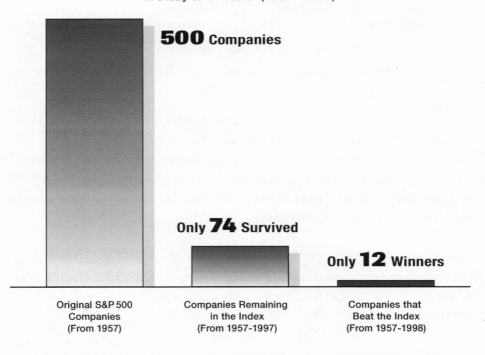

Source: Creative Destruction, Richard Foster & Sarah Caplan.

*The S&P 500 is a wonderful thing to put your money in. If some-
one said, "I've got a fund here with a really low cost, that is tax efficient, with a 15- to 20-year record of beating almost everybody," why
wouldn't you own it?*

—Bill Miller, former Legg Mason Value Trust Mutual Fund
manager, owns the longest track record in stock mutual fund
history for beating the S&P 500 for the most consecutive years (15).

FIGURE 5.5. **Legg Mason Value's Alpha (Outperformance)**

Relative to the Russell 1000 Index
30 Years: January 1, 1983 – December 31, 2012

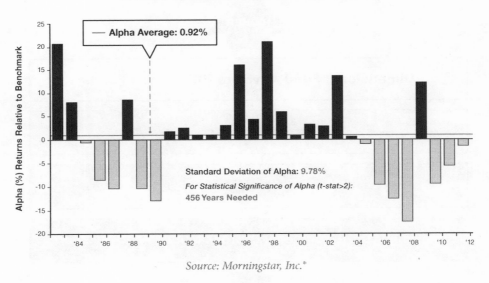

Source: Morningstar, Inc.*

Figure 5.5, *Legg Mason Value's Alpha (Outperformance) Relative to Russell
1000 Index* illustrates the track record of stock mutual fund manager and leg-
end Mr. Bill Miller, who once was named Morningstar's "fund manager of
the year" and "fund manager of the decade." Mr. Miller is credited with the
longest winning streak—beating the S&P 500 index 14 years in a row—longer
than any active stock mutual fund manager in history. At my practice, I utilize

Figure 5.5 when responding to "I-can-beat-the-stock-market" conversations. Mr. Miller *did* beat the market (on average by approximately 0.9% per year) *but* did so by taking on *materially* more risk. It was this risk that eventually did him in and caused the majority of investors in his fund to actually experience worse performance than the S&P 500. If arguably the best stock mutual fund manager in history *only did this well* over his career, and everyone else basically did worse, why would you want to play this "loser's game?"

FIGURE 5.6. **1999–2018 Hierarchy of Returns**

(Average Annual Returns)

HIGHER

Dimensional Fund Advisors (DFA) Index Funds
Index Funds
Professional Active Stock Mutual Fund Managers
Individual "Do-It-Yourselfers" Stock Mutual Fund Investors

LOWER

Source: DiNuzzo Private Wealth, Inc. (DPW)/DiNuzzo Wealth Management (DWM)

Everything that I have learned from Nobel Prize winners, empirical research, academic data, and financial history has led me to develop the simplified observation in Figure 5.6, *1999–2018 Hierarchy of Returns*. This is based on Morningstar and Dalbar data over a recent 20-year period. As you will recall from earlier, individuals' (bottom tier) dismal performance falls at the bottom of the "ladder." Next, individuals are topped by professional active stock mutual fund managers (second tier) who, on average have *underperformed* their respective benchmark index (third tier). DFA (Dimensional Fund Advisors) (top tier) in my opinion, the premier efficient market theory dimension/factor based institutional manager, has historically outperformed their respective benchmarks. I believe that DFA (Dimensional) is the new benchmark, and you should utilize this benchmark when building your portfolio.

Figure 5.7 represents Dimensional Fund Advisors' (DFA) performance versus domestic and international index benchmarks over a recent 10-year period. Relative to the index benchmarks over the last ten years, DFA has exhibited similar return premium outperformance as they have since their origination four decades ago. Please note, the outstanding performance of the indexes listed is in nearly every category. These indexes are the benchmarks that have *outperformed approximately three out of four active mutual fund managers* over the average 10-year period of time. This illustrates DFA's historical acumen in accessing all known premiums, dimensions, and factors available in the capital markets, including the Market Premium, Value Premium, Size (Small Cap) Premium, and the newly identified direct/expected Profitability Premium.

Figure 5.8, titled *Dimensional Fund Advisors vs. Vanguard: Annualized Returns by Category* illustrates DFA major equity (stock) Asset Classes over a recent 20-year period relative to Vanguard's comparable indexes. If you are a "Do-It-Yourselfer," I recommend you open your account at Vanguard and access their indexes. As I have illustrated, the standard indexes, both domestically and internationally, outperformed the active managers approximately three out of four times over a 10-year period.

FIGURE 5.7. **Dimensional Fund Advisors (DFA)**

Track Record vs. Index Benchmarks (10/1/2008 – 9/30/2018)

DFA U.S. LARGE COMPANY	+ 11.89%
S&P 500 INDEX®	+ 11.97%
DFA U.S. LARGE VALUE	+ 11.29%
RUSSELL 1000® VALUE INDEX	+ 9.79%
DFA U.S. MICRO CAP	+ 12.13%
DFA U.S. SMALL CAP	+ 12.40%
RUSSELL 2000® INDEX	+ 11.11%
DFA U.S. SMALL VALUE	+ 9.62%
RUSSELL 2000® VALUE INDEX®	+ 9.52%
DFA GLOBAL REAL ESTATE	+ 6.99%
S&P GLOBAL REIT INDEX®	+ 5.86%
DFA INTERNATIONAL VALUE	+ 4.82%
MSCI® WORLD INDEX ex-USA *(net.div.)*	+ 5.18%
DFA INTERNATIONAL SMALL COMPANY	+ 8.87%
DFA INTERNATIONAL SMALL VALUE	+ 8.51%
MSCI® WORLD ex-USA SMALL COMPANY *(net.div.)*	+ 9.04%
DFA EMERGING MARKETS	+ 5.36%
DFA EMERGING MARKETS SMALL COMPANY	+ 8.55%
DFA EMERGING MARKETS VALUE	+ 5.40%
MSCI® EMERGING MARKETS INDEX *(net.div.)*	+ 5.40%

Source: S&P 500®, MSCI®, Russell 1000®, Russell 2000®.

At no point in time throughout my book do I attempt to impugn Vanguard or their offerings. In my professional opinion, Vanguard vs. DFA is again a question of better versus best, or an A versus an A+. DFA outperformance is typically due to style purity, Small Cap, Value, and Direct Profitability tilts, and a host of other variables described throughout my book.

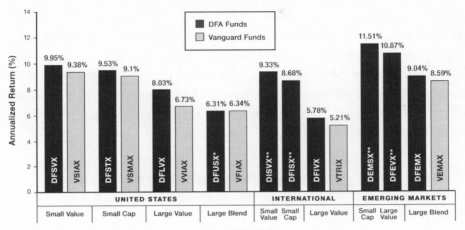

FIGURE 5.8. **Dimensional Fund Advisors vs. Vanguard:**
Annualized Returns by Category

20 Years, 6 Months: January 1, 1999 – June 30, 2019

* DFA US Large Company (backtested): 1/99-9/99 = DFLCX (closed), 10/99-Present = DFUSX.

** No comparable passively managed Vanguard mutual funds for DISVX, DFISX, DEMSX and DFEVX. All Vanguard funds are Admiral Share Class, except the International Value Fund (VTRIX), which is an Investor Share Class and is actively managed by 3 firms.

This chart starts in 1999 because it is the first full year of data for VSIAX-5/98, DFEVX-4/98, and DFMSX-3/98. VFIAX inception on 11/13/2000, alternative share class used for prior period (or since inception, if applicable). VSMAX inception on 11/13/2000, alternative share class used for prior period (or since inception, if applicable). VSIAX inception 09/27/2011, alternative share class used for prior period (or since inception, if applicable). VEMAX inception 06/23/2006, alternative share class used for prior period (or since inception, if applicable).

Past performance does not guarantee future results. Performance may contain both live and back-tested data. Data is provided for illustrative purposes only, it does not represent actual performance of any client portfolio or account and it should not be interpreted as an indication of such performance. IFA utilizes standard deviation as a quantification of risk, see an explanation in the IFA glossary. Returns are net of mutual fund fees, include reinvestment of dividends and capital gains but do not include the deduction of IFA's advisory fees, transaction costs or taxes. A client's return will be reduced by the amount of advisory fees charged by IFA and any other expenses, and the inclusion of IFA's advisory fees would have a negative impact on client account performance. Dimensional Fund Advisors generally has smaller weighted average market caps in their mutual funds than other funds. Smaller companies are riskier than larger companies and that may be an explanation for the higher returns.

Source: *©2019 Index Fund Advisors, Inc.* (IFA.com)

Hypothetical Diversified All Index Portfolios vs. S&P 500 Index

Historically, hypothetical diversified All Index Portfolios vs. S&P 500 Index have illustrated the history of diversified All-Index portfolios from a *risk-adjusted* perspective. Both the S&P 500 Index and the hypothetical Diversified All Index 70/30 portfolio examples achieved an annualized rate of return of approximately 10% per year over the last 50 years. More importantly, however, the s&p 500 did so with *higher risk* than the 70/30 portfolio. If you simply wanted to match the rate of return for the market, you could have done so with less risk with a Diversified All Index portfolio of approximately 70% in stocks and 30% in bonds. However, if you were comfortable with the level of risk in the s&p 500, you could have built a 100/0 portfolio. This portfolio contains 100% in Diversified All Index *stock* funds/Asset Classes and returned approximately 12% per year over a recent 50-year period. The goal of Diversified All Index portfolios takes advantage of a Nobel Prize-winning observation known as Modern Portfolio Theory (MPT), which combines higher volatility investments with Asset Classes with lower correlations to build an optimal risk-adjusted portfolio.

FIGURE 5.9. **Conventional Indices Limit the Investable Universe**

As of June 30, 2019

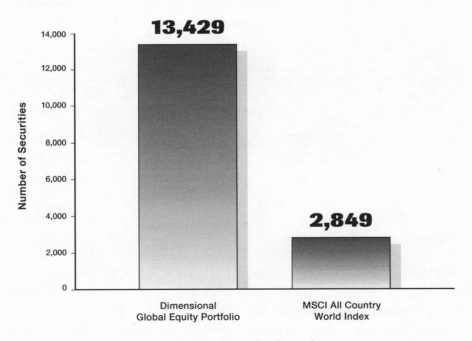

Source: Morningstar, Inc. ®, MSCI®.

In Figure 5.9, *Conventional Indices Limit the Investable Universe* you see one example of DFA's advantage and unique approach to index investing. The DFA Global Equity Portfolio has a small fractional ownership in over 13,000 securities across the globe whereas the MSCI All Country Index, one of the national benchmarks, had only approximately 2,800 security holdings in their portfolio. The additional securities enable DFA greater access to the various premiums that are available, resulting in a higher expected rate of return.

FIGURE 5.10. **Types of Investment Management**

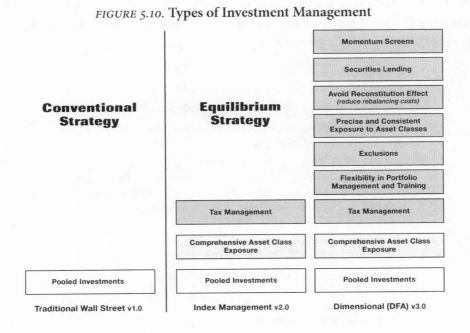

Figure 5.10, *Types of Investment Management* illustrates the various "generations" of investment management available in mutual funds. The conventional strategy, listed as version 1.0, is the traditional Wall Street "pooled investments," representing active mutual fund management which has been available for decades. In the 1970s, indexed mutual funds (listed as version 2.0) became available to the public. In addition to being pooled investments, they also had comprehensive Asset Class exposure and tax management options

available. The third column, "Dimensional (DFA) version 3.0," lists the benefits that have historically resulted in DFA's higher performance. Starting at the top those benefits are: the momentum screen that DFA incorporates in their algorithms for their portfolios (momentum refers to the ascending or descending rate of acceleration or deceleration regarding a specific security and its price), securities lending practices, avoiding the reconstitution effect, DFA's precise and consistent exposure to Asset Classes, academic exclusions, and flexibility in portfolio management and trading. I am often asked, "To what do you attribute DFA's outperformance?" The answer is found in DFA's Enhanced Dimension/Factor investment management style which blends these six value-added capabilities *among many others.*

FIGURE 5.11. DiNuzzo Private Wealth, Inc. (DPW)/DiNuzzo Wealth Management (DWM) Investment Philosophy

Investment Philosophy: Value Added, Efficient Market Investing

Enhanced Index Asset Management
- Believes that in liquid markets, prices reflect all available information
- Focuses strategies on the dimensions of higher expected returns
- Adds value through portfolio design and implementation

Index Management
- Allows commercial benchmarks to define strategy
- Tethered to a benchmark, reducing flexibility
- Accepts lower returns and increased trading costs in favor of tracking

Traditional Active Management
- Attempts to identify mispricing in securities on a consistent basis
- Often relies on forecasting techniques to pick securities and/or time market
- Generates higher expenses, trading costs and excess risk

At the top of Figure 5.11, *DiNuzzo Private Wealth, Inc. (DPW)/DiNuzzo Wealth Management (DWM) Investment Philosophy* you see that the "big picture" of my investment philosophy at DiNuzzo Private Wealth, Inc. (DPW)/DiNuzzo Wealth Management (DWM), is based on adding value and Efficient Market investing. Starting at the bottom of Figure 5.11, you notice elements of active management, which attempt to identify mispricing in securities on a consistent basis. As I have said, "no one has tomorrow's newspaper." Finding these misplaced securities on a *regular* basis is next to impossible. In addition, techniques such as forecasting, market timing, and picking individual securities generates higher expenses, trading costs, and excessive risk.

The next level is index management and it is a material improvement over active management. Indexing allows the investor to target commercial benchmarks in order to define their strategy. However, being tied to commercial benchmarks *reduces flexibility.* DFA and I believe that investors are accepting lower returns and increasing their trading costs in favor of *myopically tracking a commercial index benchmark.*

At the top, my investment strategy is *enhanced* index Asset Class management. I believe that in liquid markets, prices reflect all available information, and no one would or should maintain a consistent advantage over other market participants regarding "Price Discovery." I focus my strategies on the dimensions (Market exposure, Value, Small (Size), and Direct Profitability) in order to achieve expected higher returns. I believe that the key is adding value through portfolio design and implementation.

What you observe in Figure 5.12, *100% Stocks/0% Bonds: "Maximum Aggressive Growth"* is a representation of a 100/0, 100% stock portfolio with all Dimensional Fund Advisors (DFA) Institutional *stock* mutual funds. I label this portfolio at DiNuzzo Private Wealth, Inc. (DPW)/DiNuzzo Wealth Management (DWM) as a "Maximum Aggressive Growth" portfolio. As you can see when you look at the holdings, we own the same Asset Classes in all of our portfolios, albeit at different percentages. This illustration shows the maximum growth percentages, with US Large Company and Large Value at 20% each, moving on down through all of our other equity/stock exposures. This portfolio has captured the Value and Small Cap Premiums as well as the benefits of international diversification.

FIGURE 5.12. 100% Stocks/0% Bonds: Maximum Aggressive Growth

GENERAL ASSET CLASS		SPECIFIC INDEX	
40.0%	**U.S. Large**	**20.0%**	DFA U.S. Large Company Index
		20.0%	DFA U.S. Large Cap Value Index
20.0%	**U.S. Small**	**10.0%**	DFA U.S. Small Cap Index
		10.0%	DFA U.S. Small Cap Value Index
10.0%	**Real Estate**	**10.0%**	DFA Real Estate Index
20.0%	**International**	**5.0%**	DFA International Large Company Index
		5.0%	DFA International Large Value Index
		5.0%	DFA International Small Company Index
		5.0%	DFA International Small Cap Value Index
10.0%	**Emerging Markets**	**3.0%**	DFA Emerging Markets Index
		3.0%	DFA Emerging Markets Value Index
		4.0%	DFA Emerging Markets Small Cap Index
0.0%	**Fixed Income**	**0.0%**	DFA 5-Year Targeted Credit Bond Index
		0.0%	DFA 5-Year Global Bond Index
		0.0%	DFA Intermediate U.S. Investment Grade Bond Index
		0.0%	DFA Intermediate World ex.U.S. Bond Index

FIGURE 5.13. 70% Stocks/30% Bonds: Aggressive Growth

GENERAL ASSET CLASS		SPECIFIC INDEX	
28.0%	**U.S. Large**	**14.0%**	DFA U.S. Large Company Index
		14.0%	DFA U.S. Large Cap Value Index
14.0%	**U.S. Small**	**7.0%**	DFA U.S. Small Cap Index
		7.0%	DFA U.S. Small Cap Value Index
7.0%	**Real Estate**	**7.0%**	DFA Real Estate Index
14.0%	**International**	**3.5%**	DFA International Large Company Index
		3.5%	DFA International Large Value Index
		3.5%	DFA International Small Company Index
		3.5%	DFA International Small Cap Value Index
7.0%	**Emerging Markets**	**2.1%**	DFA Emerging Markets Index
		2.1%	DFA Emerging Markets Value Index
		2.8%	DFA Emerging Markets Small Cap Index
30.0%	**Fixed Income**	**7.5%**	DFA 5-Year Targeted Credit Bond Index
		7.5%	DFA 5-Year Global Bond Index
		7.5%	DFA Intermediate U.S. Investment Grade Bond Index
		7.5%	DFA Intermediate World ex.U.S. Bond Index

In Figure 5.13, *70% Stocks/30% Bonds: "Aggressive Growth"* you are looking at an all-DFA "maximum *risk-adjusted* growth opportunity." This portfolio provides you with maximum growth potential while still providing conspicuous downside protection and risk mitigation. The goal: to approximate the performance of a 100% stock portfolio, such as the S&P 500, and also achieve approximately 1/4 to 1/3 *less risk*. In short, this is the last and highest Asset Allocation in which you can make as much money as possible *and* still receive sophic risk mitigation benefits. This is basically, for a maximum growth/risk-adjusted portfolio, "as good as it gets."

FIGURE 5.14. 50% Stocks/50% Bonds: Balanced Growth

GENERAL ASSET CLASS		SPECIFIC INDEX	
20.0%	U.S. Large	10.0%	DFA U.S. Large Company Index
		10.0%	DFA U.S. Large Cap Value Index
10.0%	U.S. Small	5.0%	DFA U.S. Small Cap Index
		5.0%	DFA U.S. Small Cap Value Index
5.0%	Real Estate	5.0%	DFA Real Estate Index
10.0%	International	2.5%	DFA International Large Company Index
		2.5%	DFA International Large Value Index
		2.5%	DFA International Small Company Index
		2.5%	DFA International Small Cap Value Index
5.0%	Emerging Markets	1.5%	DFA Emerging Markets Index
		1.5%	DFA Emerging Markets Value Index
		2.0%	DFA Emerging Markets Small Cap Index
50.0%	Fixed Income	12.5%	DFA 5-Year Targeted Credit Bond Index
		12.5%	DFA 5-Year Global Bond Index
		12.5%	FA Intermediate U.S. Investment Grade Bond Index
		12.5%	DFA Intermediate World ex.U.S. Bond Index

In Figure 5.14, *50% Stocks/50% Bonds: "Balanced Growth"* you see a typical maximum withdrawal (retirement) Asset Allocation portfolio when clients reach age 70½ and begin IRS mandated Required Minimum Distributions (RMDS). This portfolio is represented by 50% equity (stocks)/50% fixed income (bonds). This is the classic equity (stock) exposure for your "Wants" (Risk

Tolerance) Money Bucket, to pay for your elective/discretionary "Wants" expenses in retirement. Here, your primary objective is to "play defense first," and also to typically place this portfolio on a Glidepath to typically decrease stock exposure into the future. Please note, in certain limited cases the stock exposure Glidepath would be increasing, and Ascending Glidepath modestly over time. For the 50% stock/50% bond portfolio in all DFA index bench-mark funds, the first thing that surprises many readers is that they are not giving up as much as they initially think on the return side of the portfolio. Again, *the risk protection is of equal and/or greater importance* than just the performance of the portfolio. You will see the additional material benefits of the 50/50 portfolio when taking withdrawals into account, versus individuals who are invested 100% in stocks, when I focus on this mission-critical topic. It will be a real eye-opener!

When you stop, reflect, and review the three major and most common Asset Allocation "mile markers" to fit investors' needs during the "accumulation" years, "decumulation" years, and their "Legacy" planning years regarding their beneficiaries, heirs, and charities, these are also the three Asset Allocations most commonly applied to meet these distinct challenges. Regarding the 100/0 "all growth" portfolio, you noticed the significant benefits of index-ing versus active management, and also the material benefits of accessing the worldwide premiums that are available through DFA—in my preference, the top index benchmark-based manager. The following portfolio regarding maximizing risk-managed growth is a 70/30 All-Index portfolio, which pro-vides us with the highest potential growth rate while sustaining downside protection. The final and equally most important investment strategy is for typical retirement *withdrawal portfolios*, and I have achieved success in this arena through the 50/50 All-Index portfolio. This portfolio portrays the over-all strategy to maintain "balanced growth" through your retirement years, while also "playing defense first."

Our history of Modern Finance progressed from traditional stock picking to the Efficient Market Theory, which holds that all the information regarding the value of a security has been analyzed by millions of highly intelligent market participants and is reflected in its current price...“Price Discovery.” This favors passive, diversified, and enhanced index investing and explains the failure of so many traditional actively managed funds. Dimensional Fund Advisors (DFA) has historically provided even higher returns by excelling at focusing on Market Exposure, Value, Size, and Direct/Expected Profitability Premiums/Dimensions/Factors, as well as proprietary trading techniques and portfolio design.

REBALANCING
RULES FOR BUYING AND SELLING YOUR INVESTMENTS

Once you have established your allocation, you are left with the financial equivalent of gardening…rebalancing…the benefit of rebalancing stock portfolios is closer to ½% (per year). Rebalancing forces you to buy low and sell high.
    —Dr. William J. Bernstein, *The Four Pillars of Investing*

Advisor Alpha/Gamma defines the future of complex technique(s) and processes available in the comprehensive toolboxes leading Wealth Managers possess and will utilize to improve their clients' financial life management. A current leading-edge example would be the "DiNuzzo Financial Wellness LifePlan™." This collective expertise requires a talented, deep, and broad Wealth Management team and client household relationship. Going forward, these tangible Wealth Enhancement benefits will obliterate the antiquated traditional stockbrokers' "one trick pony" hubris of attempting to add value solely in/by (failed) attempts to just manage money and attempt to outperform the stock market.

—P.J. DiNuzzo

Following Benjamin Franklin's observation that "a penny saved is a penny earned," it follows that 1% less (per year) in expenses for you and your family equals 1% more in higher annual (total) return.

—P.J. DiNuzzo

We are what we repeatedly do. Excellence comes not from our actions but from our habits.

—Aristotle

When asked what he considered man's greatest discovery, Albert Einstein replied without hesitation: "Compound interest."

—Charles Ellis, *Investment Policy*

With self-discipline, almost anything is possible.

—Theodore Roosevelt, 26th President of the United States

PORTFOLIO REBALANCING

This chapter will cover the remaining topics needed to achieve "Alpha Alpha/Gamma" for your "investment experience" and retirement income planning, beginning with portfolio rebalancing. Portfolio rebalancing provides a significant reward for *disciplined*, long-term investors. If performed correctly, it mandates "selling high and buying low." Most significantly, it helps to remove emotions from the equation. Rebalancing a portfolio is initiated primarily by Asset Classes (e.g., US Large Cap stocks, International Large Value stocks) that have grown beyond their "target policy allocation." This causes me to give them a "haircut" (selling high) and take profits which are then reallocated to the most *underperforming/slower growing* Asset Class, hence "buying low."

FIGURE 6.1. **Disciplined Portfolio Rebalancing: Buy Low/Sell High**

Hypothetical 5-Year Period

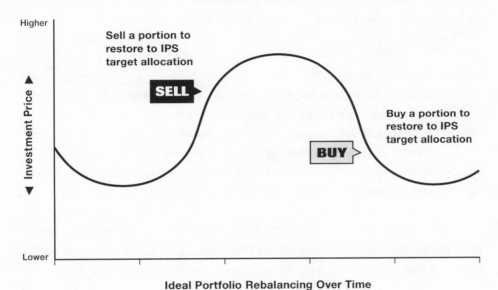

Ideal Portfolio Rebalancing Over Time

As Dr. William Bernstein has observed, the dynamic benefit of a *systematic rebalancing strategy* is that it "forces you to buy low and sell high." Additionally, this solves the problem of conflicting emotions, which terminally causes individual investors to make bad decisions. Correct rebalancing trades generally require investors to do the opposite of what they *feel* like doing. Remember… what is comfortable *rarely* leads to a successful investment experience.

When you view my "The Investing Rollercoaster™" image in the next chapter, you will witness the emotion challenges causing individual investors to consistently make bad timing decisions regarding their investments. As you can see in the above image, you want to sell a *minority* portion of your investment(s) at or around their height to restore your target allocation—e.g., "selling high." Conversely, you want to buy a portion of your investments at or around their nadir to restore them to your target allocation—e.g., "buying low."

As you can see, this rules-based process allows us to *stay focused* over time and avoids your emotions whipsawing you from peak to valley and exposing you to one of the root causes of bad investment decisions…emotions-based overreaction.

Emotionally, rebalancing is quite challenging because what I recommend causes you to act in a *counterintuitive* manner by always initiating an action that is in direct opposition to your "gut feeling." Over the years I have heard questions during rebalancing like, "Why are we selling an Asset Class investment that is up 20% and/or buying one that is down 5% on the year?" Be patient, my friend. Over time, this contrarian discipline which results in selling high and buying low can materially enhance your wealth.

Portfolio rebalancing is simply selling shares of Asset Classes which have appreciated *above* their upper target limit and reinvesting the proceeds in underperforming Asset Classes which are materially *below* their lower target limit.

Foregoing portfolio rebalancing results in three things: leaving money on the table, increasing your risk exposure, *and* lowering the risk/reward balance in your portfolio. This would violate my number-one rule—to manage every element of your retirement income process (at every fork in the road) *within our control* in order to place the odds of success in your favor. Control what you can control.

My rebalancing calculations are based on our Investment Policy Statement (IPS) and Investment Plan (IP), both of which are focused on Strategic Asset Allocation application. For example, consider a 60/40 split with 60% equities (stocks) and 40% fixed income (bonds and cash). One potential rebalancing rule, "tier 1," would be to set a trigger at a 10% maximum or minimum move relative to your policy Asset Allocation. This would mean if in your 60/40 portfolio, 60% *plus* 10% would be an *upper limit* of 70% and on the other hand, 60% *minus* 10% would be a *lower limit* of 50%. So, if the portfolio were to grow larger than a 70/30 or below a 50/50, it would trigger a rebalancing event. If these stated levels were breached, your rebalancing rules would require you to identify and reinvest the excess growth of the outperforming Asset Classes *into* the underperforming Asset Class(es).

Another method of rebalancing is a "hard rebalance." Former Vanguard chairman, Jack Bogle, often discussed this in its simplest form. Considering a typical portfolio with an Asset Allocation of 60% Total Stock Market Index and 40% Total Bond Market Index, you should audit your portfolio, e.g., every January. If the allocation were 63% in stocks and 37% in bonds (63/37), then you would sell 3% stocks (equities) and buy 3% bonds (fixed income). A hard strategy such as this would generally only apply, due to tax implications, to tax-deferred accounts such as IRAs, 401(k)s, and 403(b)s, along with tax-exempt accounts such as Roth IRAs.

THE HIGH COST OF FAILING TO REBALANCE YOUR PORTFOLIOS: PHILIP AND SARAH REVISITED

In chapter 3, I introduced you to Philip and his wife, Sarah. The couple had been following an 80/20 investment strategy. When they came to see me in 2009, they had 82% of their money in stocks and 18% in bonds, and when the Great Recession hit in 2008, they lost so much value in their portfolios that Philip had to cancel his retirement, vowing to work until his portfolios had regained their pre-2008 value.

Philip and Sarah's situation is not uncommon, but it's not always due to an improper Asset Allocation strategy. When the couple began investing many years earlier, say, when they were in their 20s, their strategy probably made a lot of sense. However, they had failed to adjust their risk/reward target as Philip got closer to retirement, *and* they weren't rebalancing their portfolios to match the new target.

Even if Philip and Sarah had been following a 50/50 strategy—which, considering Philip's age, would have made more sense for them at that time—they could have ended up, years later, with 80% in stocks and 20% in bonds *simply because they failed to rebalance their portfolios.*

Consider this: As the value of stocks and bonds change, within as little as ten years' time, 50% in stocks could grow to 70% while 50% in bonds could drop to 30% of your investment portfolios. This typically would jeopardize your plan by taking you out of your ideal risk/reward target zone.

In Philip's case, he had enjoyed a bull market from the end of 2002 until the end of 2007. His stock portfolio grew, but so did his exposure to risk, and when the Great Recession struck, his portfolios suffered a devastating loss, costing him and his wife four years of relaxation, enjoying life in retirement.

Whether you have the wrong risk/reward target for your age, *or* you fail to rebalance your portfolios quarterly—or at *least* every year—you may not have the correct Asset Allocations for your planned retirement. It's easy to become lackadaisical or indecisive regarding this critical task—i.e., riding a bull market too long, or being paralyzed by a market that's in the doldrums—but failing to rebalance your portfolios could catch you off guard when you least expect it, taking years off your retirement.

I worked with Philip and Sarah to create a customized DiNuzzo Financial Wellness LifePlan™ that included a three-tiered strategy with three tax "buckets," as well as three unique Asset Allocations that are monitored through rebalancing opportunities on a daily basis. By approaching this challenge IN Gratitude, regardless of the circumstances, I helped put Philip and Sarah on a path to retirement so they would not have to suffer through this experience again.

My rebalancing strategy is tempered if the assets are in a nonqualified (taxable) account in which we want to, as a rule, minimize trading. At my firm, I apply a "higher level" (Tier 2) rebalancing strategy based on Asset Class "tolerance bands." Tolerance bands are represented as an allowable range above or below the target percentage, and possess a minimum/maximum threshold. I typically utilize a 20% "band" on each stock or bond Asset Class in the portfolio. For example, if your target for DFA US Large Value Institutional Asset Class (in our IP and IPS) is 10%, then applying my 20% minimum/maximum would indicate that any value greater than 12% on the upside or below 8% on the downside would trigger a trade requirement.

Even with "hawk-like" attention, these band exceptions only result in approximately 1 to 4 rebalancing trades per year in the entire portfolio. My goal is to be vigilant *but* trade as little as possible.

I can do this with confidence due to my belief in Efficient Market Theory, regression to the mean (in other words, over time deviations up or down will average out), and my understanding that we *cannot* add value by timing the market. My Strategic Asset Allocation coupled with the Efficient Market Theory (indexing), along with a higher level "tolerance band" based rebalancing strategy, adds value to the investment process by:

1. Having a straightforward system to maintain your IPS (Investment Policy Statement) and IP (Investment Plan) mandate

2. Maintaining your risk/reward profile and diversification

3. Serving as an emotional ballast as part of "Behavior Coaching" to help you through wide market emotions during upward "bull" and downward "bear" scenarios

Regarding rebalancing for self-directed investors (DIYers), a calendar approach is often the best technique. Many individual investors will make a notation to rebalance every January or when they file their taxes in March or April. Some even do so on the week of their birthday. It is helpful to identify a *consistent* calendar period to rebalance your portfolio if you plan to do so on an annual basis. Choosing a time of year when you tend to be slower at work can prove to be beneficial, because you are able to rebalance your portfolio in a more relaxed environment. For example, if you are a CPA who specializes in individual tax planning and preparation, you would not want to rebalance during the January through April period when you are working peak hours.

Once again, Nobel Prize-winning research is the foundation of my rebalancing strategy, as it is related to Modern Portfolio Theory (MPT). MPT is all about constructing a broadly diversified multiple stock and bond Asset Class portfolio with acceptable risk/reward characteristics based on your volatility/risk profile and, most importantly, your unique time horizon.

Rebalancing:

- Keeps us within our Asset Allocation risk limits
- Provides modest excess portfolio return
- Provides "emotion management" and discipline

LOW FEES AND LOW EXPENSES

If, as Benjamin Franklin was quoted as saying, a penny saved is a penny earned, then 1% lower in fees and expenses for Mr. and Mrs. Jones equals 1% more in total return for Mr. and Mrs. Jones. That means more money in their pockets. Active managers, as opposed to my Efficient Market Theory (index-ing) approach, are much more expensive. Actively managed funds have materially higher overall expenses within their funds. The four layers to mutual fund costs are as follows:

1. Expense ratio (Operating Expense Ratio (OER))
2. Commissions
3. Bid-ask spread
4. Market impact costs

These total average expenses for active mutual funds including all "loads" and fees have often been estimated to be over 2%. The average expense ratio alone for the average US stock mutual fund is over 1% and the additional expenses of commissions, bid-ask spread, and impact costs often approach an *additional* 1%. These expenses are even exorbitantly higher for US Small Cap Stocks, International stocks, and Emerging Market stocks with ascending expenses, in that order. The total expenses for indexed funds, such as DFA and Vanguard, in addition to the expense ratio for commissions, bid-ask spread, and impact costs, are *wafer-thin*, due to their inherent structure.

It is important to remember that low fees and low expenses are *vital to your overall wealth enhancement*. The investment profit you keep is equal to your investment gain *minus* all expenses, fees, and taxes. Lowering these aggregate costs allows you to keep more of the profit your investments have achieved.

The importance of keeping fees and expenses as low as possible is illustrated on the following chart, and relates back to my image covering mutual fund Operating Expense Ratios (OER). Simply put: *fees matter*. Over long periods of time, high management fees and related expenses can be a significant drag on wealth creation. Passive (index) investments generally maintain significantly lower fees than the average actively managed investment simply by minimizing trading costs and eliminating the cost of researching stocks. A mere 1% difference in expenses over a 30-year period, based on a 7% annualized rate of return, results in an eye-popping difference! With a 3% fee resulting in an overall portfolio after 30 years of a value of approximately $3.2 million vs. a portfolio with a total 1.5% fee of approximately $5 million. The additional millions of dollars is a dramatic example of the importance of fees.

The greatest enemies of the equity investor are expenses and emotions.
—Warren Buffett, from *The Little Book of Common Sense Investing* by John C. Bogle

FIGURE 6.2. **Fees Matter**

(Assumed 7% Annualized Return over 30 Years)

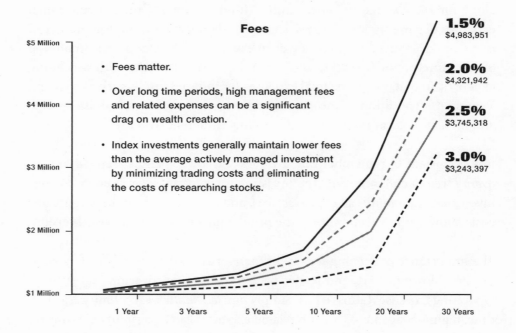

Many retail investors have total expenses of 2%, 2.5% or even 3% overall. And it is very intuitive that fees matter, especially over long periods of time, as high management fees and related expenses subversively hinder wealth creation.

A major impediment to maximizing your performance is abnormally high mutual fund expense ratios. Professor and Nobel Laureate Eugene Fama has been lecturing for decades that one of the only variables in active mutual fund managers which provides a statistically significant probability of predicting future performance is active managers with abnormally high expense ratios. Empirical research has consistently indicated that *the higher a mutual fund expense is, the lower total return the manager has historically produced.* A low expense ratio is the single most important variable which can be identified for most mutual funds outperforming similar funds. Each dollar you save represents a dollar that goes into your bank account. When building your portfolio, you want to seek investments which have no front-end loads, no back-end loads, no 12b-1 fees, minimum trading expenses, and low annual Operating Expense Ratios (OER). Additionally, you want to steer clear of commissioned salespeople who have an inherent conflict of interest. Often the "product" they are trying to sell you is in their best interest because it pays them the greatest compensation or commission (caveat emptor!).

The investment which is in the broker's best interest is predominantly not in your best interest, as it is typically the highest commission item paying the broker the most money. Almost universally, this is never a good fit in your portfolio. High commission-oriented brokers spend their days convincing investors to buy high commission investments and/or to trade them with a high frequency. This is exactly the opposite of my stated goal. You want to eliminate as much "inherent conflict of interest" in managing your portfolio by selecting a Wealth Manager or financial advisor who has a *Fiduciary Standard* and code of ethics, is serious about them, and places your best interest first.

> *We need a mutual fund industry with both vision and values; a vision of fiduciary duty and shareholder service, and values rooted in the proven principles of long-term investing and of trusteeship that demands integrity in serving our clients.*
>
> —John C. Bogle, *Enough: True Measures of Money, Business, and Life*

FIGURE 6.3. **Actively Managed Mutual Funds Have Higher Expenses**

Data as of December 31, 2017

	Average Expense Ratio (%)	Average Turnover (%)	Estimated Total Cost (%)
Dimensional Equity Funds	**0.32**	**8.8**	**0.42**
Active Equity Funds	1.05	85.0	2.35

Source: Morningstar, Inc.

When viewing Figure 6.3, *Actively Managed Mutual Funds Have Higher Expenses* please remember I have presented the *average* US and international *individual* (single) stock mutual fund Operating Expense Ratios (OER). The "DFA bar" is the weighted average of the eleven (11) US, International, and Emerging Markets DFA institutional stock funds I typically implement in constructing a 100/0 all-DFA, all-stock portfolio.

Let's assume you are going to pick your own mutual funds. If you just have an inventory of all mutual funds in the market, all active mutual funds, and if you just pick a random one as if you threw a dart at a board with their names, the average equity mutual fund expense would be 1.05%.

After avoiding the obvious detrimental high expense, high fee, "total return eaters"—i.e., front-end loads, back-end loads, 12b-1 fees, surrender charges, high turnover, and redemption fees—I want to turn your cost-saving attention to trading costs.

I am often asked to explain DFA's (Dimensional's) outstanding performance in their index benchmark-based Asset Classes, and Figure 6.4 *Dimensional's Value Added through Trading* is helpful in understanding one portion of DFA's "value add." Trading costs are one of the next largest areas for us to keep as low as possible and DFA has historically done exceptionally well in this influential portfolio management area.

FIGURE 6.4. **Dimensional's Value Added Through Trading**

Third-Party Trade Cost Results Across All Market Segments

| | TRADING COSTS *(gain / loss)* | | |
STRATEGY	Median Peer	Dimensional	Dimensional Rank[1]
US Large Cap Trading	-24 bps	+33 bps	98%
US Small Cap Trading	-67 bps	+99 bps	100%
All Developed Markets Trading[2]	-45 bps	+80 bps	100%
All Emerging Markets Trading	-60 bps	+80 bps	100%

ITG POST-TRADE ANALYTICS™ ALPHA CAPTURE℠ – 1 Year Ending September 30, 2012

1. Percent of peer universe Dimensional outperforms in terms of trading costs
2. US trading included in results only for portfolios with global mandates

DFA's trading technology and techniques have historically added material value for their shareholders and to my portfolios. This has been true both domestically with both Large and Small Cap stock funds, and internationally with Non-US Developed Markets and the Emerging Markets. DFA is a *prodigious trading force* in many of these markets, and their patient, technical, and opportunistic approach has historically enhanced our Asset Class returns.

> *Wall Street with its army of brokers, analysts, and advisers funneling trillions of dollars into mutual funds, hedge funds, and private equity funds, is an elaborate fraud.*
>
> —Michael Lewis, Conde Nast Portfolio, "The Evolution of an Investor," December 2007

Additionally, analyzing "Net Expense Ratios" across multiple Asset Classes, we again see the benefit of a low expense strategy. Since its inception, DFA's mutual fund Operating Expense Ratio (OER) fees have unfailingly been among the very lowest in their respective Morningstar categories.

DFA has consistently ranked in the *lowest* 10% in expenses relative to their peers. In most cases, they are in the single-digit percentiles.

Perhaps of more tangible and practical benefit is DFA's "Net Expense Ratio" versus the 50th percentile (average) mutual fund. If you were to perform the research you would see, DFA is in many cases 1% (or more) *lower in expenses* than the average mutual fund. This is a valuable benefit for individuals hiring my firm, as, again, for a material number of our new clients' DiNuzzo Private Wealth, Inc. (DPW)/DiNuzzo Wealth Management (DWM) Wealth Management fee plus DFA's Operating Expense Ratios (OER) are less than just what they were paying for the expenses in the mutual funds they owned before they met us with no Wealth Manager, advice, or guidance.

FIGURE 6.5. **Dynamic Withdrawal Strategy: Portfolio Withdrawal Percentages**

By Equity Allocation and Number of Years Remaining

YEARS REMAINING	EQUITY ALLOCATION				
	20%	30%	40%	50%	60%
5	20.0%	19.9%	19.9%	19.8%	19.9%
10	10.4%	10.4%	10.5%	10.5%	10.5%
15	7.2%	7.3%	7.4%	7.4%	7.5%
20	5.7%	5.8%	5.9%	5.9%	6.0%
25	4.8%	4.9%	5.0%	5.0%	5.2%
30	4.2%	4.4%	4.5%	4.5%	4.7%
35	3.8%	3.9%	4.1%	4.1%	4.3%
40	3.5%	3.6%	3.8%	3.8%	4.0%

Figure 6.5, *Dynamic Withdrawal Strategy: Portfolio Withdrawal Percentages* represents approximate safe rates of withdrawal and the math component associated with our semiannual or annual client "Progress Meetings." Capital Markets, life, milestones, goals, and objectives are not monolithic and static. I feel that an ongoing customized dynamic withdrawal strategy is one of the many benefits of working with a Fiduciary Wealth Advisor who specializes in retirement income planning and building our DiNuzzo Financial Wellness LifePlan™.

This illustration can serve as a "thought provoker" and assist in determining your annual withdrawal rate during retirement based on the probability of your portfolio surviving and your mortality expectations. Retirement income planning is not as simple as just utilizing a static 4% per year withdrawal rate over your lifetime.

YOUR "LAS VEGAS" ACCOUNT: TONY REVISITED

Recall Tony from chapter 4, the man who had invested 70% of his money in General Motors stock. It's not unusual for a person to own stock in the company they work for; the concern is, it's *especially* not unusual for a person to own an *excess* amount of company stock, which creates a "concentrated position." Again, people are typically more comfortable owning their employer's company stock than they are investing in a company they're less familiar with.

The comfort level they feel is a false sense of security, however, and your company's stock can suffer the same fate as other companies, as we saw with Tony's GM stock.

I see this same situation happening over and over again with people who are determined to trust an inordinate percentage of their investment to their company's stock. My advice to anyone who insists on purchasing individual stocks and/or concentrated positions is to put a ceiling on the percentage—ideally, no more than 5% of your total investment assets. For example, if your total investment assets—*all* investment accounts, including bank accounts—are $1 million, my recommendation is to never have more than $50,000 in your "Las Vegas" account for these types of purchases.

Why do I refer to this as a "Las Vegas" account? Because investing this way is a gamble. You want to invest your hard-earned life savings intelligently, with the best risk/reward trade-off available within a broadly diversified strategy. You can reduce your risk by putting a limit on how much company stock you have in your portfolio but remember that *every company will eventually go out of business.* It's not an "if" but a "when." Even the greatest businesses in the world don't last forever. It was not so many years ago that General Motors, Bethlehem Steel, and Sears, Roebuck and Company were three of the largest companies in the United States. For any readers growing up in these companies' heyday, the thought of them ever going bankrupt would have seemed impossible, but they all have.

So if you're thinking of loading up on Facebook, Apple, Amazon, Netflix, Google, or another company that you work for or you think is "hot" right now, remember the example of General Motors and these other companies.

The companies I mentioned may not go out of business in our lifetimes, but they will have their ups and downs. No company is infallible or immune to the "creative destruction" in open and free markets and the constantly changing, ultra-competitive business environment.

TAX-AWARE PORTFOLIO MANAGEMENT: ASSET LOCATION OPTIMIZATION, TAX LOT IDENTIFICATION, AND TAX LOSS HARVESTING

FIGURE 6.6. **Asset Location**

Potential Benefits: Maximize After Tax Returns

TAXABLE ACCOUNTS (Individual, Joint)	TAX-DEFERRED ACCOUNTS (IRAs)	TAX-EXEMPT ACCOUNTS (Roth IRAs)
Tax-Managed U.S Large	1-Year Fixed Income	Emerging Markets
Tax-Managed U.S Large Value	2-Year Global Fixed Income	Emerging Markets Small
Tax-Managed U.S Small	Short-Term Government Fixed Income	Emerging Markets Value
Tax-Managed U.S Small Value	5-Year Global Fixed Income	International Small Value
Tax-Managed U.S International Large Value	Total Bond Market Fixed Income	International Small
	REITs	
	Commodities	
(Typically Tax-Managed Equity Asset Classes)	*(Asset Classes, mostly bonds, which produce the highest taxable distributions)*	*(Asset Classes with the highest expected rate of return)*

The focus of the image in Figure 6.6, *Asset Location* is maximizing your after-tax retirement income. When we look at the three broad account types (e.g., taxable), when looking from left to right, you observe taxable accounts followed by tax-deferred accounts, and finally tax-exempt accounts. Taxable accounts are typically individual or joint accounts. Tax-deferred would normally contain IRAs. And, tax-exempt accounts would typically contain Roth IRAs.

In taxable accounts, when Asset Location is a good fit, we want to hold growth assets that have inherent tax-management or Tax-Aware characteristics. As you can see, funds that I have available through DFA that are included in my typical "tax sensitive" portfolios are tax-managed: US Large Cap, US Large Value, US Small Cap, US Small Value, and International Large Value, and/or DFA core funds.

Tax-deferred/IRA accounts would typically contain all of our bond funds, and REITs (Real Estate Investment Trusts) Asset Classes. Finally, our Roth IRAS would typically hold our highest expected growth with Emerging Markets, Emerging Markets Small, Emerging Markets Value, International Small Value, and International Small.

We are all familiar with the philosophy of Asset Allocation and diversifying our investments across numerous Asset Classes. The topic of Asset *Location* addresses this question: Within our portfolios, are there any accounts in which we can rearrange the investments to better maximize our long-term, after-tax wealth accumulation? In the image above, I have given a basic illustration that equity Asset Classes eligible for preferential capital gains treatments would be allocated to your taxable brokerage accounts, while bonds/fixed income that generate ongoing ordinary income are best placed in your IRAS/retirement accounts. Placing equity Asset Classes, in some cases, into IRAS is unfavorable *because it converts desirable long-term capital gains rates on their growth into ordinary income treatment.*

INDIVIDUAL STOCKS VS. INDEX STOCK FUNDS: GRANDPA BOB

Bob is a retired teacher with two grown and married children who have children of their own. His wife had predeceased him five years before he came to see me. Bob's four grandchildren are his pride and joy, and as a Family Steward, he's determined to give them a good financial start in life.

During our DiNuzzo Financial Wellness LifePlan™ meeting, I discovered that Bob appeared to be in reasonably good financial shape. He had a Roth IRA, a solid Social Security income, and a small pension. In fact, due to his IRA's Required Minimum Distribution, he had a 10% monthly cash flow surplus.

When Bob's wife passed away, he had approximately $100,000 in his Roth IRA account, and he had invested 100% of it in a handful of individual stocks and stock sector Exchange-Traded Funds (ETFs). Five years later, when he met with me, his account had lost 45% of its value, dropping to just $55,000. If Bob had simply invested 100% in a broadly diversified stock index portfolio, he would have had approximately $150,000 when I met him.

The average individual investor, buying individual stocks, averages 2% to 3% less in performance on those stocks than the index benchmark of that stock's Asset Class. If you're buying large stocks, the typical individual investor averages 2% to 3% less per year, over time, than if they had invested in a Standard & Poor's (S&P) 500 Large Cap Index or a Russell 1000 Index fund. If you're investing in individual small cap stocks, the typical investor averages 2% to 3% less per year than if they had invested in the Russell 2000 Small Cap Index. On par, this is true across the board, yet I am regularly visited by people who choose to ignore the capital markets' efficiencies, believing they can "outsmart the market" by picking their own stocks or sectors.

The $100,000 Bob missed out on in just five years of leaving his money in the wrong investment could have paid for a grandchild's college education. It could have provided his grandchildren with down payments for their first homes. The lost opportunity, when you consider the possibilities of where that money could have been used to benefit Bob's family, could have had an enormous, lasting effect on his grandchildren's quality of life. These are the situations that sadden me the most when I meet with investors who think they can outsmart the market, because they're typically never aware of the big picture probabilities and the long-term effects of their decisions until it's too late.

When I meet clients, I always try to get to the point—as soon as I can—that what has occurred prior to us meeting is water under the bridge. There's no sense in dwelling on it, but you need to acknowledge what went wrong, own it, and then have a cathartic moment when you realize what's done is done, but it's in the past now so you can put it behind you. This is the first day of the rest of your life, and an opportunity to rectify your investment plan so you won't have to repeat your mistakes and compound the consequences.

Bob weathered a storm that could have weighed him down financially, but now he has a winning DiNuzzo Financial Wellness LifePlan™ that's properly structured and fully diversified. He's out of harm's way and together we are maximizing his financial life management, striving for his Best-Life so he can enjoy retirement and provide for his children and grandchildren.

The Asset Location decisions I am discussing for equity Asset Classes are highly sensitive as to exactly how tax-efficient they are, and how much dividend income and annual turnover we anticipate in the portfolio and need to be analyzed on a case-by-case basis.

When considering the factors of expected return, tax type and efficiency, it is advisable to rank our Asset Classes in an Asset Location "priority list." Our goal, if it is a good fit, is to place the highest return/efficient investment on one end of our spectrum and the highest return/inefficient investments at the other end. Once our Asset Location priority list has been established, we can implement an outside-in approach where the highest return efficient investments are biased toward the taxable brokerage account and the highest return inefficient investments are biased toward the IRA/retirement accounts. By utilizing an outside-in approach, we can attempt to assure that the highest priority investment with the greatest wealth impact will be placed in the proper account(s). Research has indicated that the potential portfolio return benefit of optimal Asset Location is at approximately 0.10%–0.25% per year.

The comprehensive benefit of making optimal Asset Location decisions is, in reality, difficult to measure, because it depends on what we measure against. It is difficult to assume what we may have done in the absence of these additional location decisions. The benefit of our potential Asset Location also varies depending on the scope of accounts available, and their underlying assets. If you have exclusively taxable accounts or exclusively IRA accounts, there are no Asset Location benefits available. Because we have no possible decisions available.

In conclusion, Asset Location represents a potential "free lunch" opportunity for wealth enhancement by being able to implement a more tax-efficient manner to maximize our long-term wealth growth throughout our individual portfolios if executed properly.

You must also remember that Asset Location is a hybrid methodology. This hybrid methodology will result in your various Asset Location account types having materially different performance. Challenges I have encountered regarding Asset Location strategies are when members of a household are uncomfortable with the varying performance and underperformance of one spouse's account vs. another even though it may be in the best interest of the entire household. The overall hybrid portfolio must carefully consider how to trade all of these accounts in harmony regarding tax efficiency. Rebalancing challenges also emerge if there are insufficient assets in specific account types and this obstacle must be agreed upon before initiating this process.

Investors have two prevalent aversions: losing money and paying taxes. While I can't control periodic market declines, I can assuage them through diversification and rebalancing. Similarly, although I can't ensure that you will never pay taxes, they can potentially be minimized through Asset Location optimization, tax lot identification, and Tax-Loss Harvesting, capital gain harvesting, Roth IRA Conversions, and "income smoothing"(tax bracket management). These are the significant tax management strategies that can potentially save you money and add significant value to our relationship. Through education and quantification, we can get excited about saving money regarding taxes.

Strategies for Tax-Aware portfolio management include but are not limited to:

1. Asset Location Optimization: Current taxes may be reduced by shifting ordinary income-producing bonds from taxable accounts to IRAs. Future taxes may be reduced by shifting appreciating securities to taxable accounts (where gains can be taxed at capital gains rates) from IRAs (where gains would be taxed at ordinary rates). Future taxes may be avoided permanently by holding highly appreciated securities in Roth IRAs.

2. Tax Lot Identification: Capital gains may be minimized during the rebalancing process by choosing high cost lots. Although clients with capital loss carryovers might not notice the savings in the current year, tax lot identification can help to preserve the loss carryovers for use when rebalancing gains are unavoidable.

3. Tax Loss Harvesting: Tax loss harvesting seeks to recognize losses by selling loss positions solely for tax purposes. Tax loss harvesting produces capital losses, or "Deferred Tax Assets," that can be carried forward indefinitely until used up, thereby offsetting future gains realized from rebalancing (both short term and long term) or more typically annual capital gain distributions.

4. Capital Gain Harvesting: Can potentially save investors substantial amounts of capital gain taxes primarily by harvesting gains in current years when future tax rates are expected to be higher. Our primary "sweet spot" for this strategy is the time after a client has retired and before they initiate IRA Required Minimum Distributions (RMDS) at age 70½. Harvesting gains in low income years is very powerful.

5. Bracket Management: This is another tax savings strategy which I also refer to as "Income Smoothing." We use Income Smoothing to obtain the maximum benefit of tax rate arbitrage. I want to reduce taxable income in high income years by maximizing available deductions and then shifting income into lower income years.

Secondly, I want to increase income in low income years by deferring deductions and increasing taxable income to fill up the lower brackets.

6. Roth IRA Conversions: These have a number of advantages over traditional IRAs. Roth IRAs can lower overall taxable long-term income, offer tax-free growth rather than tax-deferred, have no Required Minimum Distribution (RMD) at age 70½, and benefit from tax-free withdrawals for beneficiaries after the death of the owner. During our client's "sweet spot" I mentioned above we are often performing a strategic mix of Capital Gain Harvesting and Roth IRA Conversions.

Asset Location optimization and tax lot identification are tax-saving strategies that don't require movement in and out of funds; however, by definition, Tax-Loss Harvesting requires such transactions. To carry out Tax-Loss Harvesting, loss positions are sold. Wash sale rules disallow loss recognition if the same, or substantially identical securities are purchased within 30 days of the sale. Because of this, we must either stay out of that position for 30 days, or purchase a similar position (that is not substantially identical). In the event of market growth within the 30 days, this "replacement" security should be appropriate for long-term holding. A potential indirect consequence of mass Tax-Loss Harvesting activities is the creation of unstable cash flows in or out of mutual funds. This can harm fund shareholders who desire relatively stable cash flows in order to minimize the impact of frictions from excessive trading resulting in higher expenses. For this reason, I have sought input from Dimensional Fund Advisors (DFA) as to the optimal Tax-Loss Harvesting activities that will not hurt fund shareholders. There are two primary issues to be considered when approaching Tax-Loss Harvesting with DFA Funds: timing and dollar amounts. To avoid extreme cash flow movements with DFA Funds, we pursue opportunistic Tax-Loss Harvesting on a periodic basis, rather than solely at year end. Additionally, DFA prefers to be forewarned by approved advisors anytime $1 million or more will move in or out of any particular fund. I communicate with my DFA regional director regarding such trades.

FIGURE 6.7. **Tax-Loss Harvesting Discipline**

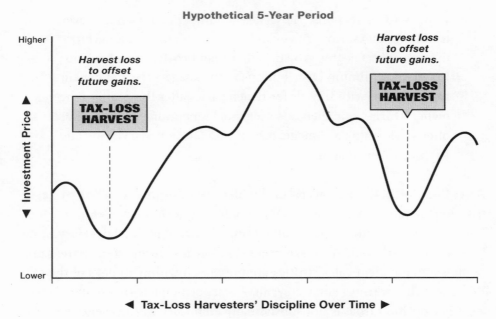

In Figure 6.7 *Tax-Loss Harvesting Discipline*, I am illustrating an often-overlooked portfolio management tool to maximize long-term after-tax portfolio growth—Tax-Loss Harvesting. Realized capital losses serve a value as a tax planning resource and can be utilized as a Deferred Tax Asset because of their ability to reduce current and future taxes.

Tax-Loss Harvesting through the recognition of losses allows you to offset gains produced by capital gain distributions or desirable portfolio rebalancing. Losses can be carried forward indefinitely until they have been utilized to offset future capital gains and a portion of your income. This strategy must be coordinated with your tax advisor for optimal results.

I recommend the following Tax-Loss Harvesting strategies:

- Take advantage of Tax-Loss Harvesting *on an opportunistic basis*, not solely at the end of the year.
- Choose an appropriate alternate DFA Fund as the replacement security when harvesting tax losses.
- Harvest losses only when the benefits are material.
- Notify DFA in advance of fund movements of $1 million or more.

The benefits to the first strategy are twofold: DFA Funds will not get hit all at once with transactions at the end of the year, and clients will reap greater tax savings by periodic Tax-Loss Harvesting.

With periodic Tax-Loss Harvesting, it is possible to recognize losses, even during upmarkets. Tax losses should be recognized when:

1. The loss is material. The materiality of the loss can only be based on client preferences and our judgment. Typically, materiality is expressed as a fixed dollar amount for a percentage of the client's portfolio. Because even short-term losses will likely eventually offset long-term gains, the tax benefit should be calculated based

on the long-term capital gain rate, currently ranging from 0%, 15%, and 20% for most investors.

2. The percentage loss is material. The percentage is significant to ensure that daily price fluctuation doesn't turn a planned lost transaction into a gain. Typically, a 10% loss minimum should be required for Tax-Loss Harvesting.

3. An appropriate replacement fund exists. As previously noted, since the replacement fund might appreciate, it is important that such fund be appropriate for long-term holdings. A plan to simply sell the replacement fund after 30 days may negate the harvesting transaction if the market has increased in the interim.

4. The value of the tax savings is significant compared to transaction costs. Finally, the tax savings should be significant compared to the cost of the transaction. A good rule of thumb (based on the DFA's tax-managed strategies) is that the savings must be at least eight times the cost. I wish to acknowledge with gratitude the assistance and input regarding tax aware portfolio management primarily to Sheryl Rowling, CPA, a national expert in this field, along with the assistance of Glen Free and Jeff Cornell, both of DFA.

SET YOUR RETIREMENT ASSET ALLOCATION WITHDRAWAL GLIDEPATH: REVIEW ANNUALLY AND RELAX

Research shows—unequivocally—that investors who work with financial advisors are significantly more ready for retirement.
—Bob Reynolds, President & CEO, Putnam Investments & Great WestLifeCo., US

The case highlights the wide gap and opposing roles of a broker who is permitted in law to further his and his firm's interests at the expense of customers, and a fiduciary who is required in law to put his clients' interests first. This is at the core of why the fiduciary standard is important.
—Knut A. Rostad, Committee for the Fiduciary
Standard, as quoted in *Wealth Manager*

Another key to enjoying your investment experience is to put your withdrawal portfolio(s) on a custom Glidepath that steadily reduces your exposure to stocks as you approach retirement and during retirement.

The above quote by Bob Reynolds sums up my philosophy throughout my book as your "financial life planning coach." I want to help you relax into a comfortable retirement by providing you with a world-class strategy for you and your family. It is the essence of everything I am attempting to accomplish. As I mentioned earlier in the book, there are three types of investors: Do-It-Yourselfers, Validators, and Delegators. I do recognize that a minority percentage of investors are Do-It-Yourselfers, but my focus is on the majority of investors who are delegating some, most, or all of their portfolio to a competent Wealth Manager with whom they are aligned philosophically. My goal is for you to implement the specific recommendations I have enumerated throughout my book for lifelong personal finance success.

FINDING YOUR GLIDEPATH

*"I mix up latitude and longitude…
how can I possibly find my Glidepath?"*

As in every key thus far, my plan is to help you wade through the confusion and customize a time-honored strategy to proactively protect yourself from common emotional investment mistakes. One of my key tenets for your success is establishing your retirement Glidepath Asset Allocation, which is the percentage of stocks vs. bonds in your portfolio(s) according to your "Wants" (Risk Tolerance) and "Needs" (Risk Capacity) buckets.

A "Glidepath" portfolio resets its Asset Allocation mix (stocks vs. bonds) in its portfolio according to an agreed-upon time period that is customized for each individual investor. My DiNuzzo Financial Wellness LifePlan™ Glidepath strategy has real, tangible, positive benefits, in that it will relieve your anxiety, your uncertainty, the knots in your stomach, and those questions in the back of your mind that keep on clawing away at you: Am I in good shape? Do I have enough? Am I withdrawing a safe number from my portfolio? Is my portfolio going to last? Do I have enough money to retire? How much can I afford to withdraw? What tax bracket am I going to be in? What is my effective tax rate going to be? What's a safe percentage rate of withdrawal? A solid Glidepath strategy for the portfolios you will be withdrawing from during retirement will address all of those objectives so that you can relax and enjoy the fruits of your life's work.

Practically speaking, *your Glidepath will dictate your Asset Allocation* (percentage of stocks and bonds). For example, while you may have had 80% in stocks and only 20% in bonds when you were in your 20s, by the time you retire at approximately age 65 and need to take withdrawals from your portfolio, you typically would want to target 50% in stocks and 50% in bonds. This pre-structured strategy will protect you tremendously from the emotional volatility and suboptimal returns they produce.

Once your Asset Allocation and Glidepath strategy are in place, the potential for mistakes in your investment process over the course of your lifetime significantly decreases. To illustrate this, stand at the end of your dining room table and extend your arm straight out from your chest, palm down. Walk along the table toward the other end, slowly lowering your hand, simulating the landing of an aircraft. This is a good visualization of what you want to do with your investment portfolio Glidepath. You want to approach the descent slowly over time and systematically decrease your exposure to stocks.

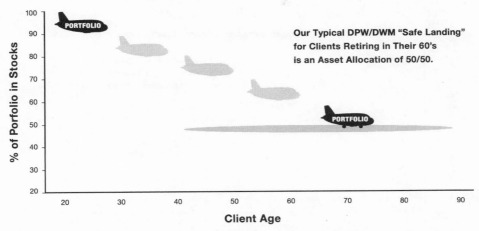

FIGURE 6.8. DPW/DWM Retirement Income Portfolio
DiNuzzo Descending Glidepath™

For Your Precious Retirement Income Cash-Flow Cargo

Source: DiNuzzo Private Wealth, Inc. (DPW)/DiNuzzo Wealth Management (DWM)

As illustrated in Figure 6.8, DPW/DWM *Retirement Income Portfolio DiNuzzo Descending Glidepath™*, the altitude of the airplane represents the percentage of the portfolio in stocks. When you are in your 20s, you may have 80%, 90%, even 100% in stocks. As you get closer to needing to take *withdrawals* from your portfolio(s), you need to *reduce your exposure* to stocks in order to lower your volatility and risk. At age 50, approximately 70% to 60% or less of your portfolio should be in stocks. At age 60, where you are looking for the green light for a safe landing, approximately only 60% to 50% of your withdrawal portfolio(s) should be in stocks.

Now consider what would happen if you had 80% of your portfolio in stocks the year you intended to retire and initiate withdrawals. Can you imagine trying to descend from 80% in stocks to your target level of, let's say, 50% in one year? It would lead to a *crash landing*, and unfortunately, that is what happens to hundreds of thousands of other individual investors across the United

States. Needless to say, these individual investors typically have to continue working for years past their original intended retirement date.

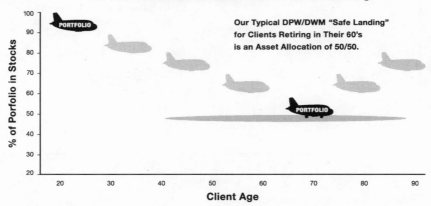

FIGURE 6.9. DPW/DWM Retirement Income Portfolio
DiNuzzo Ascending Glidepath™

For Your Precious Retirement Income Cash-Flow Cargo

Source: DiNuzzo Private Wealth, Inc. (DPW)/DiNuzzo Wealth Management (DWM)

In Figure 6.9, *Retirement Income Portfolio DiNuzzo Ascending Glidepath*™ you can observe the same Glidepath strategy until the point of inflection for portfolio withdrawals but with a distinctly different concept from that intersection forward. In some cases with clients who are not spending their RMDs and/or have a higher than usual Risk Tolerance I will continue to modestly increase their exposure to stocks over their lifetime.

In Figure 6.10, *Results Summaries: DFA vs. S&P 500 Index*, illustrating the S&P 500 as a proxy for individuals' 100/0 portfolio(s) provides tremendous insight into the danger of taking withdrawals from a portfolio too heavily weighted in equities (stocks). Again, as a reminder, the S&P 500 index has outperformed the supermajority of all individuals' stock mutual funds and individual stock positions over this period, so I am being generous in using this as the benchmark for the average individual.

FIGURE 6.10. **Results Summaries: DFA vs. S&P 500 Index**

January 2000 – October 2018

HYPOTHETICAL ALL DFA INDEX (50/50) PORTFOLIO*

Beginning (Retirement) Portfolio Value:	$1,000,000
Initial Annual $45,000 Retirement Portfolio Withdrawal:	4.5%
Annualized Standard Deviation	7.69%
Annualized Return:	5.32%
Ending Value of $1,000,000 Portfolio:	$1,249,965

*Hypothetical Returns are less 1% investment management fee and expense ratios.

S&P 500® INDEX (100/0) PORTFOLIO**

Beginning (Retirement) Portfolio Value:	$1,000,000
Initial Annual $45,000 Retirement Portfolio Withdrawal:	4.5%
Annualized Standard Deviation	14.41%
Annualized Return:	5.26%
Ending Value of $1,000,000 Portfolio:	$522,527

** Reminder: The S&P 500® outperformed the *super-majority* of all active
stock mutual fund managers over this period of time.

In the "Results Summaries from January 1, 2000 to October 2018," you will see the key data from my analysis. As we observed, this period was dramatically below the S&P 500's 90-year long-term track record average of approximately +10% per year with annualized return "growth" of only +5.26% per year. Below, we see the disastrous results of being too heavily invested in stocks and taking what initially appeared to be a "reasonable" withdrawal ($45,000) of 4.5% based on the initial portfolio value of $1 million. The starting value of $1 million on January 1, 2000 is now only $522,527 on October 31, 2018. This is an accurate representation of what happened to many investors over the past 18+ year period. And though some may suggest that the individual could have lowered their withdrawal, we know that in reality this generally is not an option for most retirees. *This is a catastrophic result* and one that could have easily been avoided, primarily by starting with a much more appropriate Asset Allocation, such as 50/50. This 100% stock portfolio has eaten into muscle and even bone, and now the original 4.5% withdrawal ($45,000 divided by $1 million) is in a death spiral at approximately 9% (the $45,000 withdrawal divided by the $522,527 current portfolio value).

As a reminder, an ideal withdrawal percentage rate during retirement starting in your 60s would be approximately 4% and should ideally not exceed 5%, especially during the first 10 years of retirement. One of the inherent flaws of this "strategy" (100/0) is that unless the market is constantly at new highs when you liquidate positions to provide for withdrawals, you are selling when your stock positions or stock mutual funds are down, *permanently* locking in some kind of loss or lost growth opportunity by not ever allowing those holdings to rebound.

In Figure 6.10, you also see a more appropriate retirement withdrawal Asset Allocation at 50/50 to fund your "Wants" (Risk Tolerance) bucket, for your discretionary expenses. Analyzing the same exact time period, we now see under our "Results Summaries from January 1, 2000 to October31, 2018" a potentially life-altering, improved result. You now observe that even after withdrawals of $3,750 per month for 214 months, totaling $802,500, that the portfolio balance on October 31, 2018, is at $1,249,965. Comparing the $1,249,965 portfolio value to the 100/0 s&p 500 portfolio value of $522,267 is the epitome of this entire exercise. As I have stated throughout my book, we can be very successful if we *control what we are able to* and continually place the probabilities for success in our favor.

You must not jeopardize an entire lifetime of hard work in retirement by getting the withdrawal Asset Allocation decision wrong. Hundreds of times over the past 30+ years, in prospective client consultations, I have encountered individuals who invested too aggressively regarding their withdrawal portfolio(s) in retirement. Even if you don't plan on taking withdrawals from certain portfolios, in certain cases (such as IRAs) you will have "forced" withdrawals at age 70½.

As an illustration and "stress test" for this above scenario, I have chosen a hypothetical individual who would have retired on January 1, 2000, and their subsequent "experience" through October 31, 2018. This period is excellent as a "sensitivity analysis" as it contains two of the worst bear (down) markets since the Great Depression. Since we have experienced this recently, and there have been other similar periods in the past, we certainly cannot rule it out in the future. You will notice that the 100/0 portfolio never came close to recovering from the 2000–2002 "tech-wreck" and the 2008–2009 "Great Recession" financial meltdown. As a review, in the case of both portfolios, the 100/0 S&P 500 index and a 50/50 DFA All-Index benchmark-based portfolio, I am starting in the example with a portfolio of $1 million, an annual withdrawal of $45,000, and an initial withdrawal rate of 4.5% per year, or $3,750 per month from the portfolio.

The Benefits of a Glidepath Strategy

A Glidepath strategy offers the following benefits:

1. Establishes a process for selecting an appropriate Asset Allocation for every one-year, five-year, and 10-year period of your life

2. Allows for reasonable flexibility within your unique plan

3. Protects you from market timing mistakes

4. Provides comfort through lowering stress and anxiety by building a customized financial life plan tailored for success for you and your family/household

5. Helps you avoid common "emotional" investor mistakes while working, and especially approaching and during retirement

Establishes Appropriate Asset Allocation for Every Key Period of Your Life

One of the major accomplishments of establishing a distinctive "Glidepath" for yourself and your family will be that you will have a unique process that will provide you with comfort in knowing where you will be every year of your life. A 10-year period would illustrate where you would be in your 20s, 30s, 40s, 50s, 60s, and through retirement. The process for selecting that Asset Allocation is going to be the Glidepath.

The Glidepath is going to be one of the beneficial tools you will be able to devise and utilize, which will leverage the hard work you put in earlier by building your Personal Balance Sheet (PBS), Retirement Cash Flow Statement (RCFS), and then ultimately building your DiNuzzo Money Bucket Stack Analysis™ (DMBSA™). Your "Needs" (Risk Capacity) bucket is followed by your "Wants" (Risk Tolerance) bucket and, ultimately, your "Dreams/Wishes" (Legacy/ Quality of Life) bucket. You have already designed an Asset Allocation range for all major purposes of your savings and portfolios that you accumulated during your lifetime, so now you can simply apply a Glidepath strategy onto your "Wants" (Risk Tolerance) and "Needs" (Risk Capacity) buckets. As stated earlier, if you have excess savings, the "Dreams/Wishes" (Legacy/Quality of Life) bucket will be at a higher growth level because that will be for your beneficiaries and heirs, as well as any potential charities.

Allows for Flexibility

It is important to build in reasonable flexibility within your DiNuzzo Financial Wellness LifePlan™. As we all know, things happen in life, and we are faced with many changes throughout our lifetime. These changes may require the flexibility to make a slight course correction, but you should not need to veer very far off of your Glidepath during retirement.

For example, an individual may have saved more money than they needed and had a moderately above average market period during their accumulation years when they were doing their heaviest savings. They have the flexibility to choose a portfolio that is slightly more aggressive. So instead of having a "Wants" (Risk Tolerance) bucket with 50% in stock and 50% in bonds, they may be able to have a strategy with 60% in stocks and 40% in bonds if their Investor DNA allows them to be a slightly more aggressive investor. On the other hand, if individuals have gotten ahead of their plan and are more conservative, they may allow themselves the flexibility to be more conservative with their "Wants" (Risk Tolerance) strategy. Rather than having the standard 50/50 stock/bond ratio, they may easily be able to achieve their financial goals through a 40% stock and 60% bond allocation through retirement. The beauty of this flexibility related to our Glidepath is that we can view our Glidepath as a lifetime of spanning the distance from coast to coast.

For example, when going from the West Coast of the United States to the East Coast, you will not have to make any sudden decisions over the course of the 3,000-mile trip. Why? Because with my Glidepath, you will always be able to see clarity on the horizon, both visually and through this "financial instrumentation." I have designed a full financial instrument panel in which you can monitor every key variable that you need to track. You will not be under the pressure at any time on your Glidepath, to make any abrupt changes in your philosophy, strategy or implementation.

Protects You from Market Timing Mistakes

The protection from market timing errors that your investment Glidepath offers is arguably *the number one* benefit of establishing your investment Glidepath. In the Dalbar research I discuss throughout my book, I illustrate numerous scenarios, along with decades of data showing that individuals *dramatically* underperform the broad market indexes. Emotion-based market timing is one of the chief culprits causing individual investor's underperformance. With my Glidepath, you have an ironclad strategy to eliminate the emotional component of the investment decision-making process regarding how much stock you should have in your portfolio and the percentages of stock exposure. Over the course of a lifetime, nearly every investor is faced with the challenge of avoiding market timing mistakes. With the Glidepath, you basically have a blueprint…not just an idea, but an actual blueprint…for exactly how to handle your unique financial life plan.

For example, if you are 5 years away from retirement, and your "Wants" (Risk Tolerance) Glidepath "safe" landing is a 50/50 portfolio (50% in stocks/50% in bonds) and if you are 55% in stocks 5 years before retirement, you will not easily be pulled by the "siren songs" of the stock market, because you will have your eyes on the prize. You will understand that you will not want to do something such as increase your stock exposure to 60%, 80%, or even 100% in your withdrawal portfolio five years prior to retirement. It will be crystal clear where you are, how and why you got there, *and* where you are going. The paramount reason individual investors make market-timing mistakes by dramatically increasing or decreasing their stock exposure, is that they simply do not have a philosophy, a strategy, and a plan. You, on the other hand, now have a world-class plan.

Creates an Individualized Plan

As I discussed earlier, developing a customized DiNuzzo Financial Wellness LifePlan™ for you and your family/household provides immeasurable relief from financial stress and anxiety. This, of course, is one of the ultimate benefits of the Glidepath. Of over 300 million people in the United States, there will be no one else who will have a plan from start to finish that is the same as yours. When we look at individual investor mistakes directly related to this topic, the emotional whipsaws he or she feels internally generally produces the wrong reactions.

Helps You Avoid Common Investor Mistakes

Finally, your unique Glidepath will help you avoid common investor mistakes while working, and especially, when approaching retirement. For example, when you are in your 40s and have a 60/40 portfolio (60% stocks/40% bonds) for your "Wants" (Risk Tolerance) (withdrawal) solution, you understand how that protects your downside as well as has the appropriate expectation for success from a total return perspective for the portfolio over your lifetime. Again, seeing where you are on your personal Glidepath for that portion of your portfolio, which will provide withdrawals later in retirement, eliminates a tremendous amount of emotional discomfort. Once you tune in to the frequency of the benefits of developing Glidepaths for each appropriate withdrawal Money Bucket, which we identified in our DiNuzzo Money Bucket Stack Analysis™ (DMBSA™), it will all come together and you will understand where you should be on these various Money Bucket Glidepaths. Remember, regarding your "Dreams/Wishes" (Legacy/Quality of Life), you can maintain a 30,000-foot cruising altitude throughout your lifetime (60/40 to 100/0).

FIGURE 6.11. **Discipline of Index Investors**

Hypothetical 5-Year Period

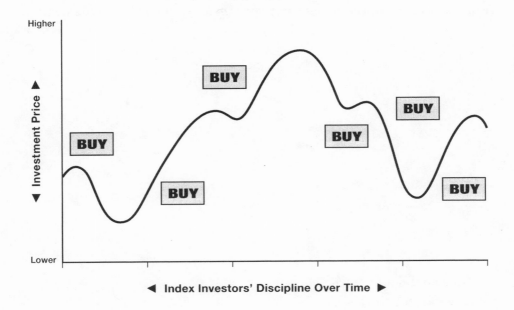

◄ **Index Investors' Discipline Over Time** ►

In Figure 6.11, *Discipline of Index Investors* I am presenting a hypothetical five-year period and my investment philosophy implementation which will lead you to long-term success. This is a pure "invest and relax" illustration. My prescribed philosophy allows you to avoid the pitfalls and investment caveats listed throughout my book. The philosophy, strategy, and plan implementation are transparent, empirically rigorous, and has been proven, in my opinion, as the optimal strategy for success. We *will not be making any market timing decisions*, but rather buying consistently throughout our lives. Although our stock exposure on average will shrink over our lifetimes, it is still the same concept and keys for success.

Put the portfolios that you will withdraw from during retirement on a "DiNuzzo Financial Wellness LifePlan™" Glidepath that slowly reduces your exposure to stocks over time scheduled to intersect with your retirement. This gives you the confidence that you are following your proactive investment plan and protects you from making counterproductive emotional errors. In the years approaching retirement, this also protects you from dramatic market swings. Set your Glidepath and enjoy your smooth landing into retirement!

MANAGING YOUR EMOTIONS
WITH A PLAN AND DISCIPLINE

When you feel tempted, unsure, unsettled, anxious, or as though you have lost your investment philosophy "anchor" because you were exposed to media noise, or some investment "talking head," take a breath and review my investing mental health emotional checklist. Ask yourself a few simple questions:

1. *Does this individual I'm listening to manage money for a living?*
2. *Is it a material amount of money?*
3. *Do they have a public track record vis-à-vis an appropriate index benchmark?*
4. *Is the track record longer than a decade or two?*
5. *And finally, is it a successful risk-adjusted track record?*

At first, you will be surprised that over 99% of the individuals that you see on TV, listen to on the radio, have read in social media or print fail this simple checklist. After a while, you won't be surprised anymore.

—P.J. DiNuzzo

Viewing investment (and personal finance) challenges through a "microscope" when they should and can only be observed and interpreted accurately via a "telescope" is a certain recipe for anxiety and failure.

—P.J. DiNuzzo

Individual investors consistently overreact to the media noise, news, and market movements. Short-term market movements and returns are classic "noise" and consistently "surprising" while long-term movements and returns (for example, over 20 years) never are.

—P.J. DiNuzzo

We can and should relieve our personal finance anxiety by "standing on the shoulders of giants" and not attempting to reinvent the wheel. There are proven philosophies, strategies, methods of implementation, and resulting discipline, successfully applied for decades and decades by the largest, best, and brightest institutional portfolios and managers. Let's emulate them, relax, and experience an achievable inner peace.

—P.J. DiNuzzo

The investor's chief problem—and even his worst enemy—is likely to be himself.
    —Benjamin Graham (1894–1976), legendary American investor, scholar, teacher, and co-author of the 1934 classic, *Security Analysis*

In the short run, the stock market is a voting machine but in the long run, it is a weighing machine.

—Benjamin Graham

There are no dependable ways of making money easily and quickly either in Wall Street or anywhere else.

—Benjamin Graham

Owners of stocks...too often let the capricious and irrational behavior of their fellow owners cause them to behave irrationally. Because there is so much chatter about markets, the economy, interest rates, price behavior of stocks, etc., some investors believe it is important to listen to pundits—and, worse yet, important to consider acting upon their comments.

—Warren Buffett

It's human nature to find patterns where there are none and to find skill where luck is a more likely explanation (particularly if you're the lucky [mutual fund] manager). Mutual fund manager performance does not persist and the return of the stock picking is zero.

—Dr. William Bernstein, *The Intelligent Asset Allocator*

The most important key to successful investing and financial independence is learning to properly manage your financial emotions.

If you were to look at the "What We Do" section of our firm's website, you would notice that we list dozens of points of value that we provide for our clients. Emotions management/behavior coaching is at the very top of the list. It is also in a tie for the #1 most important topic in my book. Surprised?

Many people assume that preparing to be successful investors has nothing whatsoever to do with emotions, other than dealing with a bit of anxiety.

Initially, investors assume that success or failure is determined by something "numbers" related, regarding performance, annual rates of return, and average rates of return over time. However, Vanguard, Morningstar, top investors, economists, and Nobel Laureates confirm that the real key to investment success is *proper emotions management/behavior coaching*. This is all the more true for retirement investing and income success.

Behavioral scientists have been studying individual investors for decades. Historically, Nobel prizes were awarded in the quantitative sciences—i.e., the math portion of investing. However, that has changed over more recent decades, with more Nobel prizes going to those immersed in *behavioral* science. After numerous decades, behavioral scientists have noted that individual investors performed significantly lower than the indexes and the market in which they were invested. For example, if they were invested in large cap stocks, they were significantly underperforming the s&p 500 Index.

The study of behavioral science has produced a tremendous amount of insight into investment techniques and the process of investing which has improved the results for the average individual. Understanding human behavior and the mistakes made by other individual investors is *mission critical*.

But I'm different than the rest, you may be thinking. Beware! Not appreciating basic human behavior and commonly repeated mistakes inevitably will lead you down the road to failure. Regardless of superior intellectual talents, observation skills, or hard work, the fact remains that individual investors have been making the same mistakes year after year and market cycle after market cycle. This chapter will help you understand your emotional behavior as an investor, know what risks to guard against, and provide proactive solutions for common areas of failure and underperformance.

YOUR INVESTOR DNA

> *The investment business is a giant scam. Most people think they can find managers who can outperform, but most people are wrong. I will say that 85 to 90 percent of managers fail to match their [index] benchmarks. Because managers have fees and incur transaction costs, you know that in the aggregate they are deleting value.*
> —Jack R. Meyer, from *The Little Book of Common Sense Investing* by John C. Bogle

The investor who permits himself to be stampeded or unduly worried by unjustified market declines in his holdings is perversely transforming his basic advantage into a basic disadvantage.
—Benjamin Graham, *The Intelligent Investor*

Your Investor DNA is your very human tendency to look at the stock market in a vacuum, judging it only according to your own lifetime of experience and what you can immediately perceive, rather than heeding generations of objective financial data. Because we all inherit this Investor DNA, we have a herd mentality that leads more and more financial "sheep" into the wrong pasture.

Your Investor DNA is the source of most of the unhelpful emotions about investing. You must understand your Investor DNA and learn to manage these destructive emotions if you want to keep history from repeating itself in your own financial situation. Only by doing so can you chart a course to retirement income success.

Here are several characteristics of your Investor DNA that will keep you following the wrong herd every time:

The Mars vs. Venus Tendency: Plowing Forward Before Consulting Data and History

Numerous research studies state that women are better investors than men! Why? First and foremost, women exhibit better "buy and hold" tendencies. When faced with a situation they do not fully understand or comprehend, women tend to pause and gather more information so they can acquire a deeper understanding. Men, when facing the same situation, are apt to myopically put their head down and plow forward, testosterone fully engaged, without delving into the matter any further. Dr. Terrence Thomas Odean, Professor and Chair of the Finance Group at the Haas School of Business at the University of California, Berkeley, completed a study of approximately 60,000 individual investors over an entire decade, in all 50 states and across all demographics. The only statistically significant information he could produce from his research was that *women are better investors than men*. He cites the above reasons.

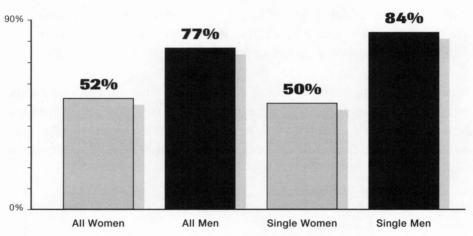

FIGURE 7.1. **Boys Will Be Boys**

Annual Turnover (%)

Source: Barber and Odean (2001) Quarterly Journal of Economics.

Overall, individual investors exhibit three negative-return-producing tendencies: decision biases, limited attention, and emotionally based "buy and hold" decisions. One "decision bias" occurs when individuals (typically men) display an unusual amount of overconfidence. Overconfidence breeds material sub-performance primarily through too much trading. Another decision bias is referred to as "recency bias." Recency bias results in individuals who consistently chase performance. I often refer to individuals chasing performance in more simplistic terms, such as consistently arriving late for the party.

The next individual investor flaw is "limited attention." Individual investors are easily distracted by "shiny objects" and typically gravitate toward buying

attention-grabbing stocks. Attention-grabbing stocks have often risen tremendously regarding their price. The second limited attention deficit is that
individual investors typically ignore fees. Ignoring fees when they are one of
the best predictors of your portfolio's correlation to future performance is
flawed, to say the least.

Regarding emotional "buy and hold" decisions, on one hand, individual
investors tend to buy in bubbles. Bubbles occur when a certain investment
rises to dramatic heights, thus drawing the attention of individual investors,
who then typically buy it at excessively high prices.

The final emotional challenge is that individual investors hold on to their losers entirely too long because they often find it more comfortable to ignore
reality. Because they haven't actually sold the underperforming asset, individual investors rationalize that they haven't lost any money yet. This produces
an out-of-sight, out-of-mind mentality toward the losers in their portfolio.
Such rationalizations are another contributor to their consistent investment
underperformance relative to the available stock market indexes.

FIGURE 7.2. **Mutual Funds: Money Pours into Last Year's Winners**

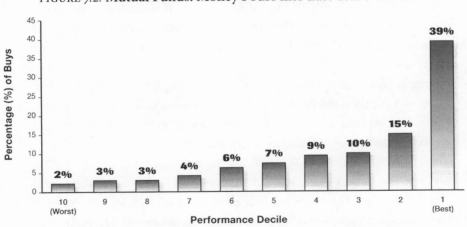

Source: Barber, Odean, and Zheng.

Figure 7.2, *Mutual Funds: Money Pours into Last Year's Winners* reflects Professor Odean's research that individual investors are exceptionally emotional and tend to trade excessively. As I previously mentioned, recent positive performance attracts individual investors as a moth is attracted to a flame. As I indicate throughout my book, individual investors who consistently arrive late to the party consistently end up empty-handed, with subpar performance.

WHY FEAR (AND GREED) ARE ENEMY #1 TO YOUR INVESTMENT STRATEGIES AND ACHIEVABLE DINUZZO FINANCIAL WELLNESS LIFEPLAN™ SUCCESS: GREG AND AMY

Imagine being in a room with two large "emotional magnets" on opposing walls. Painted on each magnet is only one word: *Fear* on one magnet, and *Greed* on the other. If not properly understood and managed, these powerful emotional magnets will pull you, unknowingly and potentially uncontrolled, from one end of the room to the other over your entire life. This is what the typical individual contends with, and giving in to one or the other of these destructive emotions will undermine the best intentions of any individual investor.

Greg is an architect and Amy is a real estate agent. They are excellent savers, have no children, and had several million dollars in their 401(k) accounts. At the outset of the 2016 presidential election, the couple was invested 60% in stocks and 40% in bonds.

When Trump was elected president, Greg and Amy were so distraught and full of fear, they took all their money out of stocks—*and stayed at 0% stocks for over two years.* These types of emotional decisions typically result in financial losses that are never recovered.

This situation is not found solely on the Democratic side of the aisle. Likewise, when Obama was elected president in 2008, a number of registered Republican prospective clients I met with were so concerned, they had liquidated some, most, or *all* of their stocks or stock mutual funds, fearing the worst for the economy.

Fear is an equal opportunity enemy when it comes to undermining your investment strategy. Whether you're a Republican, Democrat, Independent, or politically agnostic, giving in to fear can end up costing you hundreds of thousands of dollars, as it did for Greg and Amy, and other individuals, partners, and couples who I have met with over the decades after succumbing to these emotional drivers.

When your "gut" is telling you something about the market, it's usually wrong, on average two out of three times. So, even when it's right, it's typically a random accident. When it comes to your life savings, don't listen to your gut. Instead, rely on historical data and have a plan which will guide you to never, *ever* give in to Fear.

The very first time I talk to a prospective client, I ask if they have ever heard of the phrase, "science versus art." Our job as Wealth Managers relies on equal parts Science (as in *numbers*) vs. Art (as in *emotions management*). At least 50% of the interactions we have with prospective and existing clients are purely of an emotional content and have nothing to do with "numbers." Considering the continuous bombardment of unsubstantiated and often conflicting and confusing opinions the typical investor is subjected to via TV, social media, print media, and other sources, it's not surprising that emotions around financial investments can run high.

The challenge that causes these disasters and which the typical individual continually runs into is not having a philosophy and core belief from which they can develop a strategy. With a core belief-based strategy in place, however, the investor can then ultimately implement a customized investment plan that places them in the best position possible, not only from the numbers perspective, but also from the emotions management perspective, which would preclude them from ever being in this position. In Greg and Amy's case, the challenge going forward is proactively managed within the context of their collaborative and, customized DiNuzzo Financial Wellness LifePlan™.

Willingness to Take Illogical Risks with Your Money

The neural activity of someone whose investments are making money is indistinguishable from that of someone who is high on cocaine or morphine.

—Jason Zweig, *Your Money and Your Brain*

Another characteristic of our Investor DNA is significant risk-taking, or gambling. As a behavior, gambling is obvious when a person goes to a local casino or partakes in some other risky behavior. Most often individuals will state they are doing it just for entertainment purposes. But a small percentage of the population has a significant and deep-rooted issue with a gambling instinct that manifests itself in investing. (Again, I am referring mostly to men here.)

I have always advised not to appropriate any more than 5% of your investment portfolio in what I refer to as your "Las Vegas" account(s). By this I mean a trading belief, a hunch, a hot stock tip, a backyard "over the hedges" conversation with your neighbor, or any other kind of extreme active management stock picking or market timing outside the principles and processes I outline in my book. Again, if an individual has a $1 million portfolio of total investment assets, they should *not* allocate more than $50,000, or 5%, to such "Las Vegas" type investments.

The stock market is not a perfect mechanism, but it is the *best* and premier mechanism for "Price Discovery" and valuing investment assets. And although not perfect, the imperfections are not discernible enough to be exploited by any investor on a *consistent* basis. Thus the vast majority of investors' portfolios underperform relative to the appropriate benchmark index.

Choosing to Ignore the Past

Practically speaking, individual investors should treat the market as unbeatable and realize that when they try to beat it because it is inefficient, they are likely to injure themselves, rather than gain at the expense of another.

—Meir Statman, Professor of Finance, Santa Clara University, and author of *What Investors Really Want*; "Meir Statman: Amateur Investors Expect Impossible," sf *Gate.com*, November 16, 2010

One of the benefits we have in the capital markets and stock market is the tremendous amount of data and history at our disposal. We have comprehensive and tedious records dating back to the 1920s, in addition to a significant amount of good data going back approximately 170 years to the mid-1850s. Over the last 100 years, the stock market has averaged over 9% return per year. Astonishingly, the average individual investor has often only achieved a rate of return of approximately *one-half to two-thirds* that rate. Professor Daniel Kahneman and other behavioral scientists have received Nobel prizes for their work in this arena. Yet far too many investors ignore their findings. Individual investor results have been dismal.

Even though there is an enormous amount of data regarding the capital markets and financial markets illustrating that individuals consistently, decade after decade, make similar mistakes and dramatically underperform market indexes on a regular basis, history repeats itself because many investors simply continue to ignore the past. They view it as a liability. In contrast, we want to take the history that is available and turn it into an *asset* for those of us in the investing process. Those who choose to ignore the past are truly doomed to repeat it.

One primary objective of my book is to help you improve your investment knowledge and utilize this historical data wisely. Investment history produces valuable feedback regarding human error, particularly as it relates to emotional failures in individual portfolios. In other words, the historical data clearly demonstrates the widespread practice of making the wrong decisions at the wrong time based upon *emotions*. That's why one of the "fathers" of successful investment management, Mr. Benjamin Graham, stated, "The investor's chief problem—and even his worst enemy—is likely to be himself." In other words, individual investors sabotage themselves over their lifetime, and their own emotions serve as the largest impediment to investment success.

WHY GREED IS ALSO ENEMY #1 TO YOUR INVESTMENT STRATEGIES AND ACHIEVABLE DINUZZO FINANCIAL WELLNESS LIFEPLAN™ SUCCESS: ALICE

Alice is a hospital administrator who, despite my best advice, insisted on investing 100% of her retirement portfolio in stocks. This was during the late 1990s, and she was seeing tremendous returns on her investments. I tried to work with Alice, but like many investors during this time, she allowed her investment strategy to be undermined—not by Fear, but by its counterpart: *Greed*.

I could not take on Alice as a client because I could see the writing on the wall. She was destined to pay for this critical error in her investment strategy, and when the NASDAQ lost 80% of its value and the broad stock market plummeted 50% between March of 2000 and November 2002, she did.

You might think the toughest time for a Fiduciary-based financial advisor is when the markets are down and we're in a bear market, but it's often equally difficult for individuals to maintain discipline during a bull market, when clients are clamoring to take advantage of more growth opportunities than is prudent. From the mid- to late-1990s, and any other time we've enjoyed a bull market, I've been somewhat impugned and even maligned by investors who think they "know better" than the market. It physically pains me to see individual investors give in to Greed, because I know that it typically doesn't end well, and for people such as Alice, it's often even devastating.

Fear and Greed are clearly your enemies, and your gut knows nothing of historical financial data. Adopt an investment strategy based on logic and you can save yourself many years of grief in the future.

Believing "It's Different This Time"

Insanity: doing the same thing over and over again and expecting different results.

—Albert Einstein

This is the tendency where, even after understanding market data over time, investors convince themselves that "this time will be different." Thus they behave in a manner incongruent with decades, or in some cases, a past century, of financial data. As it has been said, the market never repeats itself exactly, but it certainly rhymes. "Mr. Market" can be a cruel and expensive teacher, and your goal is to take time to study the available lessons for success, and avoid the potentially destructive life-altering "tuition."

Believing You See Patterns Where There Are None

Toss a coin; heads and the manager will make $10,000 over the year, tails and he will lose $10,000. We run [the contest] for the first year [for 10,000 managers]. At the end of the year, we expect 5,000 managers to be up $10,000 each, and 5,000 to be down $10,000. Now we run the game a second year. Again, we can expect 2,500 managers to be up two years in a row; another year, 1,250; a fourth one, 625; a fifth, 313. We have now, simply in a fair game, 313 managers who have made money for five years in a row. [And in 10 years, just 10 of the original 10,000 managers.] Out of pure luck...A population entirely composed of bad managers will produce a small amount of great track records...

—Nassim Nicholas Taleb, *Fooled by Randomness*

Many investors study stock market prices and perceive insights that they believe others do not. This tendency is also especially true for the male species. The data and empirical research have shown that no individual can be expected to consistently outsmart the stock market and perceive where it's going until it gets there. Research indicates that new information is *fully incorporated* into a securities market price in approximately 5 to 60 minutes.

The capital markets and prices are being reached on a second-by-second basis, as a result of *millions* of educated and informed investors pricing capital assets in an open and free market. The price reached between independent buyers and sellers in the open and free capital markets, "Price Discovery," is the best estimation of a fair market value of the underlying asset. Think of the stock market like the well-known line from the Prego pasta sauce commercial—"it's in there." All available information in the vast and incomprehensibly ubiquitous capital markets is reflected in the current price of the investment you are observing. The sauce is done, the cake is baked—the price is settled upon.

Yet individual investors often tell me they believe they have a "unique ability" to understand and see what is going on in the market, and they want to make an investment or market call based upon that *feeling*, or sixth sense, as it were. When making a market timing call, they feel led to get out of some, most, or *all* of their stock positions until they feel that "everything looks good again." These individuals typically require an upswing of about 20% or so in order for them to "feel comfortable" again and optimistic. However, missing a 20% move, no matter how you look at it—10% for two years or 6% to 7% per year for three years—is an appreciation and total return that the average individual investor can ill-afford to miss. Unfortunately, when it comes to financial assets, your Investor DNA often leads you into making the wrong decisions at the wrong time.

Moreover, when investors believe they see patterns that do not exist, they extrapolate those patterns and build on them. Worst of all, they trade on patterns they *believe* they see. It can involve certain situations when the market hits a particular price or goes above or below a certain price. As Professor Burton Malkiel and Nobel Prize winner Eugene Fama have discussed and identified for decades, market values move randomly (e.g., Dow Jones Industrial Average, S&P 500, and Russell 2000) and short-term data, over a day, week, or even months, should be viewed as nothing more than "noise." There are no active trading premiums identifiable to the average individual. Investing in the financial markets should only be done by those who have an appropriate long-term time horizon, which would be a *minimum* of five to ten years. You need to be invested for *at least* ten years to even *begin* to realize a statistically significant rate of return in the range of what most educated participants expect from the market. Conversely, if you have a lump sum of money and you are planning to, for example, purchase a new house within one to three years, your time horizon is too short to benefit from investing in the stock market, and you should avoid exposing that portion of your portfolio to the stock market.

Believing Investment Success Depends on Intelligence and Skill

Some fiduciary boards, particularly those composed largely of non-professionals, do not adequately understand the true returns, risk, and cost associated with investment in hedge funds.
> —Statement of the Financial Economists Roundtable on
> Hedge Funds, Stanford Graduate School of Business

"Okay, you don't trust my sixth sense, but my acquired and successful survival skills, instincts, common sense, and high IQ will surely help me succeed in the financial markets...won't they?"

Good question. However, many individuals incorrectly assume that successful investing is a natural ability, much like the kind many people feel they have when driving an automobile. What they don't understand is that the discipline of personal finance and investing is completely different from their other acquired skills, whether they are doctors, accountants, professors, lawyers, pilots, entrepreneurs, or engineers.

The critical mistake is assuming that since they are highly intelligent and are successful in their particular skill, trade, or career, this success and intellect will seamlessly spill over into their personal finances and investments. As I have seen time and time again, this often ends poorly. The necessary set of skills required to succeed with personal finance and investments is distinctly different from other career disciplines. What is needed first is *understanding and knowledge*, followed by *a plan to succeed in personal finance.*

The Emotional Cycle of Investing (the "Roller Coaster")

Prediction is very difficult, especially if it's about the future.
> —Niles Bohr, Nobel Laureate in physics

While the physical thrill of riding a roller coaster may be desirable, it is not something we generally seek out when it comes to our financial situation. As you can see on my following graph, market cycle emotions start off with optimism and escalate to euphoria, only to capitulate to the bottom of the hill before beginning another slow ascent. As I mentioned before, average individual investors typically are buying at the wrong time, after equities have increased, and selling at the wrong time—doing the exact opposite of the age-old adage for success of buying low and selling high. The average individual investor is, in reality, perversely buying high and selling low most of the time. As the accompanying graph illustrates, he or she is purchasing at the worst time for financial success and is selling at the bottom of a market, which is actually the maximum time for financial opportunity, but they are often liquidating some, most, or all of their positions.

> *The only time you should sell is when you need cash, or you have given up your faith in capitalism.*
> —Mark Hebner, President, Index Funds Advisors

My Figure 7.3, *The Emotional Cycle of Investing: The Investing Rollercoaster*™ represents the classic emotions the average individual investor experiences during a single business cycle, which averages about five years in the United States. Notice that the roller coaster begins with optimism and ends in optimism. In the beginning, investors are optimistic. When the stock market goes higher, they're excited, when it goes even higher, they're thrilled, and at the very top, they're euphoric. The time when individuals are euphoric has historically been proven to be the *absolute worst time* to buy stocks. When, for example, 10 people want to buy and only 1 person wants to sell, that is typically the point of maximum financial risk.

> *Investing is a strange business. It's the only one we know of where the more expensive the products get, the more customers want to buy them.*
> —Anthony M. Gallea and William Patalon III, *Contrarian Investing*

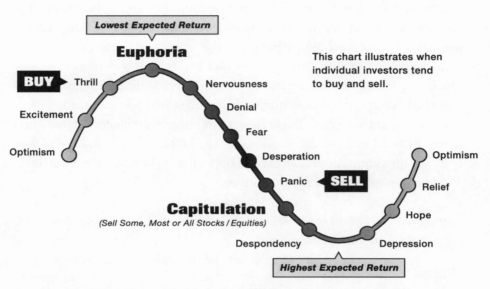

FIGURE 7.3. The Emotional Cycle of Investing: The Investing Rollercoaster™

5-Year Typical Business Cycle

Source: DiNuzzo Private Wealth, Inc. (DPW)/DiNuzzo Wealth Management (DWM)

Let's think about this in a more familiar context. Let's say you wanted to buy a sweater, and I could tell you the specific day this year when Macy's was going to mark up their sweaters, and on that day that sweater's going to cost more than any other day throughout the entire year. You of course, from a pragmatic perspective, would never go and buy the sweater on that day at Macy's, but yet that's what the average investor does in the stock market over and over and over.

Inevitably, when the market comes down, there's anxiety, denial, fear, desperation, and panic. The word in my Figure 7.3 that should stand out in bold face is *capitulation*. Capitulation is when individuals get off of the roller coaster, which means selling all, most, or some of the stocks or stock mutual funds in their portfolio. When individuals make market timing calls, regarding when to get out of the market and get back in, they have empirically been proven to be *wrong approximately two out of three times.* This is the result of trying to time the market and thinking that you can see something that all these other tens of millions of other highly educated and well-capitalized investors can't see. The idea that you can see a stock that's mispriced that, again, these tens of millions of other highly intelligent investors cannot, is just pure folly.

The market generally goes down a little bit more after people capitulate and they're despondent and depressed—yet this is the point of maximum financial opportunity. This point would have been in February/March 2009, October/November 2002, and October/November 1974.

To get back to the roller coaster, we are now at the nadir of the cycle. This is when the people who have capitulated and have gotten off the roller coaster are beginning to say that they will get back in the market when it either "feels good" or "it's obvious that it's okay" to get back in. Unfortunately, as I previously stated, the market generally has to move up 20% to 25% before individuals start to "feel good" or it's "obvious." The problem is that by then they've missed that opportunity. Again, if the market moves up 24% from the time they sold to the time they went back in, 24% divided by three is 8%, or three years of an 8% average rate of return.

But the truth is that the nadir is paradoxically the point of *maximum financial opportunity.* This is the inverse of my earlier example, as there may be 10 sell orders for every one buy order. So if 10 people, for example, want to sell Microsoft stock at a specific moment when the market's open during the course of the day, and only one person wants to buy Microsoft, the simple laws of supply and demand are going to kick in. Fundamentally, the price is going to get driven down because there are significantly more sellers than buyers.

Yet the headline of the October/November 1974 issue of a famous national magazine stated that "stocks were dead," and the lead article was dedicated to a plethora of reasons why you would be stupid to buy stocks, and that bonds are where you should put your money. Based on what we know about the nadir of the roller coaster, if you were alive in 1974, that would have been the best point of entry into the stock market in your lifetime, yet the media was directing you to act in exactly the wrong manner.

Right at the point of maximum financial opportunity, the media tends to make its most dire and negative predictions. They offer precisely the opposite advice for investment success, whether it's on the radio, on TV, in magazines, in newsletters, in newspapers, or via the internet or social media.

It can be an emotionally traumatic experience for individuals paying attention to this "media noise" to try to be successful investors. I remind our clients and prospective clients repeatedly that our genetic, base survival instincts are completely useless when it comes to investing. They are simply incorrect most of the time. Historically we've survived for millennia relying on our heightened sensitivity to risk and risky situations. These instincts helped us survive in the wild, but are a disaster when they make us constantly *overreact* to perceived risk in the capital markets.

> *Investors should remember that excitement and expenses are their enemies. And if they insist on trying to time their participation in equities, they should try to be fearful when others are greedy and greedy when others are fearful.*
> —Warren Buffett, 2004 Annual Report of Berkshire Hathaway

In Figure 7.4, *Succumbing to "The Emotional Cycle of Investing"* we're looking at another one of the culprits in the below-average performance for individual investments. The bar on the far left-hand side shows us that over the recent 48 years, the total return of the stock market of the S&P 500 was 9.8%. The bars to the right-hand side of the Figure indicate the average return for individual investors who missed only the single best day in the market over these 48 years, then the five best days, and so forth, up to the 25 best single days in the market. So if you only miss the 25 best days, or less than one best day per year, you're now at an annualized rate of return of 4.5%. And although that may sound decent, if you look to the right of that, one month of risk-free US Treasury Bills, comparable to one-month CDs, yielded 2.8%. So you did less than 2% better per year than a one-month CD and the amount of risk you took on was *massively* disproportionate because you had money in the stock market.

FIGURE 7.4. **Succumbing to "The Emotional Cycle of Investing"**

Daily: January 1, 1970 – December 31, 2017

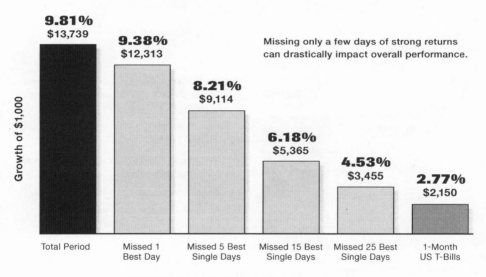

S&P 500® Index Annualized Compound Return

Sources: CRSP®, Bloomberg, S&P's Index Services Group and Ibbotson Associates, Chicago.

On one hand, it's very easy to internalize the challenges and the problems associated with timing the market when this is how much you can lose if you time the market wrong. On the other, this should give you a sense of the cost of getting "on and off" the investment roller coaster repeatedly in the first place. "Mr. Market," as we have seen, can be a cruel and unforgiving teacher.

Surprise! The returns reported by mutual funds aren't actually earned by mutual fund investors.
    —John C. Bogle, *The Little Book of Common Sense Investing*

People exaggerate their own skills. They are overoptimistic about their prospects and overconfident about their guesses...
    —Professor Richard Thaler, University of Chicago,
        in *Investment Titans* by Jonathan Burton

FIGURE 7.5. **The 1998–2017 Dalbar Study**

Annualized Investor Return *vs.* Benchmark (%)

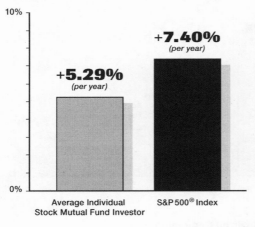

The Dalbar Study measures the results of the market annually with the average results that individual investors have obtained.

From 1998–2017, the S&P 500® Index annually returned 7.40%.

However, the average stock investor only made 5.29% annually. Why?

Because investors:

1. **Lack Investment Knowledge and**
2. **Lack Self-Control and Discipline.**

Source: Dalbar, Inc.

Dalbar, Inc., a financial services market research firm based in Boston, Massachusetts, has been a leading research organization in the area of investment behavioral science and investment emotions. Over this recent 20-year period, they have identified that the average individual investor utilizing active mutual funds and working without an advisor has achieved a rate of return of approximately *only two-thirds* of the stock market benchmark index, the S&P 500. This dramatic underperformance is a result of a number of emotional blunders and mistakes. First, average individual investors consistently arrive late for the party and leave early, as you saw previously with the emotional cycle of investing. In addition, they "purchase returns," which means that when they are making an investment decision, they take a look at past performance, and "chase performance" by buying mutual funds that have performed well over the last one, three, or five years. Subsequently, those funds generally underperform in the next one-, three-, or five-year period of time, causing individual investors to sell their fund rather than "buy and hold," which is the desired recipe for success. Additionally, the average mutual fund investor only holds their fund positions for an average of approximately three years. In contrast, I recommend holding your stock position, when exposed to the proper indexes and premiums in the market, for literally the rest of your life, and of course, typically, decreasing in percentage over time.

Figure 7.5 shows the data from a study done by Dalbar. If you look at the left-hand side of the Figure, you see that the average return of self-directed/Do-It-Yourself equity investors over a recent 20-year period, managing their own portfolios, was 5.29%. Compare this to the graph on the right, which shows that if you had simply bought and held the 500 largest companies in the United States during this recent 20 years, your rate of return would've been 7.4%. (Just as a reminder, the S&P 500 includes the largest, safest stocks, such as Apple, Microsoft, IBM, Coca-Cola, Pepsi, Walmart, McDonald's, Boeing Aircraft, Exxon, etc.)

Now, this large of a gap does not come from individual investors making just one or two mistakes. To create this kind of a gap over the recent 20 years, the average individual investor has had to make multiple if not dozens of mistakes. This gap is what I call the *"Emotions Gap."*

The reason that individuals had an average return of 5.29% while the market was 7.4% is because they have gotten on and off of the "investment roller coaster," with either all, most, or some of their stock mutual fund investments, at the wrong times.

My point is that "market timing" is a loser's game. Author Charles Ellis said as much in his book titled *Winning the Loser's Game*. Ellis was a fan of professional tennis, and he knew that conventional wisdom at the time stated that the best tennis players were superior athletes because they could hit a shot better, return better, etc.—and thus were generally able to outperform their competition. But when Ellis studied this phenomenon in more detail by charting and analyzing every shot, he found that the most common trait and the highest correlation to success was *making the fewest errors*.

THE PROBLEM WITH "MARKET TIMING": MAX AND ELEANOR

Max and Eleanor are retired college professors. They have a solid retirement plan, with complete coverage through Social Security, TIAA traditional fixed annuity income, and IRA accounts. Their Required Minimum Distribution on their IRA accounts actually provides the couple with 130% coverage of their expenses, so they have a monthly 30% cash flow surplus.

During our second meeting, the Plan Presentation, I examined Max and Eleanor's investing history more deeply. They had been getting in and out of the market every few years and had made decisions that cost them money three out of four times. Typically, individual investors who rely on their emotions and attempt to time the market when they make their buy and sell decisions have been found to be incorrect and make mistakes two out of three times. In this anecdotal example, Max and Eleanor had missed the mark 75% of the time.

When the market is at its lowest point, its nadir, you are not likely to buy based on market timing because the typical individual investor is not comfortable that it's going to go up at that point in the cycle. More likely, they will get into the market after it's up about 20% or more and they begin to have confidence that it's on solid footing and will continue to go up. But at that point, the typical individual investor has already missed a 20% return on their investment.

Likewise, timing the market will not tell you the best time to sell. Stocks will be going down, but until they've gone down a certain percentage, the typical investor will most likely hang onto them and then sell them too late, after they've lost a material amount of value.

I've seen this happen with prospective clients hundreds, if not thousands, of times. It's what I refer to as "coming to the party late and leaving the party early" and it's the bane of individual investors, but avoidable with a disciplined plan.

When I estimated the lost opportunity in Max and Eleanor's portfolios due to their knee-jerk market timing reactions, the number was so large that I was not looking forward to sharing that information with them. In fact, I dreaded it. However, I knew that they would likely continue this pattern of getting in and out of the market, and continue, in their retirement, to pilfer away a potentially massive amount of growth.

The bottom line is, though I speak in terms of stocks and bonds, risks and rewards, and dollars and cents, the true importance of a solid investment strategy is the effect the outcome has on a person's quality of life. The goal of the DiNuzzo Financial Wellness LifePlan™ is to guide you, provide advice, and protect you from Fear, Greed, and all other emotional enemies challenging your financial portfolios so that you ultimately can live your best and most meaningful life.

Success in the stock market requires the same approach. You want to "play defense first" and make the fewest errors—not initially attempt to outperform the market or other investors. Here's how I explain this approach to our clients: I tell them that throughout the investment and retirement planning process, we're going to walk on a long journey and encounter a couple dozen forks in the road along the way. At each juncture, we'll have a choice between the path on the left and the path on the right. We always want to choose the path that has the *highest probability* of success.

For example, if we come to the first option in investing and retirement income planning success, and the path on the right has an 85% probability of success and the left has a 70% probability, we're going to go through the path on the right. Success depends upon knowing the probabilities at this myriad of junctures and choosing the best probabilities at every fork in the road. And the two investment paths before you at the beginning, this question of active investing versus index investing represents a huge, and potentially life-altering, fork in the road.

> *In investing, what is comfortable is rarely profitable.*
> —Robert Arnott, Chairman, Research Affiliates

> *Our stay-put behavior reflects our view that the stock market serves as a relocation center at which money is moved from the active to the patient.*
> —Warren Buffett, 1991 Annual Report, Berkshire Hathaway

Let's you and I take a deeper look at the implications of the study I referenced in Figure 7.6, *The 1998–2017 Dalbar Study: Annualized Investor Return vs. Benchmark (%)*. For decades, most people had thought that if a mutual fund manager was achieving a rate of return of 8%, then everyone who owned that fund would also have an 8% return.

When queried as to how this could be happening, Dalbar has historically cited nine reasons. They said reason number one was extraordinarily significant. Reason number two was a distant second. And reasons number three through nine were even further behind. So it really comes down to number one: individual investors *lack investment knowledge*. Number two, individual investors *lack self-control and discipline*. Now, these are very significant. If you lack specific knowledge in anything, you're going to have an extraordinarily difficult time being successful at it. And it certainly follows that you're also going to have an extraordinarily challenging time maintaining your discipline and your self-control if you don't possess the knowledge.

FIGURE 7.6. The 1998–2017 Dalbar Study

Annualized Investor Return *vs.* Benchmark (%)

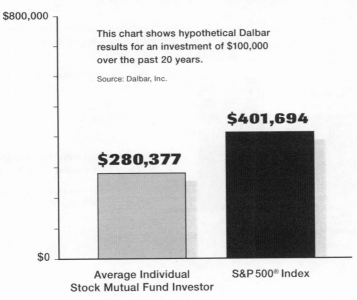

This chart shows hypothetical Dalbar results for an investment of $100,000 over the past 20 years.

Source: Dalbar, Inc.

$800,000

$0

$280,377

$401,694

Average Individual
Stock Mutual Fund Investor

S&P 500® Index

Source: Dalbar, Inc.

I maintain this mantra: knowledge equals comfort, and comfort builds confidence. If you don't have confidence in what you're doing, you're not going to be able to maintain your self-control and discipline. Ergo, you see the numbers in the Figure 7.6: the $100,000 the average individual "managed" grew to $280,377 over 20 years, while $100,000 in the s&p 500 index grew to $401,694.

For the distinct majority of investors in the market investing for success and preparing for retirement, this would be catastrophic for retirement income planning. You cannot afford to underperform this dramatically from what the market has to offer.

The four most dangerous words in investing are, "it's different this time."
—Sir John Templeton, *Money*, 2002

FIGURE 7.7. The 1998–2017 Dalbar Study

Annualized Investor Return *vs*. Benchmark (% and $)

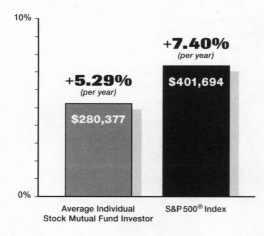

The Dalbar Study measures the results of the market annually with the average results that individual investors have obtained.

From 1998–2017, the S&P 500® Index annually returned 7.40%.

However, the average stock investor only made 5.29% annually. Why?

Because investors:

1. **Lack Investment Knowledge and**
2. **Lack Self-Control and Discipline.**

This chart shows hypothetical Dalbar results for an investment of $100,000 over the past 20 years.

Source: Dalbar, Inc.

My next image, Figure 7.7 *The 1998–2017 Dalbar Study: Annualized Investor Return vs. Benchmark (% and $)* presents both the percentage and dollar returns for the average individual stock mutual fund investor over a recent 20-year period. The aggregate analysis is a supplemental eye-opener. Again, I recommend pausing to contemplate the implications of these results on your life, family, household, and personal finances. As we move through the multiple steps throughout the following chapters, all my recommendations and advice are focused on helping you succeed—and avoiding the average individual investor's abysmal results.

Fund investors are confident that they can easily select superior fund managers. They are wrong.
   —John C. Bogle, *The Little Book of Common Sense Investing*

FIGURE 7.8. The "Emotions Return Gap"

The Annualized and Aggregate Underperformance of "Do-It-Yourselfers"

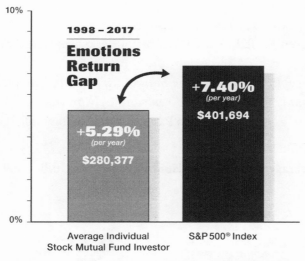

Source: Dalbar, Inc.

Figure 7.8, *The "Emotions Return Gap"* sums up very succinctly my teaching points regarding the prior three Dalbar images and "identifies" the culprit: individual investors' *emotions*. This illustrates the aggregated effects of "Do-It-Yourselfers" mistakes and errors. Emotions have cost individual investors an incomprehensible amount of money and quality of life. The contrast is startling, attention-grabbing, and saddening. This image refocuses attention on Dalbar's #1 reason regarding underperformance by individual investors: lack of investment knowledge. Additionally, the government financial regulatory body FINRA produces national research assessing individual investor education levels approximately every five to ten years. Consistently, their research's conclusion is an approximate "grade" of C or lower for the average individual. Knowing your enemy is well over half of the battle, and I will implement this newfound knowledge and use it to your advantage to drive your investment portfolio's success.

Our favorite holding period is forever.
—Warren Buffett, letter to Berkshire Hathaway shareholders, 1988

Inactivity strikes us as intelligent behavior.
—Warren Buffett, Annual Report of Berkshire Hathaway, 1996

Let other people overreact to the market…if you can stay cool while those around you are panicking. You can surely prevail.
—James Pardoe, author, *How Buffett Does It*

FIGURE 7.9. **Average Mutual Fund Holding Period for Individual Investors**

1998 – 2017

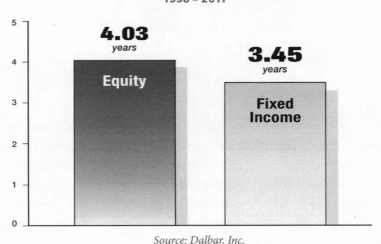

Source: Dalbar, Inc.

A residual observation regarding the inadequacy of individual investors' investment behavior is the sub-standard amount of time they keep and possess their holdings, once purchased. The individual investor holds onto their typical stock or bond mutual fund for only approximately three to four years.

By contrast, as you will observe throughout my book, you want to hold onto your positions (e.g., US Large company stock index, US Small company stock index, International Large Value stock index, etc.) literally for decades. Albeit, on average, you will typically lower your overall percentage exposure to stocks over time.

Individual investors consistently *overreact* to the media noise, news, and market movements. Short-term market movements and returns are classic "noise" and consistently "surprising" while long-term movements and returns (for example, over 20 years) *never are*. For four decades, my mantra at our practice has been one of the market metaphorically going through the four seasons and associated weather patterns (spring, summer, fall, and winter) throughout every business cycle in the United States' history. Considering that the average business cycle from start to finish is approximately five years, the most alarming realization is that at no point in time does the average individual investor with their three- to four-year mutual fund holding period remain invested for long enough periods to realize the return benefits of the financial markets they are trying to access.

Consistent historic appeals by many firms, such as mine, along with industry giants such as Jack Bogle, Warren Buffett, and Nobel Laureate Eugene Fama, have unfortunately had little effect on the masses. As a result of jumping on and off of the "emotional cycle of investing roller coaster" with all, most, or some of their investments (mostly due to media noise and a lack of investment education), the average individual investor is abandoning their investments at the wrong time and not holding them long enough to succeed.

If I have noticed anything over these 60 years on Wall Street, it is that people do not succeed in forecasting what's going to happen to the stock market.

—Benjamin Graham, legendary American
investor, scholar, teacher, and author

FIGURE 7.10. **Are Your Emotions Helpful in Predicting the Past? (Part 1)**

25 Years Ending December 31, 2012

		Rank	Total Return
AAPL	Apple, Inc.	?	?
XOM	Exxon Mobil	?	?
HOG	Harley-Davidson	?	?
JKHY	Jack Henry & Assoc.	?	?
MCD	McDonald's Corporation	?	?
NEM	Newmont Mining Corp.	?	?
ROST	Ross Stores, Inc.	?	?

Let's assume you possess one of those cheesy Hollywood time machines you see in the movies or on TV. Knowing what you know now about the economy and which companies have done well, if you could go back in time and invest in those companies, which would you invest in? Which of the companies in Figure 7.10 do you think did the best over this recent 25-year period?

The difference between luck and skill is seldom apparent at first glance.
—Peter L. Bernstein, *Capital Ideas: The
Improbable Origins of Modern Wall Street*

FIGURE 7.11. **Are Your Emotions Helpful in Predicting the Past? (Part 2)**

25 Years Ending December 31, 2012

		Rank	Total Return
AAPL	**Apple, Inc.**	**4**	**5,345%**
XOM	**Exxon Mobil**	**6**	**1,851%**
HOG	**Harley-Davidson**	**3**	**14,987%**
JKHY	**Jack Henry & Assoc.**	**1**	**34,989%**
MCD	**McDonald's Corporation**	**5**	**2,263%**
NEM	**Newmont Mining Corp.**	**7**	**112%**
ROST	**Ross Stores, Inc.**	**2**	**24,032%**

Source: BasisPro™.

If you are like most people, you may have thought Apple would have done the best over this period of time: it's one of the largest stocks in the stock market and it's grown phenomenally. But out of these seven companies I have listed here, Apple ranks number four over this period of time. It's not even in the top three. Do you know who is in the top three? Harley-Davidson. I've been in hundreds and hundreds of consultations, and I can't tell you how many times I've heard, "I didn't buy Apple when I should have bought Apple," or "I bought Apple and I sold it." Apple, Apple, Apple—that's all investors historically have complained about. I've never heard an individual say, "Wow, I should have bought Harley-Davidson, or Ross Stores, or Jack Henry!" During this particular 25-year period, most of us only heard that Apple had gone up over 5,000%. Harley-Davidson had gone up close to 15,000%.

This helps to illustrate how detrimental it can be to subjectively make investment decisions relying on your feelings and emotions. The better example is the one that ranked number two, at the bottom of the page: Ross Stores. When I first saw this a few years ago, I hadn't even noticed they were in business, and lo and behold, Ross is number two, doing well over four times as well as Apple. And who would have thought that a discount clothing store would have blown away the performance of Apple? Of course, Jack Henry, a software manufacturer for community banks, is far and away number one. Finally, look at number seven. Gold. Some people may have thought that a gold mining company would have done better than Apple over this 25-year period. But the real point here is this: even if you could go back in time and pick stocks based on what you know now, generally your picks would still be poor choices.

FROM ROULETTE TO CHESS:
ANALYZING THE LUCK/SKILL CONTINUUM

It turns out for all practical purposes there is no such thing as stock picking skill. It's human nature to find patterns where there are none and to find skill where luck is a more likely explanation (particularly if you're the lucky [mutual fund] manager). Mutual fund manager performance does not persist and the return of stock picking is zero. We are looking at the proverbial bunch of chimpanzees throwing darts at the stock page. Their "success" or "failure" is a purely random affair.
—Dr. William Bernstein, *The Intelligent Asset Allocator*

Wall Street's favorite scam is pretending luck is skill.
—Ron Ross, PhD, economist, *The Unbeatable Market*

Contrary to their oft-articulated goal of outperforming the market averages, investment managers are not beating the market; the market is beating them.
—Charles D. Ellis, author of *Winning the Loser's Game*, as quoted in *The Financial Analyst's Journal*

We talk about the ability of experts to predict the future, whether the future is geopolitical or financial. And if you look at, let's say, stock picking advice specifically, you find that the experts, the people we most revere, the people that we pay the most, are generally about as good as a monkey with a dart board.

—*Freakonomics* authors Stephen Dubner and Steven Levitt

FIGURE 7.12. **Who Is the Better Stock Picker?**

Figure 7.12 hopefully makes the point. No one has a crystal ball, tomorrow's newspaper, a vision of the future, or a unique advantage over others. The open capital markets are very efficient, especially over time. The best approximation of any company's stock value is the price assigned to it by the millions of buyers and sellers in the open marketplace. I would argue that a monkey throwing a dart at the *Wall Street Journal's* stock prices has an equal chance of matching or beating a "professional stock picker" over an extended period of time.

Odds are you don't know what the odds are.
> —Gary Belsky and Thomas Gilovich, *Why*
> *Smart People Make Big Money Mistakes*

If there's 10,000 people looking at the stocks and trying to pick win-
ners, one in 10,000 is going to score, by chance alone, a great coup, and
that's all that's going on. It's a game, it's a chance operation, and people
think they are doing something purposeful…but they're really not.
> —Merton Miller, Nobel Laureate and Professor
> of Economics, University of Chicago, from the
> PBS Nova special, *The Trillion Dollar Bet*

Very little evidence [was found] that any individual [mutual] fund
was able to do significantly better than that which we expected from
mere random chance.
> —Michael Jensen, "The Performance of [115 US Equity] Mutual
> Funds in the Period 1945–1964," *Journal of Finance*, May 1968

FIGURE 7.13. **From Roulette to Chess**

Analyzing the Luck/Skill Continuum

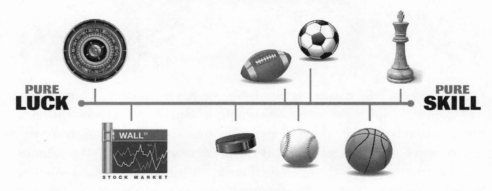

Source: Michael Mauboussin: From Roulette to Chess: A Look at the Luck/Skill Continuum.

As they say, a picture is worth a thousand words. On the left of Figure 7.13, *From Roulette to Chess: Analyzing the Luck/Skill Continuum*, based on Michael Mauboussin's book *The Success Equation: Untangling Skill and Luck in Business, Sports, and Investing*, pure luck is represented by the Las Vegas-style roulette wheel. On the right, pure skill is represented by the chess piece. Between pure luck and pure skill, there are various sports represented, indicating how much skill is involved: basketball is followed by soccer, then baseball, then football, and finally hockey. But the entire prize of this image is how close Wall Street is located to pure luck. So often when people try to "outsmart" Wall Street, they're simply "seeing patterns" where none exist. All the information you need has been baked into the price by the input of tens of millions of highly educated investors with tremendous resources. If you do outperform the market, *the primary reason is luck*. When that luck evaporates at some point in time (and it will), you'll end up underperforming.

> *Hint: Money flows into most funds after good performance and goes out when bad performance follows.*
> —John C. Bogle, *The Little Book of Common Sense Investing*

> *Buying funds based purely on their past performance is one of the stupidest things an investor can do.*
> —Jason Zweig, finance columnist for the *Wall Street Journal*

DO WINNERS REPEAT?

My graphic shown in Figure 7.14, *Do Winners Repeat?* clearly illustrates the phenomena that I have seen repeated consistently over the past four decades... top performing funds rarely repeat their performance. The chart shows on the left-hand side all the funds that were in the top 25% during the five-year period from 2002–2006 (a total of 377 funds). The question is, how many of those funds repeated their performance over the next five-year period from 2007–2011? As the right-hand side of the chart shows—only 8%! Only 8% of the funds got back-to-back "A's" on their report cards over the 10-year period. Only 10% of the original funds show up in the second quartile—I will give them a "B" for at least doing better than average during the second 5-year period. That leaves over 80% of the original funds in the bottom 50% during the second 5-year period, and 15% not surviving at all! What stock mutual funds do individuals purchase? Again, if you're thinking about buying a stock mutual fund right now, you're looking back at the last one, three, or five years. Obviously, you're not going to purchase something that's been languishing in the bottom 25% in terms of performance.

FIGURE 7.14. **Do Winners Repeat?**

As of December 2011

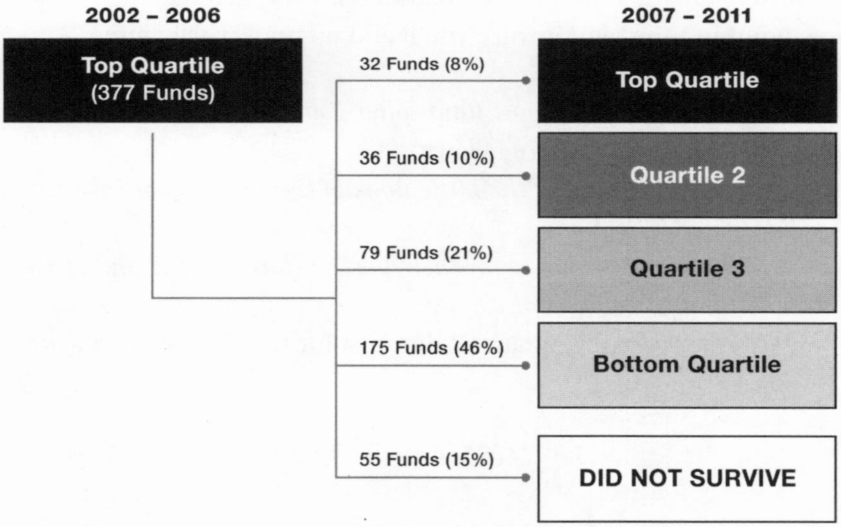

2002 – 2006		2007 – 2011
Top Quartile (377 Funds)	32 Funds (8%)	**Top Quartile**
	36 Funds (10%)	**Quartile 2**
	79 Funds (21%)	**Quartile 3**
	175 Funds (46%)	**Bottom Quartile**
	55 Funds (15%)	**DID NOT SURVIVE**

Source: Morningstar, Inc.

Additionally, you're not going to buy something that got a "B" on their report card. You're going to go and pick the top funds, the "A" funds that have the best performance, and generally people choose the best performance over the most recent five-year period of time.

My point is that people tend to invest *exactly the opposite* way they should invest. They're buying these funds when they're in spring or in summer— when they're growing strong, or in full bloom. Based on my investment "roller coaster" you saw earlier, after they buy these funds, they go into remission. They go into fall and then winter, or directly into winter.

This all goes back to my fundamental question: Do you have an investment philosophy? Do you have a strategy to implement that philosophy? Do you have an implementation plan for your strategy? Have you structured yourself to relax and enjoy success through discipline? You need to understand that all of your positions are going to go through spring, summer, fall, and winter, and you've got to recognize that from the start. Nothing is immune from this cycle. The final question is, do you have the discipline and the self-control that are necessary for success?

I have an investment philosophy. I have a strategy based upon my philosophy. I have a plan of implementation. I have discipline based on these three elements. I believe in a regression to the "mean," and I understand the cycles of domestic investments over the last 90+ years. Regression to the mean refers to the reality of the bell curve, or normal distribution. If you had a rubber band, the further you pull it, the further it's going to snap back. If something averages 10% a year, that's the mean. Regression to the mean simply describes a "magnetic pull" toward the average, and if you have several bad years in a row, with a return of 0%, 0%, and 0%, then that suggests eventually we're going to have the equivalent of 20%, 20%, and 20% returns. Even if they are going through fall or winter, we know spring and summer are coming. We're not investing willy-nilly. We're basing this on a 90+ year capital market track record. Why would you want to play that loser's game? And again, it's not that individuals elect to do this ahead of time. They listen to the media's noise, which is always playing toward *greed* and *fear*, and their emotions and lack of education get the better of them.

In addition to this, the supermajority of individuals are receiving advice from brokers and advisors who are under what amounts to a "suitability" standard as opposed to a "Fiduciary" standard. If an advisor is bound by what is akin to a suitability standard, then an investment just has to be "suitable." This requirement is significantly lower than a Fiduciary Standard. As I explained in the Introduction, our firm, since 1989, has been licensed and operated under a Fiduciary Standard and takes it very seriously. Simply put, we are legally and morally bound to tell you what we would do if we were in your shoes. Just from an intuitive perspective, why would you want to seek advice that is non-Fiduciary in nature and inbred with an inherent conflict of interest?

INVESTMENT PORNOGRAPHY

Market timing is a wicked idea. Don't try it—ever.
        —Charles D. Ellis, *Winning the Loser's Game*

It's not that stock prices are capricious. It's that the news is capricious.
        —Burton G. Malkiel, *A Random Walk Down Wall Street*

This message (that attempting to beat the market is futile) can never be sold on Wall Street because it is in effect telling stock analysts to drop dead.
        —Paul Samuelson, PhD, Nobel Laureate in Economic Sciences

Once in the dear dead days beyond recall, an out-of-town visitor was being shown the wonders of the New York financial district. When the party arrived at the Battery, one of his guides indicated some handsome ships arrived at anchor. He said, "Look, those are the bankers' and brokers' yachts." "Where are the customers' yachts?" asked the naïve visitor.
        —Fred Schwed Jr., *Where Are the Customers' Yachts?*, 1940

Starting in the 1970s, individuals began taking a more proactive role in managing their investments. The media saw an opportunity, and began to dispense all sorts of "advice" about investments, and of course, most of it unhelpful. To this day, the media continues to play on individuals' emotions to increase viewers and readers, with no consideration for investment success. Their only consideration is their own bottom line. And as I mentioned in the Introduction, as most of you are now taking on the responsibility of becoming your own FCIO, this noise factor has only increased.

The financial media's fundamental business model is *diametrically* opposed to the success of *you*, the individual investor. Every media outlet wants to get you hooked on their brand of advice. They know that the way to get you hooked is not by providing reliable information you can digest, learn from, and go on your way. Rather, they get you hooked by supporting a perspective that will require you to keep coming back for more and more "information," especially information (like stock prices) that change by the nanosecond. The goal is addiction, not sound advice. The way to do that is to excite *emotions* and create urgency—manipulating emotions is the most effective way to get people addicted to media.

In particular, the two emotions the media aim to manipulate are *fear* and *greed*. Reams of "urgent" financial advice comes out about how to change your investment strategy as a result of these "ever evolving" events. For anyone looking to the mass media for guidance, thinking it will help them or improve their investment strategies, it is a fool's errand. Beware of the emotional pull of "investment pornography."

Figure 7.15, *The Lure of Market Timing* shows how the investment world can play on an investor's greed. The chart shows the growth of $1,000 over a 70-year period across three Asset Classes and two-timing strategies. A "perfect" timing strategy would have yielded over $7 billion. (This assumes a hypothetical rebalancing scenario in which you knew in advance at the beginning of each calendar year which Asset Class was going to perform the best that year.) By contrast, a "perfectly awful" timing strategy would have produced a mere $66. But the lure of the $7 billion remains, and the idea of "missing out" plays upon investors' greed. Despite the fact that no one has a crystal ball, or tomorrow's news in advance, investors continue to put their faith in market timing strategies and consistently make bad investment decisions.

FIGURE 7.15. **The Lure of Market Timing: The Growth of $1000**

70 Year Period Ending December 31, 2010

One-Month Treasury Bills:	$16,850
S&P 500® Index:	$1,645,511
CRSP 9-10 Index:	$12,797,514
Perfectly Timed Strategy:	$7,327,825,197
Perfectly Awful Timed Strategy:	$66

Sources: S&P 500®, CRSP®, Morningstar, Inc.®

FIGURE 7.16. **Some Investment Pornography**

BUSINESSWEEK, AUGUST 13, 1979

The Death of Equities

MONEY, MAY 1996

Make Money Even if the Market Falls

In Figure 7.16, *Some Investment Pornography*, emotionally charged media titles such as these can dislodge the base of the typical individual investor and contribute to their long-term, subpar investment performance.

FIGURE 7.17. **Found: The Next Microsoft**

WORTH, JUNE 1996

Found: The Next Microsoft

On the June 1996 cover of *Worth* magazine was another emotionally charged title: "Found: The Next Microsoft." Titles like these lead individual investors to believe they can consistently beat the market by finding investment "gems" that they individually may somehow be able to access. By the way, the little-known company mentioned in this article did not come anywhere close to becoming the next Microsoft, as you may have already guessed.

The general systems of money management [today] require people to pretend to do something they can't do and like something they don't. [It's] a funny business because on a net basis, the whole investment management business together gives no value added to all buyers combined. That's the way it has to work. Mutual funds charge two percent per year and then brokers switch people between funds, costing another three to four percentage points. The poor guy in the general public is getting a terrible product from the professionals. I think it's disgusting. It's much better to be part of a system that delivers value to the people who buy the product.

—John C. Bogle, *The Little Book of Common Sense Investing*

FIGURE 7.18. **Sell Stock Now!**

MONEY, AUGUST 1997

Don't Just Sit There...Sell Stock Now!

On another *Money* magazine cover article in August of 1997 was a bold headline in red with an exclamation point, imploring you to "Sell Stock Now!" When you sit back and observe the financial "noise" we are assaulted with on a regular basis, it is no wonder that we witness the dramatic underperformance of the average individual investor. This is yet another example of such noise. If you would have sold stock at this time, you would have missed the balance of a tremendous bull market from the latter half of 1997 through the end of 1999 and into the year 2000.

FIGURE 7.19. **Everyone's Getting Rich!**

MONEY, MAY 1999

Tech Stocks: Everyone's Getting Rich!

Here, shown in Figure 7.19, was another emotionally charged title on a very popular national investment magazine. This emotional pull may have led individual investors to invest in tech stocks in mid-1999, and they probably got caught up in the "tech wreck," which occurred starting in March of 2000, just months after this magazine was on the newsstands nationwide. Basically, every parental adage that you have heard over your lifetime would apply to investing in the stock market: "there is no free lunch," "if it sounds too good to be true, it probably is," and many others. If there is a proposed "steal" investment available and it is on the cover on a national magazine, common sense should indicate that it is probably not a "steal" after other millions of investors have already read or heard about it. Or, if it was a "steal" the original finder of this information would not be sharing it with other investors for just a few bucks.

The only value of stock forecasters is to make fortune-tellers look good.
—Warren Buffett, 1992 Annual Report of Berkshire Hathaway

In financial publications, there is no shortage of stock pickers with their pick of the day, week, month, or year, and the *Wall Street Journal* is a good example. Professional stock pickers were asked to pick their 10 best and 10 worst investments for 2005. The "10 best" approximate annual return was 13% for the year, while the "10 worst" average return for the year was 19%. Financial pundits do not get attention by making small, safe predictions, but rather effusive and gregarious predictions. The problem is that individual investors tend to get caught up in the emotions of the predictions, and don't bother to take a look at that individual or firm's track record for said historical predictions. In order to succeed you must educate yourself properly and learn to look behind the veneer of financial hubris.

FIGURE 7.20. **Which Is True?**

LOS ANGELES TIMES, JUNE 18, 2008

UCLA Still Foresees No Recession

LOS ANGELES TIMES, JUNE 25, 2008

Chapman Sees US in Recession

Again, there are reliable publications that have no premeditated attempt of misleading, but nonetheless, the results of their information can be confusing to say the least. Figure 7.20 shows two separate articles in the *Los Angeles Times* in June 2008, approximately one week apart, obviously sent conflicting messages. They quoted two observations from two separate universities' economists with one stating that they foresaw no recession on the horizon, and the other stating that they saw the US already in a recession.

These types of conflicting messages create "paralysis from analysis" for individual investors.

FIGURE 7.21. **More Confusion**

LOS ANGELES TIMES, OCTOBER 26, 1999

Inflation Jitters Send Bond Yields Up Again

LOS ANGELES TIMES, OCTOBER 29, 1999

Stocks Soar, Rates Fall on Low Inflation Data

Figure 7.21 shows yet another conflict regarding investment information just days apart in 1999, again in the *Los Angeles Times* business section. One article regarding the economy states that inflation "jitters" caused bond yields to rise. Just days later, the other article states that stocks were "soaring" due to the fact that no rising inflation was being observed, the opposite of what the previous article claimed.

> *Having been an idealistic young sales-oriented fellow, I became a licensed stockbroker for one of Wall Street's most prestigious firms in the late 60s. I learned very quickly that to succeed I had to "sell my soul," and to be more than moderately successful, I had to follow the boss's program and to sell exactly what the boss wants sold—it was "the hell with the clients"…kudos for having the intestinal fortitude at* Portfolio *[magazine] to speak out about the "sacred cows" that graze along Wall Street!*
> —Peter Magurean III, "The Evolution of an Investor,"
> Conde Nast Portfolio.com reader comments, 2007

FIGURE 7.22. **Stocks Stink**

PIMCO, SEPTEMBER 2002

Stocks Stink and Will Continue to Do So Until They're Priced Appropriately

Not all market predictions are "off the wall" or promulgated by charlatans. The famous quote in Figure 7.22, *Stocks Stink* is from the article titled "Dow 5,000" by Mr. Bill Gross, one of the top bond managers from one of the largest bond mutual funds management companies. Mr. Gross felt compelled to opine that the stock market "stunk" and would continue to do so until stocks were, in his mind, priced appropriately. In September 2002, when the Dow Jones Industrial Average was at 7,591, Mr. Gross predicted that the Dow was headed down to 5000. The market cycle bottomed out two weeks later at 7,286. So not only did the market only go down a few hundred more points from when he wrote the article, it also occurred within a couple of weeks. Currently, as I am writing this book, the Dow Jones Industrial Average ("Dow") is over 26,000! Approximately only 17 years after Mr. Gross wrote this article, the market is over five times higher in value than his prediction. Individual investors need to be continually on their guard against these "siren songs."

> *The American economy is going to do fine. But it won't do fine every year and every week and every month. I mean, if you don't believe that, forget about buying stocks anyway...It's a positive-sum game, long term. And the only way an investor can get killed is by high fees or by trying to outsmart the market.*
>
> —Warren Buffett, *Fortune* magazine, "What Warren Thinks…" April 14, 2008

FIGURE 7.23. **Market Is Up—But No Reason to Buy Stocks**

WALL STREET JOURNAL, OCTOBER 10, 2002

Terrorism…War…Falling Earnings Estimates: Right Now There Doesn't Seem to be Any Reason to Buy Stocks

Dow Jones Industrial Average Price Change

Thursday, October 10, 2002	▲ +247.68
Friday, October 11, 2002	▲ +316.34
Monday, October 14, 2002	▲ +27.11
Tuesday, October 15, 2002	▲ +378.28

In Figure 7.23, you see an investment analyst quoted in a *Wall Street Journal* article ("Bears Claw Markets Yet Again, As Dow Industrials Fall Nearly 3%,") as saying, "Right now, there doesn't seem to be any reason to buy stocks." However, the Dow Jones Industrial price average change on that day was up over 247 points, followed by over 316 points on Friday, a small increase on Monday, and a very dramatic increase the following Tuesday of 378 points. As you will also see below, according to the *Wall Street Journal* this four-day gain was the best gain over four days since 1933 and "confounded investors." Don't be among the confounded!

FIGURE 7.24. **Best Four-Day Gain Since 1933**

WALL STREET JOURNAL, OCTOBER 15, 2002

Best Four-Day Gain Since 1933, Confounding Investors

In a subsequent *Wall Street Journal* article, "Stocks' Four-Day Gain: 969 Points," from October 15, 2002, you see that the market has done the exact opposite of the previous consensus prediction that the market would continue to decline. The pulled quote from this article states its essence: "Best four-day gain since 1933, confounding investors." The stock market had one of its most massive rallies in history, gaining 969 points in the Dow Jones Industrial Average over just four short trading days. Keep repeating my mantra: no one has a crystal ball or tomorrow's newspaper concerning the stock market, and attempting to outsmart the market is truly "a loser's game."

FIGURE 7.25. The So-Called "Lost Decade"

WALL STREET JOURNAL, MARCH 26, 2008

Stocks Tarnished by "Lost Decade": US Shares in Longest Funk Since 1970s; Credit Crunch Could Prolong Weakness

The first ten years of the 2000s have been commonly referred to as "the lost decade" by the financial media. And as you will see on the next couple of Figures, the observations have been dour to say the least. Sometimes these financial observations make it seem as though the individual investor had no chance during this "lost decade." But as you will see, there were exceptional outcomes which were attainable through building an All-Index, balanced Asset Allocation, systematically rebalanced, globally diversified, low fee, low expense, "buy and hold" portfolio.

Figure 7.26 illustrates draconian headlines across major economic print media over and during the first decade of this century from January 1, 2000 through December 31, 2009. There were negative articles regarding the two wars we incurred, two periods of high unemployment, two recessions, a significant housing crisis, and the largest credit market meltdown since the Great Depression. Again, with this type of consistent negative press you would think that there were no viable options available to the average individual investor. In fact, I would agree that if you were attempting to "outsmart" the stock market during this period of time, you were faced with an exceptional challenge—and the super-majority of active stock managers did underperform the market significantly.

FIGURE 7.26. **Headlines from the "Lost Decade."**

January 1, 2000 – December 31, 2009

2 WARS

"US and Britain Strike Afghanistan"
The New York Times, October 8, 2001

"Bush Orders Start of War on Iraq"
The New York Times, March 3, 2003

2 RECESSIONS

"Will There Be a Double Dip"
The Economist, August 8, 2002

"How Today's Global Recession Tracks the Great Depression"
Financial Times, June 17, 2009

2 PERIODS OF HIGH UNEMPLOYMENT

"Welcome to the Amazing Jobless Recovery"
Bloomberg Businessweek, July 28, 2003

"US Unemployment Rate Hits 10.2%, Highest in 26 Years"
The New York Times, November 6, 2009

CREDIT MARKET MELTDOWN

"Crisis on Wall Street as Lehman Totters, Merrill is Sold, AIG Seeks to Raise Cash"
Wall Street Journal, September 14, 2008

"Corporate Bond Defaults Hit Record"
Financial Times, August 20, 2009

HOUSING CRISIS

"US Home Prices Continue Record Slide"
Los Angeles Times, February 25, 2009

"2009 Foreclosures Hit Record High"
Wall Street Journal: Market Watch, January 14, 2010

Sources: The New York Times, Financial Times, Los Angeles Times, Wall Street Journal.

You will almost never find a fund manager who can repeatedly beat the market. It is better to invest in an indexed fund that promises a market return but with significantly lower fees.

—"The Blame Game," The Economist, July 3, 2003, from John
C. Bogle, *The Little Book on Common Sense Investing*, 2007

FIGURE 7.27. Hypothetical Mix: Indexed Portfolio

An Illustration

FIXED INCOME		50.0%
1.	BofA Merrill Lynch 1-Year Treasury Note Index	12.5%
2.	Citigroup World Government/Bond Index (1-5 Years, hedged)	12.5%
3.	Citigroup World Government/Bond Index (1-3 Years, hedged)	12.5%
4.	Barclays Capital Treasury Bond Index (1-5 Years)	12.5%

US EQUITIES		35.0%
5.	S&P 500 Index	10.0%
6.	Russell 1000 Value Index	10.0%
7.	Russell 2000 Index	5.0%
8.	Russell 2000 Value Index	5.0%
9.	Dow Jones US Select REIT Index	5.0%

INTERNATIONAL EQUITIES		15.0%
10.	MSCI World ex USA Value Index	5.0%
11.	MSCI World ex USA Small Cap Index (price only)	2.5%
12.	MSCI World ex USA Small Cap Value Index	2.5%
13.	MSCI Emerging Markets Index (gross dividend)	1.5%
14.	MSCI Emerging Markets Value IMI Index	1.5%
15.	MSCI Emerging Markets Small Cap Index	2.0%

Source: S&P 500®,
Russell®, Dow Jones®, MSCI®

Sources: S&P 500®, Russell®, Dow Jones®, MSCI®.

What I have been discussing throughout my book are institutional-based, time-honored investment strategies to build "all-weather" portfolios. In Figure 7.27, you see an All-Index portfolio with 50% equity/stock positions and 50% fixed income/bond positions. This is a basic illustration of a 50/50 portfolio, and on the next Figure, Figure 7.28, representing the hypothetical performance of this All-Indexed portfolio over this "lost decade." The indexes I am using are for illustrative purposes only. I am just making a basic observation of the potential "different experience" that was available over the first decade of this century. The 50/50 portfolio is very realistic in that currently my firm's average portfolio across the over $760 million as of November 30, 2019 that we manage is approximately 60% stocks and 40% bonds.

When asked what he considered man's greatest discovery, Albert Einstein replied without hesitation: "Compound interest."
— Charles Ellis, *Investment Policy*

FIGURE 7.28. **A Different Experience**

January 2000 – December 2009

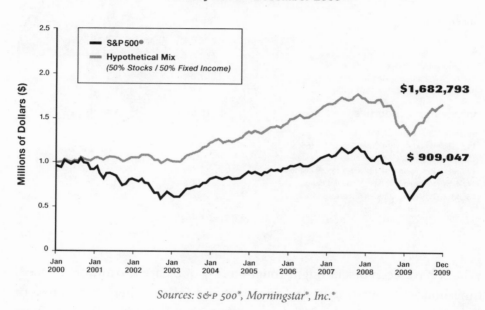

Sources: *S&P 500°, Morningstar°, Inc.°*

Figure 7.28 is the "different experience," which was available with a "balanced" stock and bond index portfolio, which was available for the first decade from January 1, 2000, through December 31, 2009. The "lost decade" as it was often referred to by the financial press. The S&P 500 starting value of $1M on January the 1st of 2000 resulted in an ending value at the decade end of slightly more than $909,000. Again, this is and has been commonly referred to as the seminal definition relating to the "lost decade" due to a massive percentage of individual investors being overweighted *vis-à-vis* the S&P 500 in the early 2000s. Most individuals are somewhat surprised at how well a 50/50 portfolio with 50% stocks and 50% bonds in an All-Indexed portfolio, globally diversified, performed during the same 10-year period of time. The 50/50 hypothetical illustration which we are looking at started with a hypothetical value of $1M, and grew during the same period to an ending value of more than $1.6M. What we are observing in my illustration are multiple benefits from very powerful investment research and strategies.

THE KEY TO EMOTIONS MANAGEMENT: KNOW YOUR VALUES

When your values are clear to you, making decisions becomes easier.
—Roy Disney, Co-Founder of Walt Disney Corporation

If you have the proper values and principles, take the time to learn from history, and gain a full understanding of the terrain before you, then your decisions won't be difficult. Oftentimes prospective clients come into one of our offices because we've been recommended by their sibling, parent, or friend, and that's good enough for them. They just want us to take over and do it for them. But even if our clients don't want to hear all this detail, we still insist on meeting with them and educating them regarding all of the principles in my book and working through our DiNuzzo Financial Wellness LifePlan™ with them. They have to understand why we're doing what we're doing, because that will help them control their emotions later, when their emotional roller coaster is taking a dive and all of a sudden they want to get off. It's much easier to follow the plan if you proactively know why you're doing what you're doing and stay committed to your core philosophy, beliefs, and strategy.

Decide to develop your values and principles based on the objective data and what's most important in the long term. What is your value system? Will you decide to follow it based on the strongest emotion in the moment, or do you value something greater that enables you to stay in control and keep your course steady?

If you develop your principles and values based on the objective data and on what's most important in the long term, you'll avoid falling off of the emotional roller coaster, because you know that in reality, you aren't on a roller coaster. You're on solid ground. And you don't need to obsessively revisit your plan and convince yourself of its merit over and over again. You simply follow it, and remain steady. In the process, you've just removed the lion's share of the anxiety that tends to characterize Financial Life Management, investing, and retirement plan challenges today.

In my opinion, there's no better plan than the one that has a successful 90+ year track record and is built upon the foundation of Nobel Prize-winning empirical research, as opposed to a plan with at best a 10-year track record that routinely underperforms the market in the long term.

The key to investing success—and particularly long-term and retirement investing success—is emotions management. Understand that your own natural Investor DNA, the Emotional Cycle of Investing, and the media's ubiquitous "Investment Pornography" will lead you straight toward financial disaster. Instead, choose now to build a solid investment plan based on "controlling what you can control" and the extraordinarily long-term available data and empirical research, not your emotions.

CONCLUSION

Deep emotions ignited over four decades ago by the disgusting and upsetting investment "advice" my now-deceased father was receiving from the financial industry has led us here today.

What began as a passion for helping immediate family and friends improve their personal finances by winding my way through the halls of academia, empirical research, and objectivity will hopefully have helped you and touched your life in a positive way. I have been successful by building my Wealth Management practice on this fundamental tenet and mantra: seek out the best and brightest financial minds, demand nothing less than pure objectivity, control what you can control, and always treat my clients exactly the same way I want to be treated. Every penny my family and I have invested is invested 100% in the same manner as investments I recommend to my clients.

No one can be an expert at everything. For example, for my own business, I have a practice management coach, a strategic management coach, and an entrepreneurial coach. Similarly, investors have historically improved their performance by hiring the right Wealth Manager or financial advisor—in other words, the right "Financial LifePlanning Coach"—and the information in my book is intended to help "coach" and "challenge" you to success. Again, I do not recommend anything for my clients that I don't do myself.

Investing, and especially investing to achieve the milestones on our quest for financial independence and a successful retirement, is a journey and like most journeys worth taking, you can't see the destination from where you stand at the beginning. Sometimes you can't even see past the first two or three turns. I wrote my book so that you would have the "keys" and a road-map to help guide you along every step of the way. We have looked at each step, each "key," in great detail, and now it is time to take a step back and look at the map as a whole.

To review, these are the *Seven Keys* that form the path from where you are to where you want to be.

1. The First Key: Are You a Do-It-Yourselfer or a Delegator?

Before you begin to get in control of your Financial Life Management, you must first determine whether you can accept guidance or if you're some-one who has to do it all on your own. Figuring out whether you're a Do-It-Yourselfer or a Delegator comes down to your Investor DNA, which you can identify by examining your strengths and weaknesses and where they align among the nine High-Net-Worth Personality Types. You can't change your DNA and you're not likely to change your personality type, either. How you proceed relies on your classification as a Do-It-Yourselfer or a Delegator. Recall that each type has a unique attitude toward their finances.

The Delegators:

- Family Stewards: *"Good financial management lets me take good care of my family."*
- Independents: *"To me, successful financial management means freedom."*
- Phobics: *"The last thing I want to talk about is my money."*

Do-It-Yourselfers:

- Accumulators: *"You can never be too rich or too thin, but being rich matters more."*
- Gamblers: *"You have better odds playing the market than in Vegas."*
- Innovators: *"Options and derivatives are the best thing that ever happened."*

Delegators or *Do-It-Yourselfers*

- The Anonymous: *"My money is my business, and no one else's."*
- Moguls: *"Being rich means power."*
- VIPs: *"There are a lot of ways to get respect, and having money is one of them."*

All of my clients are Delegators to a degree, trusting my firm with their Financial LifePlanning and portfolio investment choices. A small percentage—roughly one-quarter of my clients—are "Validators" who delegate *some* of the responsibility to my firm, while maintaining a portion of their portfolio investment and financial planning decisions. Do-It-Yourselfers make all their own decisions.

If you're a Do-It-Yourselfer, I hope you have enjoyed my book. If you are a Delegator, you now understand the distinct differences between a product salesperson/retail broker and an independent Fiduciary-based advisor, and you are ready to choose the advisor that's right for you. Choose wisely—your Financial Wellness LifePlan™ depends on it.

2. The Second (and Most Important) Key: Have a Plan

Most people think a successful DiNuzzo Financial Wellness LifePlan™, including retirement planning, only has to do with their investment strategy. The first step to planning a truly successful DiNuzzo Financial Wellness LifePlan™ is to take time to think about and set your unique milestones, goals, and objectives, both now and in retirement. Retirement is more than a lifetime of Saturdays, and a retirement plan is more than an investment strategy. First decide what a full and meaningful retirement will look like for you, including all of your major financial goals. Then make, refer to, or delegate to a professional a detailed financial roadmap checklist of everything that you will need to address to achieve those financial goals.

The DiNuzzo Financial Wellness LifePlan™ comprises both the art and science of investment planning and management, and your plan is more art because it's subjective and unique to you. Once you've created your overall vision of what financial success looks like for you, you will break this vision into the tangible milestones and goals that will make your vision a reality. From there, you can make another checklist, a financial one of all the financial contributions and investments you will make and best practices you will follow to reach your milestones and goals. This includes your personal finances and cash management, tax and estate planning, and risk (insurance), retirement, and education planning.

This prepares you for your DiNuzzo Money Bucket Stack Analysis™, where you will create a Personal Balance Sheet, Retirement Cash Flow Statement, and compare your income and expenses to identify where you rate on your financial report card.

Create Your Personal Balance Sheet

Lay the foundation of your retirement plan with a solid understanding of where you are today by building your own Personal Balance Sheet. Without an accurate accounting of your current assets, liabilities, and Net Worth in the form of a Personal Balance Sheet, you can't even begin to answer the question "Can I retire?" This is the foundation for the remaining steps. Manage this or it will manage you.

Create Your Retirement Cash Flow Statement

Capture every expected monthly expense of $10 or more on your Retirement Cash Flow Statement. Don't think of this as a budget, but as the key to being financially independent and able to relax about the future. Cash flow is critical in the retirement years because income is often fixed and there is no time to make up for even the smallest deficit. Do this ideally at least 10 years before retirement, and make the necessary adjustments in your plan while you still have time. As before, manage this or it will manage you.

Complete Your DiNuzzo Money Bucket Stack Analysis

Next, separate your investments into four "Money Buckets" to bring into focus your personal finance triangle for success: your Personal Balance Sheet, your Retirement Cash Flow Statement, and your DiNuzzo Money Bucket Stack Analysis™. Here, you identify your assets and place them in one of four "Buckets": "Cash Reserves," "Needs" (Risk Capacity), "Wants" (Risk Tolerance), or "Dreams/Wishes" (Quality of Life/Legacy). Stack your buckets with a solid foundation, understand how each one is funded, and develop a detailed cash flow plan to allocate your assets from where they currently are to where you want them to be to fulfill your goals. At this point, you will also be examining your three Tax Buckets (taxable, tax-free, and tax-deferred) and Withdrawal Buckets. This analysis may be an eye-opener for you, and it will give you a solid base for a DiNuzzo Financial Wellness LifePlan™ that delivers an investment plan based on reality and tailored to your "Wants," "Needs," and "Dreams/Wishes," now and for the future.

3. The Third Key: Strategic ("Buy and Hold") vs. Tactical ("Market Timing") Asset Allocation

Asset Allocation refers to the percentages of stocks versus bonds and cash that you maintain in your portfolios. Your choice drives growth and determines risk and is a major factor in your portfolios' success. While active mutual fund managers typically engage in a tactical approach to Asset Allocation, a strategic "buy and hold" approach that adheres to rules created to meet your specific objectives and goals is my recommendation.

In the DiNuzzo Money Bucket Stack Analysis™ described in chapter 2, you divide your money into buckets. In chapter 3, you create a customized "buy and hold" Asset Allocation and withdrawal strategy for each bucket that is appropriate for its unique purpose.

Asset Allocation drives risk and return and is the bedrock of your investment strategy. Since each Money Bucket has its own unique purpose and timeline, your allocations will vary to account for these differences. Generally speaking, a longer time horizon can weather market ups and downs and benefit from the higher returns of a stock-heavy portfolio, while a shorter time horizon requires a more conservative approach, with a greater percentage of investment in bonds. Further, the Asset Class subcategories within stocks, bonds, and mutual funds affect expected risk and rates of return. This is why, for improved results, you need to divide your portfolios into separate buckets and have individual Asset Allocation strategies for each bucket. Remember that individual stock selection, mutual fund selection, and market timing account for just a slight percentage of overall risk and return. An optimized balance of stocks and bonds considers the Efficient Frontier, a model that can maintain your current levels of return while lowering risk or increase your returns while maintaining the same level of risk.

4. The Fourth Key: Diversification to Maximize Reward vs. Risk

Your Asset Allocation strategy lays the groundwork for diversification. Fully diversifying your assets by exposing your investments to the entire universe of stocks and bonds and every desirable Asset Class maximizes that strategy. This means exposure to the entire universe of companies, appropriately weighted toward the known market premiums and Asset Classes with offsetting risk correlations. Tilt your portfolio toward the available Equity Premiums (first

Value, then Small, then Direct/Expected Profitability and Capital Investment) to maximize returns while minimizing risk. Once you have fully diversified, only two reasons exist for adding an investment to your portfolio over the rest of your lifetime: (1) to increase return, or (2) to decrease risk. You can do both with a properly diversified portfolio.

Full diversification isn't limited to one market, but takes a world view, considering Developed Markets and Emerging Markets. Surprisingly, the average active mutual fund holds a small percentage of global stocks available in this Equity Universe, and self-directed investors who purchase individual stocks tend to invest in even fewer stocks. In each case, the investor is missing out on an index of 10,000 or more companies that have a history of producing the most desirable risk-adjusted results.

Diversification within your taxable, tax-deferred, and tax-free buckets can have long-term effects on your results. Again, your time horizon is mission critical for proper portfolio management. Consider the goals for each bucket, fund them appropriately, and diversify to meet your goals with the highest returns and least risk within your timeframe.

5. The Fifth Key: Indexing vs. Active Investment Management

The history of Modern Finance has progressed from traditional stock picking to the Efficient Market Theory, which holds that all the information regarding the value of a security has been analyzed by millions and millions of highly intelligent market participants and is reflected in its current price. This favors passive and diversified index investing and explains the persistent failure of so many traditional actively managed funds. Dimensional Fund Advisors (DFA) has historically provided even higher returns by excelling at focusing on Market Exposure, Value, Size, Direct/Expected Profitability, and Capital Investment dimensions, as well as proprietary trading techniques and portfolio design.

Recall Nobel prize-winning economist Eugene Fama's research, which intimated that "active management" led to no advantage. Rather than trying to outsmart the market by choosing individual stocks or a small number of stocks such as the selections offered in "active funds," capitalize on Efficient Market Theory with index investing and a "buy and hold" strategy. The failures of active investing are many and though investors continue to be drawn to the allure of buying and selling investments based on timing, gut feelings, or hot tips, in the end, it is a loser's game and not the path to the long-term investment success that will meet your financial objectives or satisfy your life goals.

6. The Sixth Key: Rebalancing

Rebalancing your portfolio takes into account shortening time horizons for the goals of your Money Buckets, while capitalizing on opportunities for enhanced wealth and reduced risk. Leading Fiduciary-based Wealth Advisors can help you achieve "Gamma/Advisor Alpha," which has a significantly higher potential value than simply "alpha" (outsmarting the market) or "beta" (Asset Allocation) and depends on a specific and multifaceted approach to overall household wealth enhancement.

The DiNuzzo Financial Wellness LifePlan™ seeks to help investors achieve Gamma/Advisor Alpha over the lifetime of their portfolios. It removes emotions from the equation and mandates a counterintuitive approach that actually forces you to sell high and buy low, leading to enhanced wealth over time. This is accomplished mainly by selling shares of Asset Classes which have appreciated above their upper target limit and reinvesting the proceeds in underperforming Asset Classes which are materially below their lower target limit.

Rebalancing should be regular, disciplined, and consistent, while keeping the number of trades to a minimum to minimize fees and other expenses. Placing the portfolios that you will withdraw from during retirement on a Glidepath that considers your Money Buckets and Tax Buckets and slowly reduces your exposure to stocks over time accomplishes this, while helping you reach your goals. This gives you the confidence that you are following your investment plan and protects you from making counterproductive market timing emotional decisions. In the years approaching retirement, this also protects you from dramatic market swings. Set your Glidepath and enjoy your smooth landing into retirement!

7. The Seventh (and Equally Most Important) Key: Managing Your Emotions

Finances stir the emotions. You probably have a lot riding on the outcomes of your investment decisions, so it's natural to allow your emotions to take hold, affecting your best judgment. By now, you understand that emotional investing, unlike that built on historical data and empirical research, almost never results in a better outcome. Despite the facts, investors continue to be influenced by external factors such as market fluctuations.

The most important key to successful retirement investing is learning to manage your emotions. Understand that your own natural Investor DNA, the Emotional Cycle of Investing, and the media's ubiquitous Investment Pornography will lead you straight toward financial disaster. Learn to ignore your emotions and the many distractions that play upon them. When choosing a Wealth Management Firm, find one that understands the dangers of emotional investing and adheres to an approach based on establishing a solid investment plan based on objectivity, long-term data, and empirical research. A Fiduciary-based Wealth Manager can be your best defense against emotional—and potentially devastating—choices. Follow *The Seven Keys to Investing Success* and safely navigate yourself and your family to a successful retirement.

These *Seven Keys* outlined in my book are fundamental elements for a successful investment experience and DiNuzzo Financial Wellness LifePlan™. Part of financial independence and a successful retirement is relaxing into the confidence that you have made the best decisions possible based upon the best information available, and knowing that you are not going to run out of money before you run out of breath. I wish I could go back and give this book as a gift to my father, or to anyone who has suffered from the misinformation of the retail financial services market. It is information that has previously been available only to those who have institutional resources, but it has been my life's mission to offer it to you, the individual investor. I hope my book will empower you to make and enjoy smart money and Best-Life choices based on The DiNuzzo Way™ Core Principles as evidenced throughout my DiNuzzo Financial Wellness LifePlan™. I also believe we made progress in developing gratitude, appreciation, confidence, and peace of mind which can provide guidance in supporting you to live your best and most meaningful life.

THE EVOLUTION OF DIMENSIONAL

by

DAVID BOOTH, CO-CHIEF EXECUTIVE OF
DIMENSIONAL FUND ADVISORS

Dimensional evolves as the science of investing evolves, which explains why we keep such close connection to the academic community. Many, if not most, of the major advances in portfolio management over the last 60 years have come from academic research.

We believe that the best way to add value over benchmark returns is by structuring portfolios around the dimensions of expected returns. Portfolio structure, rather than the tactical shifts associated with conventional management, drives the performance of portfolios.

Clients vary in their preferences toward these investment dimensions. We work with clients to figure out what structure works best for them. Often, this involves trading off increased expected returns against costs and tracking error.

Identifying Dimensions of Expected Returns

We consider a dimension to be a factor that explains differences in returns, is persistent and pervasive, and is consistent with an equilibrium view of investing. These characteristics give us confidence that we can expect the relations observed in the past to repeat in the future.

Our fixed income portfolios are structured around two generally accepted dimensions of fixed income expected returns: term (maturity) and credit spread (quality). Our equity portfolios are based on four dimensions of expected returns that have been identified by academic research: the overall market (beta), company size (small cap/large cap), relative price (high/low), and direct profitability (high/low).

Beginning in the mid-1960s, asset pricing models have been developed to explain differences in average returns across portfolios and individual securities. Testing any model eventually produces anomalies, because no model can perfectly describe reality. But eventually, most anomalies disappear, get explained away, or sink the pricing model that revealed them.

Evaluating the Research

Our evolution parallels the evolution of research. In 1981, when we started our firm offering small cap investment strategies, the "size effect" was an anomaly. Small cap stocks had higher average returns than could be explained by the single-factor market model used at that time. Nevertheless, we felt comfortable launching a small cap fund, because the size effect was so persistent and pervasive. We didn't have a good explanation for the higher returns, but it seemed reasonable that the smaller the firm, the higher its costs of capital; and the return to an investor is the company's cost of capital.

Not long after we started Dimensional, Don Keim discovered another anomaly, "the January effect." His research showed that most of the size effect occurred in January. We could see no sensible equilibrium explanation for a January effect, so we disregarded it. As it turns out, there hasn't been a January effect since we began managing small cap strategies. This is what happens to most anomalies—they disappear when the data set is explained.

Data mining is a big concern when we look for patterns in returns. As a result, we have more confidence when patterns are persistent across time periods and pervasive across markets. The multifactor research of Eugene Fama and Ken French is a good example. When Fama and French first presented their research on the dimensions of equity returns in 1991, their evidence was based on US stocks from 1963 to 1990. Some people wondered if their results might be due to data mining, similar to the January effect. In response to that concern, Fama and French did two out-of-sample tests. First, working with Jim Davis, they collected and analyzed the data in the US from 1926 to 1962. Second, they studied the performance of stocks in developed and Emerging Markets around the world. They found the return patterns in both the pre-1963 data and the non-US data were consistent with the patterns they had observed in the US returns from 1963 to 1990. More recent returns continue to support their earlier conclusions. As a result, we are confident that the size and value factors are, in fact, dimensions of expected returns.

The Fama/French research led us to create our value strategies, which increase the exposure to low-priced stocks relative to their weight in benchmarks used by our clients. Recent research on profitability by Robert Novy-Marx has identified another measure that appears to meet our standards for a dimension of expected returns. Using a measure of gross operating margin as the gauge of profitability, high profitability firms have higher average returns than low profitability firms. Our research team has replicated his work, and, once again, we find the results persistent and pervasive around the world.

Using Valuation Models

The finding that firms with high direct profitability have higher stock returns is not surprising to most people. But to some, a higher expected return must mean greater risk.

A parallel may be drawn between direct profitability and term premiums for fixed income obligations. It is well known that buying 1-month Treasuries produces a lower return, on average, than buying 3-month Treasuries. For some investors, 3-month bills are less risky, or only slightly more risky, than 1-month bills. The higher return for the 3-month maturities is not due to mispricing; it is just the result of market forces.

Similarly, it is perfectly reasonable that equity markets have dimensions of returns that may be particularly attractive to some investors and not others. Our confidence that we have correctly identified a dimension goes up if we can connect it to a basic valuation model, such as the equation below.

$$Price = \frac{Expected\ Cash\ Flows}{Discount\ Rate}$$

The value of a stock or bond is the sum of future cash flows discounted back to present value. For example, the price of a bond is determined by the stream of coupon payments and principal repayment, discounted back at various interest rates. A high-yield bond must either have a higher coupon or sell at a lower price than a low-yield bond.

Generally, the greater the risk of an investment, the higher the discount rate and the lower the price. The discount rate is the investment's expected return. Reworking the equation above to solve for expected return gives us:

$$Expected\ Returns = \frac{Expected\ Cash\ Flows}{Price}$$

Expressing the relation this way highlights two of the dimensions of expected returns for equities-relative price and direct profitability. Higher expected returns are the result of having either higher expected cash flows or a lower price. The direct profitability dimension is tied to the numerator and the relative price dimension to the denominator. Stated another way, if two stocks sell at the same price, then the one with higher expected cash flows must have a higher expected return.

These two dimensions, relative price and direct profitability, can be combined to improve portfolio structure. For example, the explanatory power of direct profitability is fairly weak. However, when conditioned on the relative price dimension, the explanatory power becomes much stronger.

Momentum

Momentum is an example of a factor that does not meet our criteria as a dimension of returns but still impacts portfolio returns.

Research suggests that there is momentum in stock prices in most markets around the world. Stocks that have underperformed in a past period are more likely to underperform in the next period; stocks that have outperformed have a tendency to continue to outperform. If the momentum effect were large enough to trade on profitably, then it would be evidence of market mispricing.

We believe that momentum is a factor affecting returns, but it is too small and sporadic to actively induce trading. Momentum is stronger in small cap stocks than in large cap stocks, which is consistent with our view that it is best considered a trading cost rather than a trading rule. Momentum is also quite variable; in 2009, it was sharply negative for US stocks.

However, by trading carefully, it is possible to use momentum to increase returns. For example, momentum has explained most of the outperformance of our small cap strategies relative to small cap indices.

Contrast with Conventional Management

Dimensional's investment philosophy is centered on an equilibrium, or efficient market, view of public markets. In this view, the best way to add value over conventional benchmarks is to structure portfolios along the dimensions of expected returns. For equity portfolios, expected returns are increased by giving greater weight to small cap, low relative price, and high direct profitability firms.

A competing philosophy dominates conventional money management. In that view, value can be added through tactical shifts. For example, behavioral finance proponents argue that low priced stocks have higher returns than high priced stocks because of market mispricing. Interestingly, they use much of the same data to support their view that we use to support ours. Clients who want to hire a money manager to capture mispricings have a difficult challenge: First, they have to be able to identify successful managers in advance, and second, they have to hope that any such managers don't raise their fees to keep the bulk of any alpha for themselves.

We believe that our philosophy provides a better investment experience. Our approach is transparent and easy to explain because it relies on basic valuation methods and extensive empirical research, and it is validated by a long track record of implementation.

Looking Forward

Dimensional will continue to evolve as research on the dimensions of returns progresses. When we started the firm in 1981, academic research used the single-factor market model to explain average returns. The size effect was viewed as an anomaly because small cap returns were too great to be explained by beta. Nevertheless, we sponsored a small cap fund because the size effect was persistent and pervasive, and because it gave institutional investors a tool to efficiently diversify beyond large cap stocks.

In our view, the size effect went from being an anomaly to a dimension of returns in the Fama/French three-factor model, even though there is still no robust explanation of why it exists. Their research also identified the value effect as a dimension and led to the creation of our value funds.

The latest research has identified profitability as a dimension of expected returns, with highly profitable firms having higher average returns than can be explained by the three-factor model. So the evolution of financial science continues. We are very excited about this new research and will incorporate it into the investment policies of many of our existing portfolios.

—David Booth, Co-Chief Executive Officer,
Dimensional Fund Advisors

Left to right: David Booth, P.J. DiNuzzo, Rex Sinquefield, Kenneth French, and Gene F. Fama.

BIBLIOGRAPHY AND RECOMMENDED READING

Over the past four decades, I've supplemented my formal education and experience with a vast amount of written materials, some contemporary and others timeless. If you are interested in furthering your own knowledge of Wealth Management, personal finance and investment theory, and best practices, I recommend the following.

Belsky, Gary and Thomas Gilovich. *Why Smart People Make Big Money Mistakes and How to Correct Them: Lessons from the Life-Changing Science of Behavioral Economics*. New York: Simon & Schuster, 2010.

Bengen, William, P. *Conserving Client Profiles During Retirement*. Denver: FPA, 2006.

Bernstein, Peter L. *Against the Gods: The Remarkable Story of Risk*. Hoboken: John Wiley & Sons, 1998.

Bernstein, Peter L. *Capital Ideas: The Improbable Origins of Modern Wall Street*. Hoboken: John Wiley & Sons, 2005.

Bernstein, Peter L. *Capital Ideas Evolving*. Hoboken: John Wiley & Sons, 2009.

Bernstein, William J. *The Four Pillars of Investing: Lessons for Building a Winning Portfolio*. New York: McGraw-Hill, 2010.

Bernstein, William J. *The Intelligent Asset Allocator: How to Build Your Portfolio to Maximize Returns and Minimize Risk*. New York: McGraw-Hill, 2017.

Bogle, John C. and Arthur Levitt Jr. *The Clash of the Cultures: Investment vs. Speculation.* Hoboken: John Wiley & Sons, 2012.

Bogle, John C. *Common Sense on Mutual Funds: New Imperatives for the Intelligent Investor.* Hoboken: John Wiley & Sons, 2010.

Bogle, John C. *Enough: True Measures of Money, Business, and Life.* Hoboken: John Wiley & Sons, 2009.

Bogle, John C. *The Little Book of Common Sense Investing: The Only Way to Guarantee Your Fair Share of Stock Market Returns.* Hoboken: John Wiley & Sons, 2007.

Burton, Jonathan. *Investment Titans: Investment Insights from the Minds that Move Wall Street.* New York: McGraw-Hill, 2000.

Cornell, Bradford. *The Equity Risk Premium: The Long-Run Future of the Stock Market.* Hoboken: John Wiley & Sons, 1999.

Ellis, Charles D., et al. *Investment Policy.* New York: CFA Institute, 1994.

Ellis, Charles D. *Winning the Loser's Game: Timeless Strategies for Successful Investing* (7th edition). New York: McGraw: Hill, 2017.

Evans, Richard E. and Burton G. Malkiel. *Earn More (Sleep Better): The Index Fund Solution.* New York: Simon & Schuster, 1999.

Evans, Richard E. and Burton G. Malkiel. *The Index Fund Solution: A Step-By-Step Investor's Guide.* New York: Simon & Schuster, 2000.

Foster, Richard and Sarah Kaplan. *Creative Destruction: Why Companies That Are Built to Last Underperform the Market—And How to Successfully Transform Them.* New York: Currency, 2001.

Gallea, Anthony M. and William Patalon III. *Contrarian Investing: Buy and Sell When Others Won't and make Money Doing It.* Saddle River: Prentice Hall, 1999.

Gibson, Roger C. *Asset Allocation: Balancing Financial Risk* (5th edition). New York: McGraw-Hill, 2013.

Good, Walter R. and Roy W. Hermansen. *Index Your Way to Investment Success.* Upper Saddle River: Prentice Hall, 1999.

Graham, Benjamin. *Security Analysis* (6th edition). New York: McGraw-Hill, 2008.

Hebner, Mark T. and Harry M. Markowitz. *Index Funds: The 12-Step Recovery Program for Active Investors* (3rd edition). Ashland: IFA, 2013.

Ibbotson, Roger. *The True Impact of Asset Allocation on Returns.* Chicago: Ibbotson Associates, 2000.

Kahneman, Daniel. *Thinking, Fast and Slow.* New York: Farrar, Straus and Giroux, 2013.

Kaplan, Paul D. *Financial Analysts Journal.* New York: CFA Institute, January/February 2000.

Lange, James. *Retire Secure! Pay Taxes Later - The Key to Making Your Money Last* (2nd edition). Hoboken: John Wiley & Sons, 2009.

Lange, James. *The Roth Revolution: Pay Taxes Once and Never Again*. New York: Morgan James, 2011.

Loeb, Gerald M. *The Battle for Investment Survival*. Blacksburg: Wilder, 2014.

Lynch, Peter with John Rothchild. *Beating the Street*. New York: Simon & Schuster, 1994.

MacKay, Charles. *Extraordinary Popular Delusions and the Madness of Crowds*. Scotts Valley: CreateSpace, 2016.

Malkiel, Burton G. and Charles D. Ellis. *The Elements of Investing: Easy Lessons for Every Investor*. Hoboken: John Wiley & Sons, 2013.

Malkiel, Burton G. *A Random Walk Down Wall Street: The Time-Tested Strategy for Successful Investing* (9th edition). New York: W.W. Norton & Company, 2007.

Markowitz, Harry M. *Portfolio Selection: Efficient Diversification of Investments* (2nd edition). Hoboken: John Wiley & Sons, 1991.

Montier, James. *The Little Book of Behavioral Investing: How not to be your own worst enemy*. Hoboken: John Wiley & Sons, 2010.

Pardoe, James. *How Buffett Does It: 24 Simple Investing Strategies from the World's Greatest Value Investor*. New York: McGraw-Hill, 2005.

Ross, Ron. *The Unbeatable Market: Taking the Indexing Path to Financial Peace of Mind*. Ashland: BookMasters, 2002.

Ruskin, John. *The Two Paths: Being Lectures on Art, and Its Application to Decoration and Manufacture*. Victoria: Leopold Classic Library, 2016.

Schwab, Charles. *Charles Schwab's New Guide to Financial Independence Completely Revised and Updated: Practical Solutions for Busy People* (Revised edition). New York: Three Rivers, 2004.

Schwed Jr., Fred. *Where Are the Customers' Yachts? Or a Hard Look at Wall Street*. Hoboken: John Wiley & Sons, 2006.

Slott, Ed. *The Retirement Savings Time Bomb and How to Defuse It*. New York: Penguin, 2012.

Statman, Meir. *What Investors Really Want: Discover What Drives Investor Behavior and Make Smarter Financial Decisions*. New York: McGraw-Hill, 2010.

Surowiecki, James. *The Wisdom of Crowds*. New York: Anchor Books, 2005.

Swedroe, Larry E. *The Only Guide to a Winning Investment Strategy You'll Ever Need: The Way Smart Money Invests Today*. New York: St. Martin's, 2005.

Swedroe, Larry E. *Wise Investing Made Simple: Larry Swedroe's Tales to Enrich Your Future*. Shrewsbury: Charter Financial, 2007.

Taleb, Nassim Nicholas. *Fooled by Randomness: The Hidden Role of Chance in Life and in the Markets* (2nd edition). New York: Random House, 2005.

Tweddell, Jerry and Jack Pierce. *Winning with Index Mutual Funds: How to Beat Wall Street at Its Own Game.* New York: AMACOM, 1997.

Zweig, Jason. *The Little Book of Safe Money: How to Conquer Killer Markets, Con Artists, and Yourself.* Hoboken: John Wiley & Sons, 2009.

Zweig, Jason. *Your Money and Your Brain: How the New Science of Neuroeconomics Can Help Make You Rich.* New York: Simon & Schuster, 2007.

DiNuzzo Private Wealth, Inc. (DPW)/DiNuzzo Wealth Management (DWM) uses Modern Portfolio Theory (MPT), including the work of Nobel Laureate Eugene Fama and Kenneth French, and many empirical studies to guide its selection of funds and construction of DiNuzzo Private Wealth, Inc. (DPW)/DiNuzzo Wealth Management (DWM) Index Portfolios. The following studies are particularly relevant:

Barras, Laurent, Olivier Scaillet, and Russ Wermers. "False Discoveries in Mutual Fund Performance: Measuring Luck in Estimating Alphas." *The Journal of Finance* (forthcoming).

Brinson, Gary P., L. Randolph Hood, and Gilbert L. Beebower. "Determinants of Portfolio Performance." *Financial Analysts Journal* (1986).

Fama, Eugene and Kenneth French. "Common Risk Factors in the Returns on Stocks and Bonds." *Journal of Financial Economics* (1993).

Fama, Eugene and Kenneth French. "The Cross-Section of Expected Stock Returns." *The Journal of Finance* (1992).

Fama, Eugene and Kenneth French. "Size and Book-to-Market Factors in Earnings and Returns." *The Journal of Finance* (1994).

Fama, Eugene and Kenneth French. "Value versus Growth: The International Evidence." *Journal of Finance* (1998).

Goyal, Amit and Sunil Wahal. "The Selection and Termination of Investment Managers by Plan Sponsors." *The Journal of Finance* (forthcoming).

Graham, John and Campbell Harvey. "Market Timing Ability and Volatility Implied in Investment Newsletter Asset Allocation Recommendations." *National Bureau of Economic Research Paper #4890* (1995).

Markowitz, Harry. "Portfolio Selection." *The Journal of Finance* (1952).

Sharpe, William. "Capital Asset Prices: A Theory of Market Equilibrium Under Conditions of Risk." *The Journal of Finance* (1964).

Stewart, Scott D., John J. Neumann, Christopher R. Knittel, and Jeffrey Heisler. "Absence of Value: An Analysis of Investment Allocation Decisions by Institutional Plan Sponsors," *Financial Analysts Journal* (2009).